SAS OPERATION BULBASKET

SAS OPERATION BULBASKET

Behind the Lines
in Occupied France, 1944

by

Paul McCue

Pen & Sword
MILITARY

First published in Great Britain in 1996 by
LEO COOPER

Republished in 2009 by
Pen & Sword Military
an imprint of
Pen & Sword Books Ltd
47 Church Street
Barnsley
South Yorkshire S70 2AS

ISBN 978 1 84884 193 2

Printed and bound in England
by CPI Antony Rowe, Chippenham Wiltshire

Pen & Sword Books Ltd incorporates the imprints of
Pen & Sword Aviation, Pen & Sword Maritime, Pen & Sword Military,
Wharncliffe Local History, Pen & Sword Select,
Pen & Sword Military Classics and Leo Cooper,
Remember When, Seaforth Publishing and Frontline Publishing

For a complete list of Pen & Sword titles please contact
PEN & SWORD BOOKS LIMITED
47 Church Street, Barnsley, South Yorkshire, S70 2AS, England
E-mail: enquiries@pen-and-sword.co.uk
Website: www.pen-and-sword.co.uk

THIS BOOK IS DEDICATED TO THE MEN OF

B SQUADRON,

1ST SPECIAL AIR SERVICE REGIMENT

WHO PARTICIPATED IN 'OPERATION BULBASKET'

CONTENTS

Appendices:

INTRODUCTION AND ACKNOWLEDGEMENTS

Four years ago I completed a book on what was essentially a local history subject – the chronicle of fifty years at a little-known airfield in southern England. As a project to fill my spare time, it was more than successful. When finished, I put down my pen and vowed never again.

And yet. Filed away in some recess of my mind was a throw-away comment from one of the former RAF aircrew I had traced. Seemingly, in the summer of 1944, his squadron had flown two unusual operations deep into Occupied France. While not possessed of the full details, he had nevertheless been aware that the attacks had been in retribution for some dark deed of the enemy – in effect, a private war. He wished he had known more, and so did I.

This, then, was the lead which I eventually felt compelled to pursue. Despite the original source of my information, the story was soon revealed not to be simply an air force matter, but to be part of a much more complex tale – an operation of the Special Air Service behind enemy lines with the involvement of the Special Operations Executive (SOE) and the French *Résistance*. By one of those strange coincidences of research which now no longer surprise me, one of the SAS officers involved proved to be the father of a former school friend. The die was cast and I had little alternative but to continue.

Despite the fact that a number of the SAS survivors of 'Bulbasket' have died in recent years, and there are seemingly only four participants now left alive, the task has been completed and for this my special thanks must go to David Dane and John Fielding, two of those survivors. Not only were they of great assistance with their own recollections and photographs, but they were also instrumental in passing on personal papers of the late John Tonkin.

ix

The latter, prior to his death in 1995, was prevented by health and distance considerations from the involvement he would undoubtedly have desired. He nevertheless kindly gave permission for his papers to be released to me and from Australia, he provided my introduction to former members of the *Résistance* in France, especially Albert Dupont and Denis Chansigaud.

Tony Kemp, a prolific writer on the SAS, also generously provided me with his own past research into elements of 'Bulbasket' and wartime resistance in the Vienne.

The full list of those people and organizations who found the time to help me is given below and in itself reflects the variety of participants in the operation. Those who actively took part in the events of 1944 should now be able to fit their contribution into the wider context of 'Bulbasket'. Hopefully, they will also derive satisfaction from so doing.

My acknowlegements are therefore due to the following: J. Abrahams; Mrs A. Anderson; Mrs M. Anderson; *Archives Départementales de la Vienne*; P. & M. Ashley; *L'Association Nationale des Anciens Combattants de la Résistance*; Major Hon. Sir John Astor MBE ERD DL; Australian Department of Defence (Air Force Office), Canberra; Australian High Commission (Air Force Advisor), London; J. Baldwin ALA; J. M. Ballachey DFC BA LLb; P. M. Banks; A. L. Barrett; L. Bateman; E. Bellis; *Bibliothèque Municipale de Châtellerault*; *Bibliothèque Municipale de Poitiers*; *Bibliothèque Municipale de Tours*; the late J. Blanchard; M. Bodin; Air Vice-Marshal Sir Alan Boxer KCVO CB DSO DFC; D. Braddick; J. Bryce; J. L. Bulmer; J. Button; Major J. Carroll; N. Chaffey; Mlle S. Chambon; D. Chansigaud; R. F. Clement; G. Cowell, Foreign and Commonwealth Office; Commonwealth War Graves Commission; Colonel Sir William Crawshay DSO ERD TD; Miss I. Crisp; R. G. T. Crisp; Dr D. M. S. Dane FRCP FRCPath; R. J. DeBruin; R. Dumas; A. Dupont; D. Ellis; R. Everson; Air Commodore J. L. W. Ellacombe CB DFC; C. Favrelière; J. L. Fielding JP FRICS; Professor M. R. D. Foot, CBE *Croix de Guerre*; *Forres Gazette*; French Embassy (Armed Forces Attaché), London; M. Fuzeau; Prince Yuri Galitzine; Colonel P. Gaujac, French Army Historical Service; German Embassy, London; M. Gervais; R. Gough; J. Guidez; J-C. Guillon; M. Henson; Squadron Leader V. A. Hester DFC; P. Hirsch; P. Hughes; Wing Commander R. W. Iredale DFC; R. Jovelin; S. Jukes; Dr A. Kemp; B. King; J. D. Ladd; Mme V. la Raymondière; Air Vice-Marshal G. R. Magill CB CBE DFC; P. Martland; A. Martland; N. Massias; C. Mason ALA; R. & C. A. McCue; Squadron Leader E. C. Millett; Colonel J. Morgan; H. Mustard; New Zealand High Commission (Defence Staff), London; J. F. Noble; G. Ogg; P. Ogg; Air Commodore G. J. C. Paul CB DFC; E. E. Pennill; A. Peterkin; Mrs C. Peterkin; R. Picard; Brigadier J. K. Pitt OBE;

Mlle S. Plisson; Squadron Leader C. A. Pomeroy; W. G. Potter; P. Quintard; E. Ramsey DFC; J. Reid; Rev P. Ricketts; Squadron Leader E. Rideal OBE; J. Robertson; Royal Air Force Association; SAS Regimental Association; Major J. Schofield MBE; D. W. Shanahan DFC; C. Shores; G. Simmonds; Air Commodore E. B. Sismore DSO DFC AFC; Mrs E. Smith; Group Captain I. S. Smith DSO DFC; Lieutenant-Colonel I. F. Smith MBE, *Somerset County Gazette*; G. Sullivan BA ALA; S. Tomlin; the late Major J. E. Tonkin MC; J. D. Ward; C. Waugh; Squadron Leader J. Whittle DFC; M. Whittle; the late Air Marshal Sir Peter Wykeham KCB DSO OBE DFC AFC; The Imperial War Museum; The Mosquito Association; The Public Record Office; The Royal Air Force Museum; Major D. West; Gh. d'Ydewalle; 2 Group Officers' Association; 22 SAS Regiment.

For assistance with my word processing, particular thanks must also go to D. Baccas and M. Simmons.

Paul McCue
Wimbledon
January 1996.

GLOSSARY OF ABBREVIATIONS, TERMS AND RANKS

AS - *Armée Secrète*. The centre-right *Résistance* loyal to De Gaulle.

DZ - Drop Zone, for parachuted supplies or troops.

Feldkommandantur - Local HQ of the German regional military comma in France.

FFI - *Forces Françaises de l'Intérieure* - umbrella grouping of all *Résistan* fighting formations.

FTP (or FTPF) - *Francs-Tireurs et Partisans Français*. Communist bas *Résistance*.

Maquis - Originally a Corsican word for scrub - used to describe a fighti unit of the *Résistance*, both before and after the invasion.

Milice - Pro-German French Militia of the Vichy government.

OB-West - German Army Western Front HQ, based in Paris.

SHAEF - Supreme Headquarters, Allied Expeditionary Force.

SD - *Sicherheitsdienst/Sicherheitspolizei*. The Security Police of the SS.

SIS - Secret Intelligence Service - The British secret service primarily respc sible for espionage and intelligence gathering abroad. Also known M.I.6.

SOE - Special Operations Executive. British secret agency for promoting a supporting resistance movements in occupied and enemy territory.

Sonderführer - German Army interpreter.

SS - *Schutzstaffel*. Originally Hitler's bodyguard, later expanded into t armed forces of the Nazi party. The *Waffen* SS were fighting un which operated alongside the regular German Army.

WCIT - (SAS) War Crimes Investigation Team.

Wehrmacht - Regular German Army.

GERMAN - BRITISH RANKS
(as used in the text)

WEHRMACHT	SS/SD	BRITISH ARMY	R.A.F.
Feldwebel	Scharführer	Sergeant	Sergeant
Oberfeldwebel	Oberscharführer	Staff Sergeant	Flight Sergeant
Leutnant	Untersturmführer	2nd Lieutenant	Pilot Officer
Oberleutnant	Obersturmführer	Lieutenant	Flying Officer
Hauptmann	Hauptsturmführer	Captain	Flight Lieutenant
Major	Sturmbannführer	Major	Squadron Leader
Oberstleutnant	Obersturmbannführer	Lt-Colonel	Wing Commander
Oberst	Standartenführer	Colonel	Group Captain

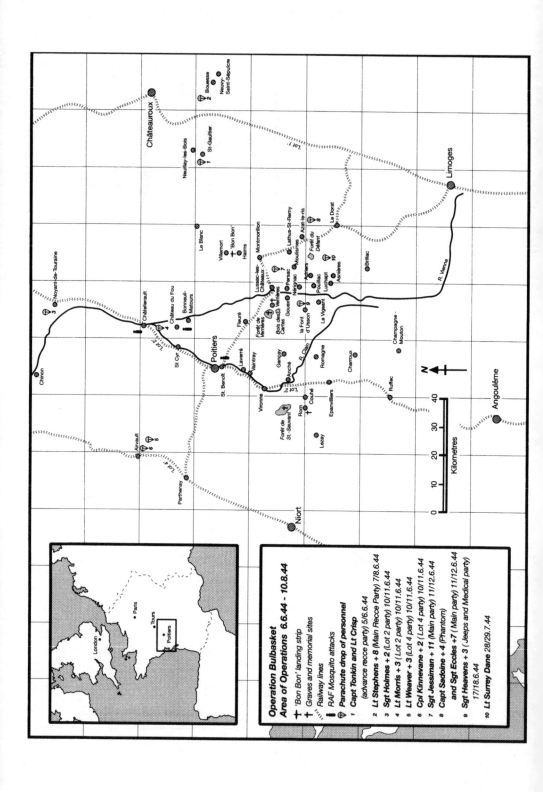

Operation Bulbasket
Area of Operations 6.6.44 - 10.8.44

✠ 'Bon Bon' landing strip

✝ Graves and memorial sites

▮ Railway lines

⊕ RAF Mosquito attacks

⊕ Parachute drop of personnel

1 **Capt Tonkin and Lt Crisp**
(advance recce party) 5/6.6.44

2 **Lt Stephens + 8** (Main Recce Party) 7/8.6.44

3 **Sgt Holmes + 2** (Lot 2 party) 10/11.6.44

4 **Lt Morris + 3** (Lot 2 party) 10/11.6.44

5 **Lt Weaver + 3** (Lot 4 party) 10/11.6.44

6 **Cpl Kinnevane + 2** (Lot 4 party) 10/11.6.44

7 **Sgt Jessiman + 11** (Main party) 11/12.6.44

8 **Capt Sadoine + 4** (Phantom)

and Sgt Eccles +7 (Main party) 11/12.6.44

9 **Sgt Heavens + 3** (Jeeps and Medical party)
17/18.6.44

10 **Lt Surrey Dane** 28/29.7.44

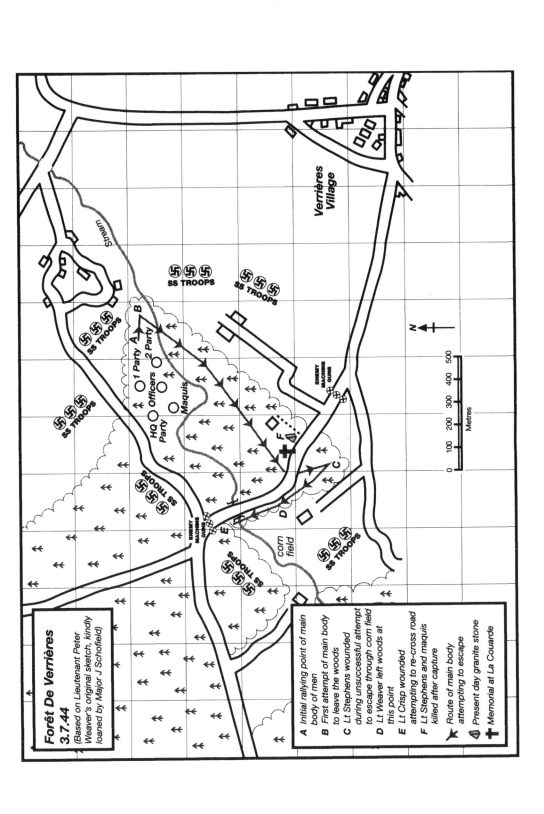

Forêt De Verrières
3.7.44

(Based on Lieutenant Peter Weaver's original sketch, kindly loaned by Major J Schofield)

A Initial rallying point of main body of men
B First attempt of main body to leave the woods
C Lt Stephens wounded during unsuccessful attempt to escape through corn field
D Lt Weaver left woods at this point
E Lt Crisp wounded attempting to re-cross road
F Lt Stephens and maquis killed after capture
✈ Route of main body attempting to escape
⬡ Present day granite stone
✝ Memorial at La Couarde

SS TROOPS

Verrières Village

Stream

ENEMY MACHINE GUNS

1 Party 2 Party
HQ ○ Officers Party
Maquis.

corn field

N

0 100 200 300 400 500
Metres

I

THE SPECIAL AIR SERVICE

The Special Air Service of today is undoubtedly among the most effective of the world's so-called 'Special Forces'. Despite the strict secrecy that normally surrounds most of its operations, present-day media coverage has meant that many of the Service's achievements have become headline news: the Iranian Embassy siege in London, covert duties in Northern Ireland and operations behind enemy lines in the Falklands and Gulf wars.

But how did the SAS find its way into today's regular British Army?

The SAS was born as one of the 'private armies' that emerged from the Second World War, and in particular from the desert campaigns of the Middle East and North Africa. Captain, later Colonel, David Stirling conceived his force in 1941 to bring havoc to the enemy's rear areas and, in little over a year, he and his nascent Service had destroyed hundreds of enemy aircraft on their own airfields and had created a legend throughout North Africa. Stirling himself was captured in February, 1943, but the SAS had by then expanded into a force of two regiments, one of them commanded by his brother Bill Stirling and the other by Paddy Mayne, David Stirling's protegé from the early days. They were among the first allied troops ashore in Sicily and Italy and had continued to build a reputation for daring operations behind enemy lines.

Early in 1944 the survivors were brought home to England and were clearly to be used in support of the forthcoming invasion of France. Less clear was exactly how. Reinforced by volunteers from Home Forces, they were designated the SAS Brigade, now some 2,500 strong, and were based at Darvel in central Ayrshire. While command of all special forces was argued over, the Brigade found itself an improbable lodger within the Army Air Corps and came under the command of Brigadier Roderick McLeod, a former regular army artillery officer, whose responsibilities consisted of the

1

two main regiments, 1st and 2nd SAS; two French parachute battalions known as 3rd and 4th SAS; a Belgian Independent Parachute Squadron (later expanded to a regiment) and supporting signals units. Of the latter, a Royal Signals squadron was to carry out headquarters duties, while F Squadron, GHQ Liaison Regiment, supported SAS parties in the field with what were known as Phantom teams. Of these, more later.

Despite being a confirmed advocate of irregular warfare, Brigadier (later General Sir Roderick) McLeod inevitably suffered when his credentials were compared with those of his predecessor. His regular army background perhaps made him less inclined to lock horns with the Army's establishment, yet this was almost a prerequisite for any leader of special forces. He had little personal experience of the type of operations in which the SAS excelled and several contemporaries believe that by the summer of 1944 McLeod was somewhat out of his depth, not only with higher command who had their own ideas on the future use of the SAS, but also with his own officers and men.

Typical of the immediate subordinates McLeod had to contend with was the commanding officer of the 1st SAS Regiment, the almost legendary Ulsterman, Lieutenant-Colonel Robert Blair Mayne, universally known as 'Colonel Paddy'. During the desert campaigns Paddy Mayne had specialized in attacks on enemy airfields far behind the lines and was reputed to have been responsible for destroying more German aircraft than the RAF. Six feet, three inches tall and and of enormous physical strength and courage, Mayne looked every inch the former amateur boxer and pre-war Irish rugby international that he was. His keen eye made him a first class marksman and his conduct in action invariably awed those around him. Normally his sensitivity, Irish sentimentality and charm made him an attractive personality. After a few drinks, however, he could be as ruthless and aggressive as when facing the enemy. He was to become one of the greatest fighting soldiers of the war, happiest when in the thick of the fiercest fighting. 'He was everything that we all wanted to be,' said one of his men.[1]

Mayne's 1st SAS Regiment had a hard core of experienced men in the remnants of the SAS's Special Raiding Squadron which had reported to

---

[1] Mayne finished the war as one of Britain's most decorated soldiers with no less than four DSOs, the Croix de Guerre and Légion d'Honneur. Despite this, his exploits, like those of the SAS in general, remained largely unknown to the public. Returning to civilian life, Mayne found it difficult to settle to his profession of Solicitor and, after several troubled years, was killed in a car accident in his home town of Newtownards, Northern Ireland.

Darvel in January, 1944. Some 130 survivors of this unit were to be the nucleus of the total strength of the Regiment's 400 men, split into A, B, C and D squadrons of 100 each. But many of the Home Forces volunteers posted to the SAS Brigade early in 1944 had no battle experience whatsoever, Trooper John Fielding being a typical example.

Early in the war Fielding had joined the Home Guard and had then been chosen for the Auxiliary Units – designed to operate in the enemy's rear as 'stay-behind' forces after a German invasion of England. The Auxiliaries were intensively trained in sabotage techniques and living off the land, but, as the threat of invasion diminished, boredom set in. Fielding's specialist training meant that his call-up for full-time army service was deferred until 1942 when the threat of invasion was finally acknowledged to be past. But in late 1943 his Auxiliary Unit background caught up with him when the SAS was looking to expand. Anyone trained in activities behind enemy lines was likely to be of use in SAS style operations and consequently many ex-Auxiliaries were approached to see if they were interested in joining. Fielding had no hesitation in volunteering and, aged 22, joined the Service on its return from Italy.

In handling the integration of untried newcomers like Fielding, 1st SAS adopted a sensible and effective approach. Those who had fought in the desert or in Italy were asked to observe the new troopers and pick out one for whom they thought they would be able to act as a mentor. Put into practice, this approach was often highly informal, as John Fielding discovered.

Queueing for his food in the mess at Darvel one day, Fielding was approached by Trooper Sam Smith, one of the veterans. Smith was a tough young Liverpudlian who had left school at fourteen and, upon joining the Army, was soon in trouble over a brawl. He only escaped a court-martial by volunteering for the Commandos and later transferred to the SAS in Egypt. One of the Regiment's 'old hands' at just 21 years of age, Smith was later to confess: 'I was in love with the SAS. It was my life'.

Now, as he waited for his meal, Smith picked out Fielding, for no better reason than he liked the look of him, and asked, 'How would you like to work with me when we go over the other side?' Fielding accepted and a partnership was forged which was to continue through France, Germany and Norway to the end of the war.

In the Scottish mountains the SAS began intensive fitness, parachute and battle training in readiness for the invasion of Europe. They did parachute drops and innumerable small party mock assaults across country in order to carry out road and railway attacks. For the latter the co-operation of the local railway company was sought and a spur line was made available so that the SAS could practice blowing it up. They taught and carried out demolitions and practised close-quarter small-arms fighting in a disused woollens factory that had pop-up full size figures of German troops. They also learned to switch from working a few days at night to daylight work and then back again. Most importantly, the Brigade had to impart that self-discipline that has always been, and still is, an essential character of SAS troops.

While the Brigade trained, argument continued over the SAS's rôle in the forthcoming invasion. Initial plans for their deployment centred on drops inland from the invasion area before D-Day. General Montgomery's 21st Army Group staff were, however, aghast at the thought that any captured SAS might compromise the coming invasion and the idea was shelved. The Brigade's part in the invasion was therefore eventually determined to be operations aimed at delaying the movement of German reinforcements to Normandy. To do so two broad methods were indicated: by setting up bases well behind enemy lines from which the SAS and the French *Résistance* would join in attacking road and railway links; and by undertaking highly mobile 'hit and run' operations against German troops. But a major stumbling block to the SAS's planned operations was the variety of different organizations and authorities who all had to give their agreement in advance to any proposed action.

Not least of the obstacles were the interests of Britain's Special Operations Executive, the SOE, which had been running agents in France for many years. SOE's job was already that of organizing and arming the *Résistance* and they were finalizing arrangements to augment their resources in France by parachuting in Jedburgh[1] teams (so-called after the Jedburgh radio sets that they used) immediately after D-Day. Jedburghs were to be three man liaison teams, normally one French, one American and one British representative, who were to operate in uniform and arrange, by radio, for arms supplies to be dropped to *Résistance* forces mobilized to fight the Germans. To their dismay, the SOE now discovered that Supreme Headquarters were planning to use the SAS for a very similar purpose and they began to lobby for the SAS Brigade's deployment to be shaped by their own Special Forces HQ in Montagu Street, London, rather than by the Army's Airborne Forces HQ to which the SAS could normally be expected to report.

In the event a compromise was reached whereby the SAS fell within the command structure of Airborne Forces, but when undertaking longer-term operations behind the lines they were expected to liaise with SOE's local agents. To the disgust of many of the SAS veterans, the Regiment's distinctive beige beret would have to be replaced by the Airborne Forces' red version for the coming campaign and this was seen as indicative of the Brigade losing its independence of action. A small headquarters unit was required to be attached to the Airborne Forces HQ at Moor Park, just on the north-western outskirts of London and today the home of the renowned golf course. Despite the restrictions that this brought, however, the SAS's Lieutenant-Colonel Collins proved to be a crucial asset there in liaising with the various services, commands and governments-in-exile.

It was confirmed that the principal work assigned to the SAS parties was to disrupt the movement and communications of German forces, by mining and generally attacking roads, railways and bridges and ambushing enemy convoys and camps. Equally important was the collection of information on enemy dispositions, and the transmission, via radio, of such details to England for possible air attack. But despite the SAS having its own trained signallers, another compromise had been forced on the Brigade in order to accommodate another special force. For radio communications support in the field, the SAS would be served by a number of Phantom signals teams attached to the Brigade. These teams were, more formally, F Squadron, GHQ Liaison Regiment, commanded by Major the Hon. J. J. 'Jakie' Astor, formerly of the Life Guards. The origins of Astor's unit dated back to 1940 when Phantom's forerunner had been set up to provide reliable communication channels from the front line in Belgium and France back to higher command. By early 1944, however, the future of Phantom was in some doubt since there was as yet no clear plan on how they could be used in the invasion. Phantom's commanding officer, Lieutenant-Colonel Mackintosh, had then shrewdly perceived that his unit could be of considerable assistance if elements were attached to the special forces and subsequently volunteers had been requested to serve with F Squadron in the SAS Brigade. Enthusiastic response to this call led to Astor forming a small headquarters unit and four patrols for 1st and 2nd SAS. In theory, F Squadron's personnel were supposed to be trained to the SAS's own high standards and could thus be absorbed as an integral part of the Brigade. For the moment Phantom's future was secured.

In finalizing proposals for use of the SAS, of crucial concern to the planners at SHAEF[1] was the speed with which the Germans would be able to rush reinforcements to the Normandy beachhead. *Generalfeldmarschall* Erwin Rommel commanded the coastal defences and knew that he must contain any invasion force on or near to the beaches until his forces could be concentrated to push the Allies back into the sea. It was therefore imperative that German units held in reserve areas should have the ability to

---

[1] SHAEF was the acronym for Supreme Headquarters, Allied Expeditionary Force.

mobilize rapidly and reach the invasion area as quickly as possible. This was even more important in respect of the armoured *Panzer* units, since it would be the weight of their firepower which could dislodge the invaders.

One German unit giving particular cause for concern to the allied planners was the 2nd SS *Panzer* Division, named *Das Reich*. Battle-hardened through bitter fighting on the eastern front, *Das Reich* had been pulled out of Russia after particularly severe losses at Kiev in November, 1943, and by early 1944 found itself in the Toulouse area of southern France with time to lick its wounds and recover its strength. This it gradually did, but not quickly enough for the Division's surviving veterans who, like their counterparts of the SAS in Britain, realized that their raw reinforcements would need vital training before they would be ready to face the inevitable invasion. Nevertheless, when the spring of 1944 arrived with still no sign of an invasion, *Das Reich's* confidence grew as fresh men and equipment brought them close to their full strength.

Such strength was awesome. With more than 15,000 fighting men and over 200 tanks and self-propelled guns, *Das Reich* was twice the size of most standard *Wehrmacht* divisions. It had six motorized rifle battalions (as compared to only four in the regular Army counterpart) in two *Panzergrenadier* regiments, the 3rd *Deutschland* and the 4th *Der Führer*, both renowned for the fanaticism of their fighting men and themselves as potent as the Division's Panther and Pz IV tanks.

SHAEF planners anticipated that *Das Reich* would be able to reach the invasion area three days after D-Day and it was therefore imperative, they argued, to drop obstacles in its path as early as possible. However, 'Overlord's' strategists would still not accept the possibility of any troops being captured and revealing details of the coming invasion. Instead, the SAS would be parachuted in as soon as possible after the invasion commenced.

Despite this revised plan, one problem had still been overlooked. The RAF's 38 Group, created to support the Airborne Forces, would already be fully committed to D-Day operations and it would not be until later in June that it was possible to drop large numbers of SAS. Thus, for the first few days after D-Day it would be the task of small advance reconnaissance parties to reconnoitre both a base from which to conduct operations and a possible drop zone (DZ) for re-supply. The essential criteria for an operating base were that it should have ample cover and a water supply. Once a suitable site was established, then troop reinforcements could be dropped and, if appropriate, jeeps. The SAS and the RAF's 38 Group had been experimenting with the viability of dropping jeeps on four huge parachutes from the bomb bays of four-engined Halifax aircraft. While exercises had eventually been successful, the principle was yet to be tested operationally.

In a SHAEF directive of 19 May, 1944, the SAS Brigade was ordered to undertake two operations aimed at establishing bases from which to interfere with the movement of enemy forces in southern France which might be sent north towards the main battle zone in Normandy. 'Operation Houndsworth', in the Morvan hills to the west of Dijon, was to be the responsibility of A Squadron of 1st SAS, while Major Lepine's B Squadron was expected to undertake a similar mission in the region east of Poitiers, close to Châteauroux. The latter operation was initially to involve just A Troop of B Squadron, commanded by Captain John Tonkin. Subject to Tonkin locating a suitable operating base, Major Lepine was then expected to lead a second group from the two remaining troops into the area.

When casting around for a suitable code-name for the operation, legend has it that Tonkin's own nickname was used as a basis.[1] The young officer had already built himself a reputation for daring operations behind enemy lines, returning on more than one occasion with dramatic, but nevertheless true, tales to tell of his experiences. His colleagues in the officers' mess had therefore teasingly christened him the 'Bullshitting Basket', feigning to be unconvinced and unimpressed by his considerable exploits. Suitably abbreviated, 'Operation Bulbasket' was chosen as the name for the latest Tonkin-led adventure.

By the time 'Operation Bulbasket' was conceived, the SAS Brigade had moved by train to Fairford in Gloucestershire to be close to the airfields of 38 Group. In contrast to regular army units, many of whom had spent many months preparing for specific duties in the invasion, the SAS moved at short notice and still with no clear idea of exactly what was to be expected of them. When they left Darvel, 1st SAS went with just their rucksacks, leaving all other effects behind so that not even the rear echelon SAS personnel would realize that a permanent move had been made. On arrival at Fairford, they entered a camp adjacent to the airfield there, ringed with a double barbed wire fence. They were greeted by Paddy Mayne who had already arrived and were uncompromisingly told that no one was to be allowed out of camp, unless in an aircraft heading for France. All necessary containers of stores and personal equipment were sent in from Station 1090, a few miles away at Down Ampney, but after that it was simply a matter of waiting, wondering about the weather and checking and rechecking weapons.

No matter what lay ahead, there could be little doubt that the young Captain Tonkin already possessed impressive credentials for any job. Aged only 23, he nevertheless had a background of having joined the SAS during the latter stages of the desert campaigns and had taken part in the landings in Sicily and Italy with the Special Raiding Squadron. Born in Singapore of old Cornish and Huguenot stock, Tonkin had been educated on the Isle of Man before taking a civil engineering degree at Bristol University. There he excelled at sport, especially rugby and shooting. When war came he wasted no time in volunteering for the Royal Engineers, but, although accepted, he was sent back to University and not recalled until January, 1941, as a lowly Sapper. Seeking a more active rôle, he was then commissioned into the Royal Northumberland Fusiliers and sent to the Middle East in early 1942. It was there, still bored and eager to find action, that he first joined the Middle East Commando and then volunteered for the 1st SAS around June, 1942. From November, 1942, to March, 1943, he had operated behind enemy lines in the Western Desert, destroying enemy supplies and carrying out long-range reconnaissance.

From July, 1943, he had helped spearhead the SAS's involvement in the landings in Sicily and Italy, participating in no less than four seaborne assault landings. In the last of these, at Termoli, Tonkin had his first, salutory, experience of rushed planning:

> 'It was another sudden job with little information and no maps. We were warned to take care as our own troops might well be there before us. In fact, the German 1st Parachute Division were there in strength. I was detailed to spearhead the thrust south to the Biferno river a.s.a.p. Penetrated too deep, too fast and by daylight was hopelessly cut off. No sign of own troops (they didn't arrive until some days later). Ran out of ammo. – was captured – very degrading!'

To Tonkin's astonishment, as a fellow-parachutist he was invited to dine with General Heidrich, the German divisional commander, who talked for hours about the Russian campaign, and how the British withdrawal from Crete began just after he had ordered his own men to start pulling out of the bloody battle. Then Tonkin was told he was to be taken to another headquarters. As he left, a German officer warned Tonkin that he was to be handed over to the special police and that the German Army could no longer guarantee his life. Tonkin immediately realized that he must escape or die, and he had precious little time to conceive a plan:

> 'When a man knows he is going to be shot, it sharpens his mind wonderfully. From then on, I really started to think.
> 'On the night of the 6th a canvas-covered three ton German

army lorry arrived with about twenty captured privates in it from the Liverpool Irish. It had a 'V' opening in the back, two SS guards in the opening and was followed by a motor cycle/side car with mounted machine gun and two men. I was promptly ordered in and we all drove north up the mountain spine along some poor roads. The guards had two stops for smoko and to exercise to get warm (it was bitterly cold and snowing lightly). At each stop, they made me report on stopping and just before starting. I noticed that they all gathered both times at the back of the truck. So after the second stop, I started to work on the ropes holding the canvas to the truck tray just behind the cab and got it loose enough to squeeze through. I told the others to count the numbers of Germans who got out of the cab at the next stop (there had been two) and to follow me if I got away. At the third stop, I reported as usual, was told both Germans had got out, so climbed *very* quietly on top of the cab. There was a nasty moment when a hand came out of the cab window and flicked a cigarette into the dark, but a third German then got out and went round to the back, so I was down on to the bonnet and away down the mountainside. As easy as that. None of the others followed me.

'About the 19th October I met up with two New Zealand privates also escaping. But luck was with us because, as we moved forward, we met a surprise British night attack coming towards us, and heard one of the leading scouts utter a typical army word when he bumped into something and hurt himself.

'And that was that.

'I know that two of my men escaped from North Italy. I don't know what happened to the remainder.'

A few weeks later Tonkin was back with the SAS but had to return to England since escaped prisoners were not permitted by the Geneva Convention to fight in the same theatre. Before his return, however, and in common with all other escaped prisoners, Tonkin was posted to a camp in North Africa for medical and psychiatric observation. He did not take too kindly to this but found a kindred soul in a fiery little Welshman who also wanted to erase the indignity of having been taken prisoner. His name was Lieutenant Tomos Stephens of the South Wales Borderers and it was not to be the last time that he encountered John Tonkin. When Stephens reached England, he remembered Tonkin's accounts of the exploits of the SAS and answered the Brigade's call for volunteers. A few months later he found himself posted to 1st SAS and became one of the Lieutenants in Tonkin's troop of B Squadron.

The confines of the sealed camp at Fairford were anathema to men like Stephens, but, after weeks of inertia, a flurry of activity broke out on the morning of 29 May. Paddy Mayne informed Tonkin that he was to be dropped with his troop of four other officers and forty men, a five-man Phantom wireless team and an RAMC corporal, near Châteauroux in the Indre. The SAS's Amended Instruction No. 6 ordered:

'You will now concentrate on building up secure bases in the area north-east of Château Chire, codename 'Houndsworth', and west of Châteauroux, codename 'Bulbasket', from D-Day onwards with a view to strategic operations against the enemy lines of communication from south of France to the Neptune area as occasion may occur, or as developments in the main battle may dictate.'

The Phantom patrol was detailed to drop in later to serve as Tonkin's main communications link; in the meantime there would be no opportunity for the SAS to even meet, let alone train with, the signallers.

Mayne also outlined three escape routes: firstly, to the Normandy beachhead; secondly, south to Spain via the Pyrenees; and thirdly, east to Dijon. The latter route involved reaching a monastery to the north-west of the town where the gardener was briefed to know a password and then pass on any escapees into a secure *Résistance* escape line.

While Tonkin was reasonably happy with his own briefing, he was horrified when he learned of the orders given to two other officers. Lieutenants Poole and Fowles, both relatively new to the Regiment, were to undertake an operation called 'Titanic' which involved two officers and four troopers parachuting into the Carentan peninsula and accompanying large-scale drops of dummy paratroops. Once on the ground their job was to create the maximum noise and confusion, thus attracting German units towards themselves and away from the invasion beaches. The experienced Tonkin judged the task practically suicidal:

'The thing that *does* stick firmly in my mind is that the two 'Titanic' officers were briefed separately but on the same day as I was. They were new to the SAS and to active service. We – the old hands amongst us – were appalled at the suicide nature of the job they had been given but successfully resolved the doubts they had by telling them what a wonderful job it was and how we were jealous. I am positive that the next day 'Titanic' was cancelled. They were so disappointed that we (stupidly) cheered them up by showing our genuine concern and relief that it was off and we had quite a few drinks at the Mess. I am also positive that the day after that 'Titanic' was put on again and I can remember the two of them coming out of Paddy's command tent as white as sheets. We were so disturbed that Harry Poat (Major and 2nd I/C) told Paddy of the circumstances. I believe Paddy told them it was volunteers only and they had the right to withdraw with honour.'

To their credit, Poole and Fowles elected to carry on and with just a handful of men kept the Germans' 915th Infantry Regiment busy for some nine critical hours during the landings on Omaha beach.

Tonkin had just started briefing his own men when another 'flap' broke out on the afternoon of 31 May. He was again summoned by Paddy Mayne and told that he would be dropped into France with just one other officer as an advance reconnaissance party. For his companion, Tonkin chose not one of his more experienced officers but 2nd Lieutenant Crisp.

Richard Crisp possessed an unusual background for a determined young officer of the SAS. As a boy the stage had been his first love and, having won a scholarship to the Old Vic Drama School at the age of sixteen, not even the German air raids on London had been able to deter him from taking up the opportunity of which he had dreamed ever since childhood. Possessed of a fine singing voice and with a natural acting ability, especially in comedy, Crisp then enjoyed what he was later to describe as 'the happiest two years of my life' during which the School was evacuated out of London to Moreton-in-Marsh in Gloucestershire. But as his eighteenth birthday approached in 1942, his army call-up grew ever nearer and Crisp agonized long and hard over his future. War was totally abhorrent to him and he could not initially conceive his being able to take up arms against the Germans. Shortly before the war his school in Salisbury had arranged to receive exchange students from Düsseldorf, but many parents had pulled out of the arrangements as tensions grew between the German and British governments. The visit of the German youngsters had ultimately foundered, but not before the young Crisp had stepped forward and, with his parents' support, offered to take three students instead of one. Only by promoting such friendships, he had reasoned, could international conflict be avoided. Now, confronted with the possibility of fighting those he had sought to befriend, as well as having to abandon his beloved acting, Crisp contemplated registering as a Conscientious Objector. Correspondence with his father, older brother and friends, reveals the emotional and moral turmoil that Crisp underwent before finally making up his mind. The evil of Hitler and the Nazis was, he resolved, an evil greater than war itself. As such, it was his duty to join the fight against this evil and consequently, albeit still with many misgivings, Richard Crisp registered for his call-up.

There then followed two unhappy years as Crisp initially found the army and military life not at all to his liking. After officer training at Sandhurst, he found himself commissioned in the North Irish Horse of the Royal Armoured Corps, but in February, 1944, his parents were surprised to receive a letter from their youngest son with the news that he had volunteered for the Special Air Service:

> 'I can't tell you more about it as I'm not allowed to. Suffice it to say I'm with the best set of people I've met in the Army, very happy and well. I hope you won't think I've gone crackers but I can't see much use going on as I was. I've got a darn sight more chance of coming through alive now anyway, tanks had their day long ago. I feel very proud to be in this Regiment.'

A contemporary of Crisp's during his SAS training was Lieutenant Leslie Bateman of D Squadron who shared a room at Darvel. Bateman remained completely unaware of his friend's acting and stage background, a past which Crisp had seemingly firmly put aside for the duration. Bateman found only a young officer whom he described as 'quiet and gentle with great courage'. The latter was undoubtedly the very quality which John Tonkin recognized when choosing a companion for the advance reconnaissance element of 'Bulbasket'.

Tonkin and Crisp were to leave at 0630 hours on the next morning, 1 June.

They consequently worked far into the night, drawing and preparing equipment, maps and money. Crisp also had to be briefed on German insignia but then, in the early hours of the morning, they received the message 'all scrubbed'. For a few hours peace returned, but later the same day, in yet another change of plan, Tonkin and Crisp were ordered up to London for another immediate briefing. A lorry and driver were swiftly provided and, together with Lieutenants Wellsted and Stewart (the advance reconnaissance party for 'Houndsworth') and Captain Mike Sadler (1st SAS's Intelligence Officer), Tonkin and Crisp were rushed up to the capital. On the way vast roadside ammunition and equipment dumps brought home the imminence of the invasion.

Once in London, a Captain joined Tonkin and Crisp as their security and briefing officer and made it clear that he would not let the two SAS officers out of his sight. They would share a hotel room and if one went to the toilet they would all go to the toilet. Tonkin accepted that the tight security measures made sense as his briefing was to contain the crucial knowledge of roughly when and where the invasion would take place and the direction of the planned breakouts.

All day of 2 June and the morning of the 3rd were spent at SOE headquarters in Baker Street memorizing the faces and code names of the agents and *Résistance* contacts of SOE's F (French) Section that they were likely to meet. Particular emphasis was given to learning the code names of Captain Maingard, otherwise known as the SOE agent 'Samuel', and the local leaders of the two main *Résistance* groups: the Armée Secrète (AS) and the Francs-tireurs et Partisans (FTP). Tonkin and Crisp were given to understand that there might be difficulties between these two factions.

Communist resistance had been organized in the German-occupied Poitiers and Châtellerault areas since October, 1940. Initially confined to the publication of anti-Nazi and anti-Vichy literature, the communists then began armed action in 1941, escalating such activity dramatically after the German invasion of the Soviet Union in June, 1941. Thus it was that the more experienced of the fighting bands of the *Résistance*, known as *maquis* groups, were to be found within the ranks of the FTP, the major communist organization.

To the east of the River Vienne in what was, until 1942, the Vichy government's unoccupied zone, a different kind of resistance was formed under the title of the 'Armée Secrète' – the AS. This was largely composed of former officers of the defeated regular French Army or officers of the Reserve and followed a more strategic path. Concerned that pin-prick sabotage operations would only serve to encourage reprisals against the civilian population, the AS concentrated instead on preparing itself to take part in open action only after an allied invasion. In November, 1942, after the assault on Dieppe and the allied landings in North Africa, the Germans occupied the Vichy zone and thus indirectly managed to swell the AS ranks. Many officers of the Vichy French Army could not stomach the total occupation of their country and so pledged themselves to the clandestine cause of the AS. Overwhelmingly loyal to De Gaulle and his Free French headquarters in London, the AS was suspicious of the communist FTP's long-term political goals, particularly post-war.

From D-Day all resistance was supposed to be co-ordinated under a unified military command structure, called the *Forces Françaises de l'Intérieure* (FFI) and responsible to the Free French forces participating in the invasion. Nevertheless, SOE anticipated that occasional friction and jealousy between the AS and FTP could still be expected and therefore recommended Tonkin to be prepared to keep them a little apart from each other.

On the ground, Tonkin was to rendez-vous with Captain Maingard by 0700 hours and in order to verify the SOE agent's identity, Tonkin was briefed to use the coded phrase, 'Is there a house in the wood?' Maingard should then reply, 'Yes, but it isn't very good.' The SOE briefing also suggested that if the correct answer were not received, then the SAS would be justified in shooting the contact. However, at one point Tonkin was able to have an informal conversation with a French agent of the SOE who was back in London between operations:

> 'Fortunately for everyone, I finally spent some hours in London with a wise old (must have been 40, but I was only 23) Frenchman with long *Résistance* experience in France who was out 'resting'. He gave me much useful advice which I recognized straightaway as being from 'the horse's mouth' and paid good heed to. Amongst a great mass of wisdom was:
> - Do not assume that the message or passwords will have been received. Until you know who 'friends' really are, hold a gun in your right hand ready to shoot and a bar of chocolate and some cigarettes in your left, both offered as a choice, then try the password, and act on the look in their eyes and not the answer you get.
> - You have two types to fear amongst the French population. Fortunately they are rare but very dangerous. They are the *Milice*, who may be in civilian clothes, and the genuine believers in the authority of the last Vichy Government who will betray you out of misguided patriotism.'

The Frenchman also recommended that poorer people were far more likely to help, as they had much less reason to keep the Germans happy. Ideally Tonkin and Crisp were told to find a small poor farm, hide up until early morning and wait for the grandmother to emerge to visit the outside toilet. This generation, with memories of the Franco-Prussian War and the 1914-18 war, would, it was thought, be the most sympathetic to the allied cause. It was further recommended that the grandmother be approached on her way *back* from the toilet when she would be in a more relaxed frame of mind. Finally Tonkin and Crisp were given the opportunity to chose from SOE's exotic array of 'secret agent' equipment – including edible paper and pens with invisible ink.

While in London on the 2nd Tonkin received further details of his railway targets from SAS Brigade headquarters. He was instructed:

'a) After establishing a base in 'Bulbasket' you will be prepared to carry out attacks on :

i) The railway Limoges-Vierzon. Attacks on this railway are not a likely requirement, but will be studied in case they are required to be cut at short notice. Such operations will be known by the code name 'LOT 1'.

ii) The railway Poitiers-Tours. You will be ready to keep this railway cut by a series of attacks and to operate generally against enemy lines of communication west of 'Bulbasket'. Such operations will be known by the code name 'LOT 2'.

b) You will study the area Tours-Orleans, south of the Loire, with a view to operating against lines of communication leading from the south to the crossings over the Loire at a later date. Such operations will be known as 'LOT 3'.'

From London the two SAS officers were taken on 3 June to Hassells Hall, an imposing Georgian mansion near Sandy in Bedfordshire, just two miles off the Great North Road and in secluded countryside. It was here that SOE's agents normally spent their final hours before being dropped into Europe from nearby RAF Tempsford. SOE were already renowned for the comforts provided for their agents and the Hall was no exception, the quality of cuisine and wine always being remarked upon by visitors. For Tonkin and Crisp, there was therefore little hardship as their 'final hours' stretched to another two days since, even at this late stage, plans continued to be cancelled or changed. A howling wind on the 4th led to a postponement but on 5 June came definite news at last – the invasion and 'Operation Bulbasket' were on, and for that very same night.

The weather was far from auspicious with a cloudy overcast and strong winds which did not bode well for a parachute drop, but within the Hall a cheerful atmosphere prevailed among the SOE agents and SAS awaiting their call to arms. Paddy Mayne paid a short visit to wish his men luck and Tonkin made sure that nothing was overlooked in his final preparations:

'We had checked and re-checked everything and packed our enormous rucksacks about fifty times (mine weighed over 80 lbs). We were instructed in the noble art of jumping from a Halifax, which is rather nasty but has the advantage of being faster and more heavily armed than a Stirling or Hudson. Finally there was nothing more to do.'

Tonkin and Crisp spent their last afternoon at Hassells Hall in the spacious drawing-room, the focal point of which was a large blackboard hanging above the fireplace. On it were listed all the operations pending, with specific instructions and times being added periodically. There was little to do other than observe the other self-contained groups in the room, usually of two, three or four people, and to ponder upon their diverse nationalities and destinations. Together with their SAS colleagues of 'Titanic' and 'Houndsworth', Tonkin and Crisp took up a number of jigsaw puzzles and were then joined in the pastime by two of the SOE agents, both attractive young women. One, Violette Szabo, was about to embark on her second and last mission into France.[1] As the evening wore on, Vera Atkins, personal assistant to the Head of SOE's French Section, sensed the growing pressure on the waiting men and women, yet recalled that Violette alone seemed perfectly calm and composed. Otherwise, there was a pervading sense of nervous tension in the room. Late in the day 'Houndsworth' was postponed for another twenty-four hours while arrangements for a reception committee were still being finalized, but for the 'Titanic' and 'Bulbasket' parties there were no further difficulties. For Tonkin, it was difficult to believe that everything was still going ahead:

'It was a horrible day for a jump. Low, dark clouds and far too strong a wind, but the complete absence of any sign of activity, our peaceful house with its jigsaw puzzles, and the general holiday atmosphere made the greatest operation in history seem completely unreal.

'We just could not realize the invasion was to start that night. We were to leave at 2000 hours for the 'drome and take off at 2200

---

[1] Violette Szabo was dropped successfully into France but was soon captured by the Germans and eventually executed at Ravensbruck concentration camp. One of Britain's most courageous agents, Violette was posthumously awarded the George Cross and was the subject of R. J. Minney's book *Carve Her Name With Pride*, later a successful film.

16

hours. We had packed in the morning so we spent the day finishing the puzzles and seeing a film. At 2000 hours the cars came for us so we just picked up our rucksacks, waved goodbye to the others and left.'

2

THE ROYAL AIR FORCE

Just two miles along quiet country lanes from Hassells Hall and close to the village of Everton, Tempsford was home to some of the RAF's most secret operations. Bordered and overlooked by the main London to Edinburgh railway line, it was an odd choice of site for clandestine undertakings, but, nevertheless, the airfield became the base of the RAF's Special Duties or 'Moon' squadrons, 138 and 161, so-called due to their night-time operations having originally been undertaken in full-moon periods to afford adequate visibility. Together, the two squadrons served both the SOE and the Secret Intelligence Service (SIS), delivering agents and supplies either by parachute drop or by landing at secretly prepared airstrips behind enemy lines.

For the SAS, and for the British Army's airborne forces in general, air transport and supply responsibilities normally rested with the troop and cargo carrying aircraft of the RAF's 38 (Airborne Forces) Group. But the demands of D-Day meant that such squadrons would already be fully committed to carrying parachute and glider-borne troops to the invasion area. The task of inserting the two SAS men some 250 miles into occupied France had therefore been picked up by SOE's F Section who had already arranged for 161 Squadron to drop a Jedburgh team in the same area.

When arriving at Tempsford from Hassells Hall, it was normal procedure for SOE's cars to have drawn blinds at their windows so that, as they entered the airfield through the station's main technical site, curious eyes could not see the mysterious occupants. The cars continued on past the RAF's offices and swung onto the concrete perimeter track which encircled the runways. A short distance further and they turned inwards from the perimeter and pulled up in front of a cluster of Nissen huts and old farm buildings, seemingly marooned on the wide open expanse of the airfield. The buildings were the last vestiges of Gibraltar Farm which had otherwise made way for the aerodrome's construction in 1941 and which stood on a site no stranger to armed forces, being astride the line of an ancient road built by Rome's legions many centuries before. It had been at Tempsford too that the later Danes had built a great fortress, only to be defeated there by Edward the Elder, son of the English King Alfred, in 916 A.D. Over a thousand years later, and Tempsford was again chosen to play a crucial role. For in the privacy afforded by the relatively isolated position, the agents and military personnel handled by SOE and SIS could make final preparations for their operations in the farm's 150-year-old barn before boarding the waiting aircraft.

At the farm Tonkin, Crisp and the three Jedburgh officers were kitted out with their parachutes and personal equipment before they waddled outside. By 1944 the operational dress of the SAS had progressed a long way from the informal kit of the desert campaigns. Standard battledress was worn, covered by the zip fastened airborne Dennison smock, a jumping helmet and rubber-soled boots. The parachute was worn on the back, and each man carried a kitbag strapped to his leg which could be released to hang below on ten feet of strong cord. Generally, there would also be a scabbard strapped to the right leg to hold a rifle or carbine; and a webbing belt, an entrenching tool, pouches and a holstered pistol.

Outside the barn a four-engined converted Halifax bomber of 'B' Flight, 161 (Special Duties) Squadron, waited, a solid dark mass against the falling night and the blacked-out airfield. Depite the weather conditions the pilot, 21-year-old Pilot Officer Kenneth Tattersall, was cheerfully confident and soon the five men climbed into the Halifax where they were each given a flask of coffee, sandwiches and chocolate and told to lie down before being covered with sleeping bags.

The Jedburgh team, code-named 'Hugh', was to be the first such team dropped into France. It was unusual in that it did not comprise the standard one British, one American and one French officer, having instead two French representatives and no American. Under SOE command, and responsible directly to Special Forces Headquarters, 'Hugh' was detailed to liaise with the local *maquis* forces of the Indre region and 'Shipwright', the existing SOE network of Captain Maingard. As such, 'Hugh' would be working in relatively close proximity to 'Bulbasket' but with no brief to co-ordinate operations. The addition of the SAS to the drop came as a late, and not entirely welcome, surprise for the Jedburgh leader, Captain W. R. Crawshay, code-named 'Crown'.[1] Bill Crawshay felt he had quite enough to think about already and last minute changes of plan, especially those which might upset

[1] Now Colonel Sir William Crawshay.

19

operating arrangements in France, were little to his liking. Realizing, however, that Tonkin and Crisp were at the whim of higher command, Crawshay and his men, Capitaine Legrand ('Franck') and Sous-Lieutenant Mersiol ('Yonne'), had made the newcomers welcome.

From the cockpit of the Halifax Pilot Officer Tattersall had only a shadowy glimpse of the figures climbing aboard before he eased his aircraft forward onto the perimeter track. As he did so, a figure out on the airfield came smartly to attention and saluted, it being the tradition of the Special Duties squadrons that an agent-dropping operation was always seen off by the respective squadron commander or, indeed, the commanding officer of the airfield. Inside the fuselage of the Halifax, the lights were switched off and the airframe shuddered as the engines were run up against the brakes. Final checks completed, Tattersall again eased the throttles forward and the aircraft rumbled down the runway. At 2307 hours, Halifax 'T-Tommy' lifted off from Tempsford's runway with its cargo of five passengers, ten containers and two packages and headed for occupied France.

As the Halifax slowly gathered height the combination of the snug sleeping bags and the soporific drone of the engines soon lulled all five men asleep. Tonkin was later to recall:

'I felt darned tired and went to sleep immediately, waking up twice, once for A.A. fire and once when the rear gunner opened up at a night fighter.'

At 0120 hours the dispatcher, Flight Sergeant Jack Corway, gently shook the parachutists awake. They finished their coffee and strapped on their bulky leg bags to the quick-release clips below their knees. Tonkin was to be the first man out, followed by Crisp and then the 'Hugh' team. He edged forward to the jump hole in the floor of the aircraft and peering out at the moonlit landscape, immediately identified the landing zone from the reconnaissance photographs he had so carefully studied back in England, an area in the Brenne marshes, some 30 kilometres south-west of Châteauroux. On the first pass, the containers were released by mistake just as Tonkin prepared to jump and so the pilot had to circle and run back in to the dropping point. The engines were throttled back and Tonkin watched for the red jump light to flash green. Suddenly the dispatcher shouted 'Go!' and dropped his raised arm. Though the light had still not changed from red, Tonkin looked down, saw open fields, and at just 300 feet pushed forward out of the hatch. It was 0137 hours on the morning of D-Day, 6 June, 1944.

The night air was warm and beautifully quiet as the noise of the Halifax receded into the distance and Tonkin had a few moments to appreciate the experience:

> 'It was the nicest exit I've ever had. Before I knew I was out of the plane I felt the 'chute tugging at my shoulders and then I was swinging in the air in bright moonlight with only a faint breeze to mar the dead silence. I lowered the rucksack and then had a look round for the other four and the containers. They were dropping into a wood and I just had time to locate my bearings before preparing to land.
>
> 'For a moment I thought I was going to land in a tree but I just missed it. My parachute caught and I came to rest with my feet just touching the ground. It was such a gentle landing that I doubt if I'd have broken an egg if I'd landed on it.'

The spot where the group landed, Les Cherpes, was close to the 'Moncousinat' farm, some five kilometres north west of the small town of St Gaultier. Almost immediately a young man ran up to Tonkin, welcoming him enthusiastically in voluble French. Remembering his briefing, Tonkin attempted the exchange of code words and was not overly surprised when the Frenchman displayed absolutely no sign of comprehension. Judging the man nevertheless friendly, Tonkin decided to continue with clearing the field as the Halifax had circled before running in again to drop its remaining supplies. It would take some time to collect everything and Tonkin was anxious that Tattersall's aircraft might have aroused the interest of the *Luftwaffe's* night fighter airfield and supporting radar near Châteauroux.

Meanwhile, Tonkin's welcomer, Narcisse Girault, had been joined by four others. His father, François Girault, was the farmer of 'Moncousinat' and was accompanied by a farmhand. The two others were members of the local *Résistance* – Lieutenant Schwatsko ('Olive'),[1] in charge of the reception party, and his second in command, Maurice Renard. Girault *père* shared Tonkin's concerns over the German airfield and warned that search parties could be expected in daylight. Quickly, everyone pitched in to roll up and hide all the parachutes. They were finished only just in time. Within ten minutes of the drop a German night fighter swept low over the area several times. In the bright moonlight the fighter was clearly looking for the Halifax bomber and any parachutists but Tattersall had wasted no time in leaving

[1] Lieutenant Schwatsko was killed by the Germans just two nights later during an exchange of shots in Eguzon.

21

the area. His return journey was eventful only in passing the huge aerial and naval armadas heading for the Normandy invasion beaches. After a flight lasting nearly six hours, the Halifax landed safely back at Tempsford.

The SAS and Jedburgh team were taken to 'Moncousinat' where Madame Girault had coffee ready for her nocturnal visitors. Then, until dawn, they dozed in the hay of the farm's barn. At around 6 am a car arrived and a dark-haired young man carrying a Sten gun climbed out. Tonkin recognized him immediately from SOE's briefing. To make absolutely certain, but unable to avoid feeling slightly absurd in the circumstances, Tonkin asked, *'Est-ce qu'il y a une maison dans le bois?'* *'Oui, mais elle n'est pas très bonne,'* answered the visitor. There was therefore no doubt; the newcomer was Captain Maingard, SOE's representative in the region and one of F Section's most successful agents.

Captain René Amédée Louis Pierre Maingard de la Ville-es-Offrans (Amédée Maingard for short) was a 25-year-old Mauritian of aristocratic background who had been studying accountancy in London when war broke out. He volunteered at once for the 60th Rifles, and it was there that SOE's talent scouts found him and asked if he would go to France. He was para-chuted into the Indre in April, 1943, to assist 'Hector', Squadron Leader Maurice Southgate, in running SOE's 'Shipwright' circuit. After Southgate's arrest on 1 May, 1944, Maingard and his equally resourceful fellow-agent, Pearl Witherington, divided the 'Shipwright' area between them and built up two of the most effective networks in SOE.

Maingard's operations to date had already entailed great risks. His major area of activity was around Châteauroux where he had a radio operator attached to him. At the end of 1943 and up to March, 1944, Maingard needed to live in Châteauroux and, incredibly, rented an attic flat in the same building as the local Gestapo HQ.[1] His reasoning was that it would be the last place they would think of looking for him – and he was proved right. Some time in March, however, he was in the flat when he saw, out of the window, his radio operator being brought in. A dilemma then arose which meant Maingard had to know if his operator talked. If the man did break, and if Maingard found out in time, he could warn the network to go to ground. But to break up the network unnecessarily would destroy months of hard work. Maingard therefore made simple signal arrangements from his window, and then stayed on in his attic on the assumption that if the oper-ator did talk under torture, then the Gestapo would come for him first and he could alert the network. It was an immensely courageous course of action to take and Maingard kept his loaded revolver ready at all times – five rounds for the Gestapo and one for himself. In the event, it took the radio operator some 48 hours to die and Maingard had no option but to listen to the poor man's tormented screams. But no hammering came on the attic door and Maingard, and his network, survived.

On the morning of 6 June he came alone to greet Tonkin's party and to take delivery of two additional radio sets which the SAS had brought for him. Tonkin also handed him a letter of introduction from General Koenig of the Free French forces in London and told him that the invasion should by now be well under way. The SOE man was taken aback by the latter news and took some convincing. Somehow, the BBC messages designed to alert Maingard had not been transmitted and for a few minutes even the SAS began to wonder if the invasion had again been postponed. The SOE agent also received new orders, brought by Tonkin from Colonel Buckmaster at SOE headquarters. Maingard was to now leave the Indre region to the 'Hugh' team, move into the Vienne *département* and locate his operating base alongside the headquarters of the local FFI commanders. The SOE base was manned by Maingard's two assistants, the brothers Hirsch. While Pierre Hirsch ('Pierrot') operated the SOE radio in a mobile transmitting post, his brother Jacques ('François') acted as Maingard's liaison officer with the various *Résistance* groups and was normally the driver of Maingard's unique car, a Matford (French Ford) with a Vickers K machine gun in place of the windscreen.

At 0730 hours, after the welcoming preliminaries were over, Maingard drove the SAS and Jedburgh officers a few kilometres to the north-east, close to Neuillay-les-Bois, where the Jedburgh team were to make contact with Colonel Paul Mirguet ('Surcouf'), head of the Indre region's FFI forces. A former refrigerator salesman from Lorraine, Mirguet was a resolute leader, determined not to be swayed by any of the petty jealousies of his different groups. He had the sole aim of creating a united, strong France and was to be described by the 'Hugh' team as 'completely selfless' in the pursuit of this ideal. Recognizing this, Tonkin and Crisp were able to relax their immediate concerns over jealousies within the *Résistance* movement and start discussions on how best to complement the activity already being organized by the FFI and SOE.

It was recognized it would be inadvisable to divide the efforts of the SAS on the two main railway lines, code-named 'Lot 1' and 'Lot 2', since the distance between the two lines was considerable and would require the SAS force to be divided for considerable periods of time. The FFI were confident that they alone could ensure that the Limoges to Vierzon line ('Lot 1') could be kept permanently cut by the *maquis* in the Haute-Vienne, Creuse and Indre regions. On the other hand, the Bordeaux to Tours 'Lot 2' line was strategically far more important, yet more easily guarded by the Germans. The countryside around it was unsuitable for harbouring large *maquis* groups and it was therefore felt that small raiding parties of SAS, directed at this line, would be the best use of resources. Tonkin accepted the logic of this reasoning and agreed therefore that his group should operate around Poitiers, some 80 kilometres to the west.

Talks were still taking place when, late in the afternoon, word reached Colonel Mirguet of enemy forces in the area. Apparently the Germans had reached the DZ only two hours after Tonkin and the others had left 'Moncousinat' and the enemy had combed the area unsuccessfully for evidence of a drop. They had then moved on to the Girault farm in the early afternoon. Despite giving it a thorough going over, everything was safely buried. The risks taken by ordinary Frenchmen such as Monsieur Girault could be immense.

As a result of the enemy activity, Maingard advised against staying in the area so that night Tonkin and Crisp moved some 60 kilometres south-east to a farm just south of Neuvy-Saint-Sépulcre. There, along with the 'Hugh' team, the SAS helped Maingard collect a re-supply drop for the *Résistance* which had been previously arranged.

On the morning of 7 June Tonkin received a radio message through the Jedburgh team confirming that his advance party, led by Lieutenant Stephens, would be dropped that night and would include Tonkin's own radio operator, Corporal Chick, with a two-way radio set. In the last hours of daylight Tonkin therefore organized a number of *gazogène* (gas burning) vehicles and shortly before midnight set off for the DZ which had been chosen some 15 kilometres to the north-west, north of Bouesse.

The operation to drop Lieutenant Stephens' party saw the RAF's 38 Group picking up responsibility for the support of 'Bulbasket' when a Stirling aircraft of 620 Squadron was dispatched with nine SAS personnel. Arrangements for the reception of such a re-supply or reinforcement drop were relatively standard practice within the SAS operating procedures. The base would be notified of the estimated time of arrival for a drop and the men, often with *maquis* help, would arrive at the DZ, conceal themselves around the field and then settle down to what could be a long cold wait. When an aircraft's engines were heard, the decision had to be made as to whether it sounded like the aircraft expected; if so, a pattern of flares would then be lit on the DZ and a code letter flashed in morse.

From the RAF's point of view, however, the exercise was somewhat more complex. The aircraft needed to fly at a specific height and the dispatcher had to take careful account of wind direction and strength if personnel and supplies were not to be scattered over a wide area. Flying slow and low, at night and over unfamiliar enemy-held territory, might sound like a recipe for disaster but the RAF never shirked the task night after night and often in highly unfavourable weather conditions.

Apart from an occasional small package, the bulk of supplies were dropped in containers and panniers. The latter were used for dropping less fragile items such as clothing, sleeping bags and tentage but were prone to bursting open on landing, scattering the contents far and wide. Containers were long cylindrical drums divided internally into cells. To simplify matters they were delivered pre-packed with code letters on the outside denoting their contents and would normally hold a mixture of clothing, rations, ammunition, weapons, 'comforts' such as rum and cigarettes, medical kit, tents and sleeping bags. Like the Halifax that had dropped Tonkin and Crisp, the Stirling was a four-engined bomber adapted to the task and could carry twenty-four such containers.

Taking off at 2240 hours from RAF Fairford, adjacent to the SAS Brigade's main camp, Flying Officer Bell arrived over the DZ just over three hours later and immediately spotted the signal lights of the ground party. At 0151 hours Bell dropped an 11 seconds stick of Lieutenant Stephens, eight troopers and nine containers from 600 feet. All landed safely and were picked up without incident, along with nearly five tons of stores in panniers. But one crucial piece of equipment was not found – the party's Eureka radio transmitting set.

The Eureka was a ground-based signal transmitter and its counterpart, Rebecca, was the receiver carried in an aircraft. The equipment was designed to pick up signals at distances of up to 70 miles. Unhindered as it was by cloud or other weather conditions, Eureka/Rebecca was of great use, in conjunction with an aircraft's radio altimeter, in locating a DZ at night and had removed dependence upon the moon periods for operations. Weighing around 20 pounds, it was not an easily portable item of equipment for the ground party but without Eureka signals to guide them, supply dropping aircraft were seriously hindered during non-moon periods.

While the disappearance of the Eureka set was to prove a severe set-back, in the short term the enthusiasm of the reinforcements more than made up for the loss. Lieutenant Tomos 'Twm'[1] Stephens was the high-spirited regular soldier from the South Wales Borderers who had met John Tonkin in a transit camp in North Africa after Tonkin's escape in Italy. Stephens, too, had been a prisoner of war and he came to France bursting

---

[1] Stephens was universally known as 'Twm', from the initials of his name – T.W.M. Stephens.

to start operations against the Germans whom he hated.

On 9 June Maingard, Colonel Mirguet, the 'Hugh' team and the SAS moved westwards to the Le Blanc area. Here Mirguet's forces seemed strongest and another conference took place where much time was spent discussing strategy and learning about local problems. The Jedburgh team was to remain in the Indre, carrying out *maquis* training and operating north of Châteauroux where they agreed to help keep the northern sector of the 'Lot 1' railway line cut. This line was already a great favourite with the *maquis*; on the night of 6/7 June they proudly reported having cut it in no less than 57 places. The SAS had also been informed that the RAF had destroyed all the bridges over the Loire and the Germans were consequently having to use the tunnel under the river at Saumur. It was therefore an important goal of the Jedburgh team to keep the railway lines cut leading to the tunnel.

Maingard, following fresh orders from General Koenig, was to leave the Indre to his helpers and move down to the *maquis* groups in the Vienne. The SAS would accompany him there and take primary responsibility for the 'Lot 2' line in the area Châtellerault-Poitiers-Angoulême, the 'Lot 1' line south of Châteauroux as required, and the line connecting the two which ran via Montmorillon. Tonkin emphasized, as instructed, the importance of petrol and railways as prime targets and, while Maingard was already well aware of this, it helped him to have British paratroop officers, in uniform, stressing the task. It was also decided that the arrival of the SAS should be actively and openly broadcast. Since the countryside was relatively open, with many villages, this decision was practically the only one anyway and Tonkin appreciated that this approach, while relatively risky, might serve to attract useful target intelligence from the local people.

Leaving the SOE Jedburgh team near Le Blanc, Tonkin and his men therefore continued on the 9th towards the south-west. Accompanied by Maingard and Mirguet and transported in vehicles provided by the *maquis*, the SAS headed to the south of Montmorillon where they were to make contact with Colonel Félix Chêne. Previously head of the AS in the Vienne-Sud and known by the code-name 'Cyclamen', Chêne had, from 6 June, 1944, been appointed by General Koenig as head of the FFI throughout the Vienne and promoted to become 'Colonel Bernard'. In addition to the operational demands of his position, Chêne was to exercise great diplomatic skills in fusing the FTP groups to his own former AS organisation.[1] At Chêne's

---

[1] Post-war Colonel Chêne continued to serve in the regular French Army, commanded a regiment in Algeria and retired as a Brigadier-General.

headquarters at the farm 'Sazas', the two regional heads of the FFI, Colonels Chêne and Mirguet, met for the first time and quickly found themselves in total accord in pursuing their fight against the Germans.

Colonel Chêne was no less supportive of the SAS than Maingard or Mirguet and arranged to attach one of his young officers, Sous-Lieutenant Albert Dupont, as an interpreter to help Tonkin for his first few days in France. Dupont had been one of the more active members of the *Armée Secrète* prior to the invasion. As early as 1941 he had been arrested and imprisoned by the Vichy authorities for spreading Gaullist propaganda and on his release in 1942 he immediately joined the AS and eventually became a liaison courier between the headquarters of Colonel Chêne and his groups throughout the Vienne. Cycling many miles around the countryside from group to group, Dupont hid his written messages between the tyre and wheel rim of his bicycle. While this method ensured safe delivery through German and *Milice* checkpoints, legibility of the messages was not helped by the thick streaks of black rubber frequently left over the scraps of paper.

The young Frenchman's attachment to the SAS was to remain indelibly stamped on his memory. He was fascinated by the new arrivals and their obvious professionalism, noting that they always carefully buried all trace of their presence, including scraps of paper, cigarette ends etc. He was let into the secret of the large buttons on the pockets of Tonkin's battledress blouse which each contained a miniature compass. In particular, he was intrigued by the small covered pipe which Lieutenant Stephens frequently smoked. The Welshman confided to Dupont that it was his good luck talisman, having kept his father safe through the 1914–1918 war. Encouraged by Dupont's efforts in English, Stephens also revealed he knew a few French words which he now attempted to improve upon. He was happy to be in France, he told Dupont, as unlike Italy where he had fought before, the countryside was similar to that in Britain and he therefore felt more at home.

At 'Sazas' Colonel Chêne arranged for the SAS to set up camp nearby and from there Tonkin went out on the 9th to reconnoitre the local countryside for a new DZ – now an urgent requirement for the impending arrival of his main party. The SAS were also taken to meet the local *maquis* group 'Amilcar', one of the first FTP units to be formed in the Vienne-Sud but by now considerably diluted in terms of communist fervour. By 1944 many more Frenchmen were seeking to take up the fight against the enemy and most simply joined the nearest *maquis*, irrespective of its political ideals. One member of the group estimated that by D-Day only some 5% of the strength of fifty men could truly be described as communists. The 'Amilcar' group was led by 'Amilcar' himself, Capitaine Robert Artaud:

'I was warned that an SAS party would arrive at my headquarters by car at around 2.30 in the afternoon. I therefore arranged that they should be received properly and from two o'clock onwards had a section ready to present arms. The SAS group were astonished and impressed to receive such a smart reception from the *maquis* . . . we set them up in a pine wood about three kilometres away from our own camp. Our task was to help them set up camp, provide means of replenishing their food supplies, protect them from attack and help with the parachute drops in order to build up arms dumps.'

It was small wonder that the SAS were astonished by the *maquis'* display of military order. Generally speaking, the British viewed the *maquis* as rather disorganized, exotic and somewhat bloodthirsty, impatient to get to grips with the enemy. But Tonkin, in unfamiliar country and with no knowledge of the language, quickly decided that the only sensible approach was to trust the *maquis* in almost everything. With their help, he selected a suitable DZ site not far from the N147 Limoges to Poitiers road, close to the house 'Montplaisir' and extending over the land of 'Le Leché', a farm managed by one of the *maquis'* helpers.

The next morning the SAS camp received a visitor who had highly interesting information for Tonkin:

'A small, very frightened and therefore highly courageous French civilian (I think he was a railway employee) arrived at our newly established base. He told us that there were eleven petrol trains on a well camouflaged and heavily guarded series of sidings about a kilometre south-west of Châtellerault.'

London had repeatedly stressed that petrol was a priority target, but Tonkin was faced with a dilemma. As many as eleven trains seemed an exaggeration; where exactly were they and how strong was the guard? If the trains were not too heavily guarded, should he defer the main party drop and attack with what he had, or defer the attack until the main party came in and risk losing the trains? If the guard were too strong – how busy were the RAF and would they be able to bomb before the trains dispersed? And what about the weather?

Whatever his eventual course of action, Tonkin realized it was essential to pinpoint and confirm the existence of the trains.

'So, Twm Stephens being a smallish, dark-haired Welshman, with a dapper moustache, we borrowed some French civilian clothes and he, the civilian and one of our highly enthusiastic *Résistance* men, who spoke about as much English as Twm spoke French, took off on pushbikes to reconnoitre. I must say that Twm looked the part of a young French farmer, but he was more than a bit caustic about riding the bike.'

With his two companions, Stephens set off on the 60-kilometre journey to Châtellerault at midday on the 10th. Before he left, a camera which Tonkin had brought with him was used to photograph Stephens in his disguise, alongside Tonkin and Richard Crisp.[1]

For Tonkin and the others the remainder of the day proved eventful. At around two o'clock in the afternoon a burst of firing was heard from about five kilometres away and the *maquis* proudly announced that four men of the 'Amilcar' group, based at 'Le Leché' to guard over the DZ area, had attacked a German convoy on the Montmorillon ta Moulismes road. Five Germans were reported killed, but it was feared that the engagement would draw further attention to the area. When the time came to go out to the DZ, however, no other enemy reaction had developed.

The main party had originally been expected to drop into the Châteauroux area on the night of 9/10 June, but had been postponed due to Tonkin's decision to move south-west, closer to Poitiers. Now, back in England, a Stirling of 620 Squadron took off from RAF Fairford to drop the SAS main party of twenty men and containers. During the flight interest had been generated among the troopers by their being joined in the aircraft by two women secret agents who parachuted onto another DZ on the way[2]. But when the Stirling reached the 'Bulbasket' DZ, the crew reported being unable to spot any signal lights in the area. The big bomber swung round for home and for the SAS aboard it was not only a disappointing anti-climax but also the first indication of the problems that would be faced by the loss of the Eureka.

It had been a frustrating night for Tonkin and his men on the 'Montplaisir' DZ. They had not even heard an aircraft and had eventually returned to camp in the early hours of the 11th. They were resting when Twm Stephens and his companions returned, very tired and saddle-sore. They had thumbed lifts for only a small part of their journey and as a result

[1] Remarkably, in view of the dire consequences had the equipment been captured, Tonkin had been equipped with a camera and film to record 'Operation Bulbasket'. Throughout his stay in France, Tonkin and his men therefore took a number of shots, including several of their French helpers.
[2] John Fielding recalled the two women agents but the official records make no mention of them; it would have been unusual to mix an SOE or SIS drop with an SAS operation.

were worn out from their pedalling. But the strenuous exercise had been well worthwhile. The young Welshman confirmed the presence of the petrol wagons and reported that they were too heavily guarded for the SAS to attack them. He could not be sure there were eleven trains, but there was certainly a huge reserve of petrol, and the railwayman was adamant that there were eleven sidings all containing petrol wagons. Stephens had made a precise note of their location and at 1717 hours that same afternoon, Tonkin had the map reference radioed in cypher back to England. An immediate air attack was requested.

From SAS Brigade headquarters at Moor Park details of the target were quickly telephoned through to the RAF's 2 Group and an outline operation plan was put together in time to alert the squadrons at 1930 hours for a low-level precision raid at dusk. Clearly the petrol trains could be moved at short notice, so time was of the essence and the plan involved Mosquito fighter-bombers at least preventing the trains from being moved. If necessary, the 'heavies' of Bomber Command could then be called in to finish the job.

The attack was planned in two stages, 140 Wing at RAF Gravesend in Kent being asked to provide six crews for an immediate take-off and 138 Wing at RAF Lasham in Hampshire required to detail a further six crews for a second attack shortly afterwards. The units chosen for the job could not be bettered, both Wings already being expert at precision attacks on pin-point targets. 140 Wing in particular had gained fame from its remarkably successful raid on Amiens prison in February, 1944, when hundreds of *Résistance* fighters had been freed after the Wing knocked the prison walls down. The Amiens raid had involved careful preparation and planning beforehand, but the attack on Châtellerault had no such advantages and the operation remains clearly focused in the memories of many of the aircrew who participated largely because of the haste in mounting it. At Gravesend, 464 RAAF and 487 RNZAF Squadron crews were briefed just fifteen minutes after the alert and were told that the target had been reported by 'a reconnaissance aircraft'.

Commanding officer of the New Zealanders' 487 Squadron (motto '*Ki te matunga*' – 'True to the end') was Wing Commander I. S. 'Black' Smith from Auckland, a former fighter and night-fighter pilot who had only arrived in Britain in August, 1939, but had subsequently managed to rise from Pilot Officer to Wing Commander in the astonishingly short time of 11 months. During the Battle of Britain Smith had flown Hurricanes and was remembered for his description of an occasion when, at the height of the Battle, he and just one other pilot were alone in the air when they sighted a formation of a hundred German aircraft. Without hesitation, 'Black' and his colleague attacked. In typical Kiwi laconic manner, Smith later described the incident thus: 'We sprayed them until our ammunition ran out and then we had to return to base'. The New Zealander had continued in this fashion when he later converted to Mosquito night-fighter operations. On 24 June, 1942, he had notched up the first two confirmed Mosquito night kills when, with 151 Squadron, he had dispatched a Heinkel He 111 and a Dornier Do 217 within ten minutes of each other. More recently, in March, 1944, Smith had led the 487 Squadron contingent of six Mosquitos on the famed operation against Amiens prison and had been first to attack and successfully breach the target's outer walls.

When 2 Group's orders reached Gravesend on 11 June Smith recalls that he was on his way to the control tower to discuss a training programme when he walked into Group Captain Peter Wykeham-Barnes, the commanding officer of 140 Wing.[1] Although 487 had no operations scheduled for that night, Wykeham-Barnes now asked Smith to provide a section of three aircraft for an immediate attack. Smith telephoned to Flight Lieutenant John Ellacombe, one of his most experienced pilots, to bomb up three of the squadron's aircraft and also to alert Flight Lieutenant Marsh, Smith's navigator.

As Smith drove quickly out onto the airfield, the sleek shapes of his squadron's aircraft came into view, dotted about the distant dispersals. There could be little doubt that for the task ahead the squadron was superbly equipped. The fighter-bomber they flew was the RAF's 'wooden wonder', the potent Mosquito.

Designed as a 'speed bomber' by the de Havilland Aircraft Company, the Mosquito was originally a private venture by the company, fitting no existing Air Ministry requirement. Soon, however, the design had an important ally. Air Marshal Sir Wilfrid Freeman, the Air Council's Member for Development and Production, had been an operational pilot in the First World War where he had first gained respect for the products of de Havilland, in particular the DH 4 bomber which he had flown. Powered by a single powerful Rolls Royce engine, the DH 4 had been fast enough to hold its own against the pace of enemy fighters. Remembering this, Freeman was an attentive listener when the same company promised an aircraft with two

---

[1] Wykeham-Barnes retired as Air Marshal Sir Peter Wykeham KCB DSO OBE DFC AFC, the family name having changed in 1955. He had joined the pre-war RAF as an apprentice and rose to become a Hurricane pilot in the Middle East, with later Mosquito intruder operations from Malta. Taking over 140 Wing in 1944 at the age of twenty-nine, he had twenty-four confirmed enemy aircraft destroyed to his credit.

Rolls Royce Merlin engines which would be capable of bombing Berlin in daylight while out-running the best German fighters.

But the Air Marshal's support had, for some time, been a lone voice. The majority of the Air Staff held little enthusiasm for what was dubbed 'Freeman's Folly', conventional thinking in 1939 still believing it was too late to consider new designs for this war and that, instead, efforts should be concentrated on improving existing types. The fact that the design was based on materials as basic as wood and glue, with manufacturing expertise provided by the G-Plan furniture company, also did little to endear it to the more orthodox thinkers of the Air Staff. Fortunately, Freeman was a man of determination and sure in his personal convictions. In the winter of 1939 de Havilland received an order from the Air Ministry for an initial batch of fifty Mosquitos, straight off the drawing board. Such an order, without even a prototype having been built, let alone flown, was a rare and momentous display of faith from a government department. Without Freeman's personal involvement, it could not have happened.

The Mosquito, in its first photo-reconnaissance variant, entered RAF service in July, 1941, and flew its first operational sortie in September of the same year. Fighter and bomber versions quickly followed and in early 1943 the FB VI, a fighter-bomber variant, commenced operations. Developed from the Mk II night fighter, the FB VI carried the same powerful nose armament of four .303-in. Browning machine guns mounted above four 20-mm. Hispano cannon. Its bomb bay could carry four 250-lb. bombs and two wing stations allowed for an additional two 500-lb. bombs or auxiliary fuel tanks to augment the Mosquito's already not inconsiderable range of 1,120 miles. The aircraft's maximum speed at altitude was 378 m.p.h. but more importantly, at low level it was usually capable of pulling away from the Germans' most effective fighter, the Focke Wulf Fw 190. It was this FB VI Mosquito which equipped 2 Group's fighter-bomber squadrons in the summer of 1944.

Turning into the dispersal area of his own Mosquito, Smith was able to benefit from a 'rapid response' technique he had developed for situations such as the one now called for. To aid the fastest possible bombing-up time, Smith had decreed that bombs should be ready laid out on the dispersals, one each side for the wing stations and four in the centre for the bomb bay. The pilot had only to taxi his aircraft over the bombs so that they could then be fused and lifted into the racks. The technique could further be enhanced according to the availability of the squadron's Chief Armourer, Sergeant Charlie Bush. Four airmen would lift a 500-lb. bomb onto Bush's neck and shoulders and, with enormous strength, the New Zealander would then simply stand up so that the bomb just clicked into place in its wing rack. Bush could service three aircraft by this method before his legs gave way and he was therefore one of the most valuable members of the squadron. Sadly, he was later killed at RAF Thorney Island.

At the dispersals Smith met up with his own navigator and the crews of Flight Lieutenants Ellacombe and Runciman who were to fly as Smith's numbers two and three respectively. The briefing was minimal as speed off the ground had been stressed as imperative and there had been no time to prepare a navigational or attack plan. Consequently, Smith simply stood by the aircraft and told the others what the target was, where it was, and how they would fly to it.

Smith and Marsh had climbed up into their usual Mosquito, aircraft 'T', when Smith noticed the Wing's Intelligence Officer standing close by. Shouting from the cockpit, the Wing Commander asked if he should expect any *flak* on the target and told his navigator to pass his map out of the window so that the Intelligence Officer could find out any details and mark the positions on the map. This Marsh did, but a minute or so later bombing-up was completed and the Mosquitos taxied out for take-off, both Smith and Marsh forgetting that the map had not yet been returned.

There was thick continuous cloud over southern England and northern France so Smith climbed his three aircraft and remained in the cloud, between six and eight thousand feet, until they reached the limits of 'GEE' signal navigational assistance, close to Le Mans. At this point Smith also reached the limit of the map he and his navigator had been using so far and therefore, easing his Mosquito to just under the cloud cover, he now asked Marsh for the target area map. It was then that the loss was discovered. The other two members of the section thought a fight was in progress as they watched arms flailing everywhere in Smith's cockpit, a frantic search of each other and the cockpit ensuing before Smith and Marsh both conceded that there was indeed no map. Smith still recalls how terse he was with Marsh until he suddenly burst out laughing, realizing how difficult it was to be angry with just a pair of eyes – all that the pilot could see of his navigator's face above the oxygen mask.

Fortunately 'Black' Smith was blessed with a short-term photographic memory for maps and could recall where the target was and its relation to other geographical features. He was also fairly familiar with the area, having flown over it before on a number of occasions. There was thus no point in trying to hand over the lead to Ellacombe or Runciman, both of whom at that moment had no better idea than their commanding officer as to their position. Letting down to ground level, Smith therefore depended on first finding the Loire and then the railway line leading south from Tours towards Châtellerault.

When he successfully located the Tours-Châtellerault railway line, Smith knew that the target would be the first major marshalling yards that they would come across to the south down this line and that it was sited on the edge of the town of Châtellerault. Sure enough Runciman's navigator obtained a pinpoint 20 miles from the target to confirm they were still on the right course and on cue the marshalling yards came into sight with the petrol trains still present. Attacking immediately, Smith bombed the northern end of the yards, Runciman the centre and Ellacombe the southern end before pulling up and around onto a reciprocal course to the north for the return journey. There was no point in hanging around as running in from the south were the Australians of Wing Commander Iredale's section who had watched and enjoyed the spectacle of 487 Squadron's bombing attacks.

Bob Iredale had thrown together a three aircraft section of himself, Squadron Leader McPhee and Flying Officer Rowell, Iredale and McPhee also having been participants in the Amiens prison raid. With no better briefing than that which 487 had enjoyed, the 464 Squadron Mosquitos took off immediately after the New Zealand unit's contingent, but flew a separate course to the target area at low level and in wide formation, thus using the opportunity to reconnoitre as great an area as possible. The only opposition encountered came just north of Bernay when Squadron Leader McPhee[1] broke radio silence to warn of a Messerschmitt Me 109 fighter closing in from the port beam. The German did not seem keen to tackle the three Mosquitos, however, and soon disappeared. To be on the safe side, Iredale led the Australian aircraft up into the cloud cover for a couple of minutes before resuming his course to the target at ground level. Approximately two miles separated each Mosquito in the wide formation adopted, thus also allowing freedom of action with cannon fire should any road or rail targets present themselves.

The remainder of the flight proved uneventful and the Australians had no difficulty in identifying the target as they made their run from the south, thanks to 487 Squadron's bombing attacks already being delivered. All three aircraft reported bombing trains, wagons, troops and motor transport in and around the yards as well as delivering cannon strafing attacks before turning north to follow Smith's formation home. Between the target and Châteaudun

---

[1] McPhee's part in this attack was mentioned in the citation for his Distinguished Flying Cross, gazetted 7 July, 1944.

the Australians remained at low level and attacked several troop trains which were stationary in sidings. An engine in motion was destroyed two miles east of Tours on the east-west railway line and Flying Officer Rowell attacked and destroyed a transport train which was heading south. The only *flak* experienced came from this train and from a single 20-mm gun on the deserted airfield at Conches. Both the 487 and 464 Squadron sections landed safely back at Gravesend between 2320 and 2325 hours.

The crews of 138 Wing's 107 Squadron at RAF Lasham had also been given a 'stand-down' from night operations on 11 June. All 2nd Tactical Air Force units were at this time living under canvas in preparation for the living conditions expected to be found when the squadrons moved to the continent. The attractions of staying within camp confines were therefore none too attractive and personnel took every opportunity to partake of 'real life' in the neighbouring towns and villages. Most of 107's aircrew had thus left the aerodrome to spend the evening in the nearby town of Alton. Soon after arrival, however, crews were called out of the cinema and various hostelries by the RAF Police who ushered them aboard a crew bus to be returned to Lasham.

Flying Officer Denis Shanahan, navigator to Flight Lieutenant Jack Whittle, recalls that briefings started immediately the crews returned, with pilots and navigators being briefed separately to save time. Whittle and the other 107 Squadron pilots were briefed by their C.O. and formation leader, Wing Commander Mike Pollard, who quickly outlined the target details and attack plans. Again, no mention was made of the SAS's involvement. Meanwhile, the navigators received route and weather details before joining their pilots and hurrying out to the six waiting Mosquitos where the armourers were still fitting wing bombs.

107 Squadron lifted off from Lasham at 2110 hours as 464 and 487 Squadrons were already heading for home. Keeping at low level and in loose formation, the Mosquitos thundered over the south coast at Littlehampton and crossed into France at St Valéry, west of Dieppe. Over France visibility worsened as drizzle began to fall and in an effort to maintain formation the Mosquitos switched on their navigation lights in the gathering gloom and climbed to 6,000 feet above what became 10/10ths cloud. After some 80 miles the cloud began to break up and the Mosquitos dropped back down to ground level. Sweeping on over nondescript countryside, the navigators picked up a good pinpoint east of Le Mans and then the River Loire itself, a beautiful sight in the late evening light and confirmation that the Mosquitos were still on track. Although it was dark by the time they approached Châtellerault, they had no difficulty in identifying the target from as far away

as 20 miles, thanks to the fires left by the two squadrons of 140 Wing. An area estimated to be 300 yards by 170 yards was in flames and smoke was already rising to 4,000 feet.

Climbing to 3,000 feet, Wing Commander Pollard called in his aircraft in turn to attack singly, allocating each Mosquito two shallow dive passes across the line of wagons, working down from those already alight. All attacks were successfully completed and, as a final gesture, Pollard personally delivered a cannon attack along the entire length of the marshalling yards. Leaving the immense oil fires well and truly stoked, 107 Squadron's aircraft headed for home individually in the certain knowledge of a job well done. The only drama came from Squadron Leader Brittain in aircraft 'J' who developed trouble in his port engine. Feathering the propellor, he nevertheless made a good landing at Lasham on his one remaining engine.

As a final postscript to the attacks, Bob Iredale's 464 Squadron crews reported the numerous trains which they had spotted between Châtellerault and Châteaudun on their return journey. 140 Wing's Intelligence Officer thought these trains worthy of further attention and consequently two Mosquitos of 21 Squadron were quickly briefed and sent off from Gravesend shortly after 2300 hours. Attacks were carried out and both aircraft returned safely.

Back in Châtellerault the town's civilian population had not escaped involvement in the dramatic attack. In the Rue Guillemot several buildings had been hit and Monsieur Duvau, a local resident, recorded the attack in his diary:

'11th June: a long air raid alert from 7.30 pm to 10 pm. Around 9.30 pm I thought I heard thunder, but then heard the noise of aircraft. Passing low and fast came three aircraft. I thought I saw roundel markings on them . . . then I heard three explosions. A large black cloud rose to an incredible height above the station . . . the aircraft returned, skimming the River Vienne and I heard more explosions and the rattle of machine guns. There is talk of eleven dead and three wounded . . . the Police Commissioner was killed as he left the house.'

'Le Glaneur', the periodical diary of Châtellerault, was unable to openly proclaim the attack's success due to the interests of the German authorities, but later carried confirmation of the raid's effect on the town:

'Last night it was the turn of Châtellerault. Suddenly, at ten o'clock in the evening, bombs fell from the sky, hitting the station and a petrol train standing there . . . an enormous mushroom cloud of black smoke formed and hung over the area and from time to time red bonfires flared up, lighting up the entire town. An hour passed and then, again, aircraft roared overhead, aiming earthwards with bombs, tracer and incendiary bullets. This time it lasted twenty minutes. Eleven dead and twenty wounded, the latter including the Mayor, Colonel Aymard, who was hit by a bomb splinter.'

Success had its price.

3

MAIN PARTY

As Wing Commander Pollard's Mosquitos were beginning their final run in to the target, some 55 kilometres to the south the SAS and *maquisards* were making their way to the 'Montplaisir' DZ to await the arrival of their main party. But as the scheduled drop time of 0100 hours approached, and Tonkin and his men stood by their unlit bonfires, a steady stream of headlights appeared on the nearby road. It took Tonkin only a few moments to realize that the advance elements of the 2nd SS *Das Reich* Panzer Division were almost upon him.

The *maquis* had warned Tonkin only that afternoon that *Das Reich* was moving north up the road from Limoges, heading towards the Normandy battlefront, but it had been decided to proceed with the drop anyway. Tonkin hoped that he would be well clear before the Germans reached the area, having no wish to tangle with the unit which had already left a trail of death and destruction in its wake. Constantly harassed by FFI forces since it had started north, *Das Reich's* patience had already been exhausted and its troops had inflicted horrifying retribution on local communities. Two days earlier the division had hanged ninety-nine men in the town of Tulle and on the 10th, in one of the most infamous crimes of the Second World War, had killed 648 civilians in Oradour-sur-Glane, less than 30 kilometres south-east of the DZ. Now making all haste to Normandy, *Das Reich* was intending to refuel from the very petrol trains at Châtellerault which were the target of the RAF. But even as the long column of lorries and half-tracks growled up the road towards 'Montplaisir', a large glow on the horizon signalled that the R.A.F's attack on Châtellerault had been successful.

Tonkin had to think quickly, and after a short debate he decided that if the signal fires were lit in a depression, they just might not be seen from the road. The DZ would also have to be cleared very quickly, with the help of the *maquis* and their bullock carts. Everyone took up their positions, one eye on the sky and the other on the approaching enemy column, and the signal fires were lit just before the deadline.

Almost dead on schedule, the SAS main party was roaring towards the DZ in two Stirlings of 190 Squadron from RAF Fairford. Since the abortive attempt of the previous night, it had now been possible to add the five-man Phantom team to the party and it was for this reason that two aircraft now roared low over the waiting reception committee. In a few moments the two bombers had disappeared but then one was heard coming back.

The Stirling which had returned to make its drop was that of Flying Officer Connel who, undeterred by the nearby road activity, had circled the DZ before making a second pass and dropping twelve men and a number of containers from just 400 feet.

Trooper John Fielding was in the main party, with Sam Smith almost too close for comfort behind him. The tightness of their dropping 'stick' led to the apex of Fielding's parachute becoming entangled with Smith's shoe, the veteran having dropped out of the floor of the Stirling immediately behind Fielding. After a few anxious moments all righted itself but Fielding then caught his breath at the sight around and below him. To one side of the drop zone the long stream of enemy vehicles in convoy could clearly be seen, their headlights stretching away into the distance. On the horizon to the north a huge fireball marked the Mosquitos' raid on Châtellerault but, worse still, the sky all around them was studded with the coloured lights of the supply containers.

From the ground the spectacle was equally alarming to John Tonkin:

'Suddenly the sky was full of multi-coloured lights – green, blue, white and red – three to a container! There must have been at least thirty-six and probably forty-five. I had never heard of this idea before, and didn't know what they were. What was for sure was that they presented a grave danger to us for, almost immediately, all the German convoy lights went out, they stopped, and we could no longer hear their engines.

'We moved *very* fast. I did not need to give any orders! Men were smashing the bulbs everywhere and we were frantically collecting Sergeant Jessiman and his 11 men who had dropped at the same time. The aircraft had disappeared and, most ominously, there was neither light nor sound from the Germans.

'We collected everything and got to blazes out of it. When we were at a reasonably safe distance, an abusive Jessiman told me it was the latest idea. The lights were each on the end of three spring-loaded arms (like an umbrella) which was held in a sleeve on each container. The intent was that, as the container parachute opened, the 'umbrella' was jerked out of the sleeve and hung by its electrical cord below the container, but unlit. On the container hitting the ground, some sort of switch was operated which lit the lights, thus enabling one to find the containers easily! Jessiman told me that base wanted me to report on their usefulness. I did so next morning but I note that my radio message is not included in the summary of messages!'

It was only later that Tonkin, on reflection, realized that the malfunctioning lights may well have been a blessing in disguise. Almost certainly the Germans must have believed themselves under air attack. The combination of low-flying aircraft and coloured lights in the sky would have seemed very similar to the target marking tactics carried out by an allied aircraft prior to bombing. The prudent reaction for the Germans would therefore have been to black out the convoy and lie low. Apparently this is exactly what occurred and the enemy would seem to have taken to the road-side ditches, wondering what fearful new weapon was being launched against them.

Sergeant Jessiman also had to inform Tonkin that the main party had only consisted of twenty SAS and the five-man Phantom team. After the departure from England of Lieutenant Stephens' group, Brigade headquarters had received a priority request from SHAEF for attacks on the railways (code-named 'Lot') west and north of Poitiers, too distant for 'Bulbasket' to reach. Two officers and twelve men, in four groups led by Lieutenants Weaver and Morris, Sergeant Holmes and Corporal Kinnevane[1], had therefore been dropped 'blind' the previous night on the vital lines, with orders to march cross-country to join Tonkin after they had carried out their sabotage. Tonkin was to transmit rendezvous points to London, which would then be re-broadcast by the BBC to the parties' radio receivers.

Tonkin very much resented this late change of plan and in his report compiled after the operation he was to complain: 'I had NOT, repeat NOT, been informed previously of this RV [rendezvous]'. Instead of an expected strength of fifty, he now had only twenty-three and was missing the fourteen men of the 'Lot' parties dropped the night before, and the five Phantom and eight SAS men who had been in the second Stirling over 'Montplaisir'. The pilot of this aircraft, Flight Sergeant Fogarty, had spotted the lights of the enemy convoy and quickly consulted Captain Sadoine, the Phantom

[1] Wartime official records used the spelling Kinnevane, the correct version is Kinnivane.

40

commanding officer. It was decided that the ground activity presented too much risk but the Stirling crews were now under orders to drop their paratroopers come what may, rather than return to England with them. Fogarty therefore flew on, his party unsettled by both the ground activity and the thought of having to drop 'blind' elsewhere. But as his dispatcher Fogarty had on board Squadron Leader Norris, one of the RAF's most experienced parachute instructors who had been responsible for training many of the SAS now with him. Calmly Norris reassured the party and readied them again for the drop. Some 25 kilometres to the south-east Fogarty spotted a suitable area of open high ground and dropped his troops and containers without further incident.

Back at 'Montplaisir' the SAS and their *maquis* helpers were quickly marching north-east, putting as much distance as possible between themselves and *Das Reich's* convoy which was showing signs of emerging from cover. Both Albert Dupont and Robert Artaud believed that one trooper had landed unconscious after knocking himself out on leaving the Stirling, but there is no mention of this in official records and the SAS survivors cannot now recall any such incident. John Fielding does remember, however, that for a moment he thought that he had broken his leg. His kitbag, designed to unclip and hang away from his leg before landing, had not done so and its weight, combined with the shock of landing, gave his leg a harsh battering.

After no more than an hour's march the *maquisards* and the SAS arrived at 'Jarrouie', a farm just south of the town of Montmorillon around which the 'Amilcar' group normally operated. This was to be the SAS's new camp for the time being and, before they bedded down, Albert Dupont had the chance to exchange a few snatches of conversation with the newcomers:

'The first I asked of them was an English newspaper and to my great joy I was given a paper printed in London the same morning.

'I asked their opinion on the likely duration of the war and one of them told me that their General Montgomery had said that the liberation of France would take two months and the war would finish in six months.

'My other role as a guide was unnecessary. Captain Tonkin was equipped with very detailed maps printed on large handkerchiefs and seemed to know the region like the back of his hand. I, the supposed guide, therefore followed his group.'

While the SAS men crawled into their sleeping bags the *maquis* guards, alert for any patrols from *Das Reich*, watched the vivid glow in the sky to the north where 2 Group's Mosquitos had attacked Châtellerault. OB-West's petrol trains, vital for the swift refuelling of *Das Reich's* movement to Normandy, had been completely destroyed.

For the local German forces there was little sleep that night. In addition to the attack on Châtellerault and the appearance of the strange lights dropped from the air near *Das Reich*, two acts of railway sabotage had been reported, one being the responsibility of the energetic Twm Stephens. After his report on the petrol trains on the morning of 11 June, Stephens had settled into a haystack for a well-deserved opportunity to catch up on his sleep. After only a couple of hours, however, he was shaken awake by Tonkin. He was ordered to blow up a road/rail bridge on the branch line south-east of Montmorillon, making sure the charge went off no earlier than 0200 hours on the morning of the 12th. This would therefore only be after the drop of the SAS main party just 15 kilometres away at 'Montplaisir'. The attack was also to coincide with Maingard and the *Résistance* cutting the 'Lot 2' line at the same time, south of Poitiers.

At 'Jarrouie' the SAS troopers were in high spirits and keen to start operations. The warm June weather and the deceptively peaceful countryside combined to give the promise of pleasant days ahead, mixed with high adventure. For many it was their first experience of a foreign land and the dangers of war seemed far distant. John Fielding remembers this first camp for the *al fresco* barbecue enjoyed by all:

> 'It was here that we killed a lamb in the farm buildings a short distance from the camp . . . it was then cooked and eaten and it was at that time, as far as I can remember, the group photograph was taken. It was also at this base that I released my pigeon which I had on my chest when I jumped, in a container, and constructed a small 'aviary' out of netting for it. I think our instructions were that pigeons could not be reliably kept more than forty-eight hours because they would lose their homing instinct.'

Certainly pigeon operations had little to commend them instead of radio communication, 'Bulbasket's' message log recording the arrival of just one pigeon-borne message. All too obvious failures were much more likely. Sam Smith released one which promptly lodged at the top of a nearby fir tree and although Tonkin, Fielding and Smith all threw stones at the bird, it stubbornly refused to fly. Captain Sadoine was no more successful at his Phantom base and was later to report:

'I wrote a message to send off by the pigeon which my No. 3 was carrying. The message being duly written and attached to the pigeon's leg, I launched the pigeon with perhaps more force than skill, for it circled us twice and made straight for the nearest big tree 50 yards away where it alighted. I believe it may still be there.'

Meanwhile Tonkin was well aware that units of *Das Reich* were still passing along the Limoges to Poitiers road and on the night of the 12th/13th Lieutenant Crisp slipped out of camp to successfully lay mines on this road in the Forêt du Défant. As Crisp returned to camp, the horizon was again lit to the north and it was later learned that RAF Bomber Command had turned their attention on Poitiers. Hundreds of heavy Lancaster bombers, led by Pathfinder Mosquitos, had raided the city's main railway station. While the station and marshalling yards were heavily damaged, so too were surrounding residential districts. 239 people were killed and 323 were wounded in the attack which lasted just twenty-eight minutes. 456 houses were destroyed and 829 damaged. The French found it difficult to understand the Allies' tactics at times like these, especially since trains were again running through the station just twenty-four hours later. A number of the SAS therefore found themselves drawn into debate on the justification for the heavy bomber raid. There was very little that Tonkin or his men could do to convince the *maquisards* that the RAF were always operating in the best interests of the French.

On the morning of 13 June Colonel Chêne arranged for the 'Amilcar' group to provide a dozen volunteer *maquisards* to be attached to Tonkin's party to facilitate obtaining food supplies, contact with the local population and to act as guides for operations at night. The Frenchmen were led by Jean Dieudonné, code-named 'Maurice', one of Robert Artaud's trusted Lieutenants. Dieudonné had been in the regular French Army since 1936 and had entered the *Résistance* forces at the age of twenty-seven. He had subsequently joined the 'Amilcar' *maquis* where, thanks to his formal military background, he was designated as the group's instructor and trainer. Already he had proved his mettle by carrying out an attack on a German convoy, killing seven of the enemy. Now he was proud to have been chosen to accompany the British and readily assured Tonkin of his co-operation at all times. Dieudonné also brought with him three cars and a small lorry, requisitioned to help transport the group as another move of camp was now necessary. With the Germans only 12 kilometres away at Sillars Camp, all the activity south of Montmorillon could not go unchallenged. On 12 June Tonkin had signalled Brigade HQ that the area was 'lousy with enemy' and he asked for jeeps to be sent as mobility was now a serious problem for his party of twenty-three. The following day he reported that 200-400 Germans were looking for them and had clashed with local *maquis* forces, inflicting several losses. The latter reported Germans patrolling within nine kilometres of the SAS base and the British therefore moved camp again that night, choosing a site on the western side of the N147 road near the village of Nérignac.

For the next few days the SAS concentrated on establishing their presence and arranging for supply drops from England. Another new DZ was found at the farm 'Primo la Coupe', near la Font d'Usson, and preparations were made for a supply drop on the night of the 16th/17th. Fires were lit from 0001 hours to 0630 hours but Pilot Officer James in a Stirling of 196 Squadron from RAF Keevil was unable to identify Tonkin's DZ and returned to England with seventeen containers still on board. More successful was Flying Officer Farrell in a Stirling of 299 Squadron, also from Keevil and aiming for Captain Sadoine's DZ to the south-east. Despite very bad weather conditions, Farrell managed to spot Sadoine's DZ twice and on the second occasion successfully ran in to drop containers.

Sadoine was later to pen a colourful description of this event:

'There was nothing clandestine about my first what the French call *un parachutage*. Once the containers were released from the aircraft there was considerable drama. Albert (the local *maquis* chief) began the proceedings by shouting 'Attention! Everyone! The *bidons* descend'. Everyone present repeated this advice to Bobo or Alphonse or Pierre, or whoever was nearest, to 'have a care that the sacred *bidons* do not crush thee!'

'Once the containers had landed, the parachute stakes were on. The winner was whoever could roll and hide away the most para-chutes before being spotted by someone else. The bullock carts then came up with much encouragement from the drivers such as: 'But come, my old one, to the *bidons* advance.' Then began the prelimin-ary discussions as to how the first container would be hoisted on to the cart and who should have the honour of commencing. I found that I had to go through the motions of beginning to hoist one end myself before, with loud cries of 'But no, my Captain! Permit!' or for example 'My Captain, what an affair!', my helpers would then get on with the job. Once, however, the drill for clearing the DZ was understood, the helpers were of the greatest value, and we succeeded one night in clearing the DZ in seventy minutes. This was very good as it included four containers that had fallen in trees.'

Reaching the same conclusion as Tonkin, Sadoine concluded that the *maquis*:

> 'should be treated unreservedly as friends and Allies . . . and the greatest trust can be put in them. Any mistakes they make are from over-enthusism and willingness to help.'

On the 17th the first of the four 'Lot' railway parties, those of Lieutenant Morris and Sergeant Holmes, reached the main group with encouraging reports of their exploits. As Jessiman had reported to Tonkin, the 'Lot' teams had been dropped 'blind' on the night of the 10th/11th by the two 620 Squadron Stirlings of Flight Lieutenant Jack and Flying Officer Gawith from RAF Fairford. Cloud cover had been 10/10ths at 3,000 feet with the result that the RAF had some difficulty in finding the DZs. Lieutenant Morris, a South African, had been dropped slightly wrong, but only some five kilometres out from the 'Lot 2' railway which was his target. One of his three men, Trooper Brown, was missing and was presumed to have suffered a parachute malfunction or 'roman candle', but, despite this setback, Morris and the two others had continued. They soon found the line and swiftly blew both tracks over a culvert a few kilometres to the south of Châtellerault.

Like Morris, Sergeant Holmes and his two men had the Poitiers-Tours stretch of 'Lot 2' as their target and had been dropped accurately some 30 kilometres to the north of Châtellerault. They removed 15-20 feet of rail under a bridge carrying the D760 road, near to Noyant de Touraine and then set off on their lengthy trek across hazardous countryside to join up with Tonkin. The distance to be covered was over 90 kilometres but Holmes, one of 1st SAS's veterans, successfully navigated his group to the main party without encountering any opposition. Tonkin was particularly happy to greet these latest arrivals as Johnny Holmes had been his jeep driver in the Western Desert and had then fought with him through Sicily and Italy.

Having received his main party, Tonkin was now left wanting in only one area – mobility. As early as 13 June Brigade had promised a drop of four jeeps on the night of the 15th/16th, and consequently, Twm Stephens, who spoke the best, if limited French, was picked to go with one of the senior *Résistance* people to recce a suitable DZ for receiving the jeeps. Camille Olivet, known as 'La Chouette', had a background as an aircraft engineer who had volunteered for the Republican cause in the Spanish Civil War, where he had helped to organize medical services. After the fall of France he had become, as a communist veteran of the fighting in Spain, a wanted man and so took up *Résistance* activities from the very beginning, firstly with the left-wing political movement, the *Front National*, in the south of the Vienne. From 1943 he had then translated his political opposition into active armed resistance with the FTP. According to Olivet's memoirs, it was he who decided that Stephens should wear civilian clothes and that they would travel by bicycle, despite Tonkin's protests that wearing civvies could prejudice Stephens' status as a prisoner of war if captured. But Olivet had objected to riding around in daylight with a British officer in uniform. So Stephens changed into an old suit borrowed from a farmer and, before setting out, was frisked by Olivet. The wily *résistant* removed some army-issue toilet paper from Stephens' pockets and bluntly told the Welshman, 'The peasants here wipe their backsides with fresh grass.'

The two men set out and, after some miles of pleasant cycling, stopped at a café for lunch. Here Stephens' accent caused some difficulties as the proprietor initially took him for a German but Olivet quietly explained the situation and all was well. In the late afternoon they arrived at 'Primo la Coupe', where the drop was planned to take place, only to discover that the area which had been suggested by Tonkin from the map was covered by young trees. Fortunately wider inspection revealed a suitable field nearby.

But the operation was then postponed on two consecutive days and it was therefore not until the night of the 17th/18th that Tonkin and his men turned up in a lorry at about nine o'clock, to be welcomed by the farmer with several bottles of home-distilled rough spirits. A complication had arisen, explained the farmer, since one of his cows was about to calve and a vet was present for the occasion. The vet's sympathies were not known for certain and much to his annoyance, he was ordered to stay at the farm until after the drop. To placate the vet's wife, a message was sent explaining that the delivery was a difficult one.

After suitable toasts to allied victory and success in the night's undertaking, everyone went outside much fortified and waited for the sound of aircraft engines, expected at 0200 hours. In the distance a German convoy could just be heard moving up the Limoges-Poitiers road, but it was far enough away not to concern the reception party.

In the event the drop was a relatively protracted affair. From Tarrant Rushton two Halifaxes of 298 Squadron carried one jeep, five containers and two men each, and two more Halifaxes of 644 Squadron each carried another jeep and six containers. From RAF Keevil Squadron Leader Angell took off in a Stirling of 196 Squadron with seventeen containers. Flying independently to the DZ, the arrivals of the five aircraft were therefore uncoordinated yet all successfully spotted the signal lights without difficulties. First over at 0159 hours was Pilot Officer Edick in Halifax 'S' of 298

Squadron, followed seventeen minutes later by Flying Officer Richards in 'H' of 644 Squadron. Only five more minutes and Flying Officer Northmore in Halifax 'M' of 298 Squadron roared over at 0222 to release a third jeep earthwards. At 0240 hours Squadron Leader Angell's Stirling deposited its containers and finally at 0244 Flying Officer Hud Nickel arrived with the last of the four jeeps.

From RAF Tarrant Rushton Nickel's Halifax had climbed slowly to altitude over the Channel – a necessity due to the light fingers of Royal Naval gunners offshore of the invasion beaches. Once over enemy-held France, the aircraft then eased down to low level, every detail of the ground visible in the bright moonlight. Back in the fuselage, noise and rushing air were ever present since the Halifax bomb bay had to be constantly open to accommodate the jeep. As they neared the DZ bomb aimer Roy Gough settled down in the perspex nose and on cue spotted the code letter flashed from the ground. The Halifax signalled an acknowledgement in return with the Aldis lamp and was soon rewarded by four fires flickering to life in the reverse 'L' shape. Running in over the fires, Gough pressed the bomb release and the jeep, together with four containers from under the bomber's wings, tumbled earthwards. A brief glimpse of the parachutes opening and the DZ was out of sight.

Below, Tonkin marvelled that the aircraft had managed not to collide and as the last jeep drifted down on its four, huge 90 foot parachutes, the reception party doused the signal fires and moved swiftly to finish their task. In preparation, four large holes had been dug in a wood close by in order to bury the cradles which held the jeeps and these were quickly covered over after filling. In addition to the jeeps and the four men, fourteen containers were also collected, holding petrol, gun mountings, spare wheels and tools.[1]

The newcomers were led by Sergeant Bob Heavens, another of the Regiment's veterans and an acknowledged expert in all things mechanical. On landing, he assembled his team of Troopers Mullen and Gray, both drivers, and Corporal Allan, the Royal Army Medical Corps orderly attached to 'Bulbasket'. Together they reported to Tonkin who enthusiastically welcomed the newcomers. Wasting no time, Heavens checked the jeeps over and, although one was found to have suffered a twisted chassis, all were

---

[1] When dawn arrived, a Fieseler Storch spotter plane appeared over the farm. A quick check by the *maquis* revealed that one of the petrol containers, fitted with red parachutes to facilitate identification and deter unwanted appropriation, had landed some way off the DZ in a cornfield and was lying in the open for all to see. Fortunately, it was hurriedly retrieved before the Storch picked it out.

pronounced ready for action. Engines roared into life and the convoy of four jeeps, along with the local vehicles already in use, turned left out of the DZ field onto a narrow farm road.

As they did so a storm of gunfire erupted. John Fielding was in the second jeep when he saw the one in front, driven by Trooper McLeod, swerve into a ditch and overturn. Recovering from their surprise, the SAS returned a withering fire at their unseen assailants, believed to be a German patrol. Feverishly they struggled to pull the crashed vehicle out with another jeep and had it righted again in a matter of moments. By a miracle no one was hit and the only injury was to Trooper O'Neill whose fingers had been crushed when the jeep pitched over. But as the SAS again sped off, the night's drama was not yet over as John Fielding recalls:

'We crossed the River Vienne and having got over the bridge, we arrived at a main road running north/south. Along this road there was a large German convoy and we laid up for a few minutes a few yards from the road and when a space occurred we drove straight through the middle of it, presumably much to the surprise of the Germans.'

Once more the SAS had dared and won. The convoy was again the *Das Reich*, the 2nd SS Panzer Division, still crawling northwards to Poitiers. It may well have been a patrol of the division which had been sent to investigate the DZ; the convoy would almost certainly have detected the aerial activity which lasted for three-quarters of an hour. But the Germans seemingly had no time to react to the SAS's desperate dash through their column and not a shot was fired.

On their return to base, the SAS carefully checked over their new transport. With additional fuel tanks, the American-built Willys jeeps had a range of some 700 miles and were fitted with the excellent and rapid-firing Vickers 'K' .303 machine gun. Proven in combat throughout the SAS's operations in North Africa and Italy, the rugged and speedy jeeps would enable Tonkin's men to range farther afield, yet would do little to lower the profile of the uniformed troopers. As the SAS were admiring their jeeps, Trooper O'Neill faced traumatic treatment for his crushed hand. While his comrades held his left hand behind his head so that he could not see, Corporal Allan swiftly amputated the two middle fingers with a pair of scissors.

The following day, 18 June, Tonkin reported the safe arrival of the jeeps. He was later to learn that this drop, and another the same night supplying four jeeps to the SAS 'Operation Dingson' team, had been the first operational test of the technique. Tonkin's radio message also noted that he had still to succeed in contacting Captain Sadoine and by now Tonkin was becoming increasingly puzzled by the non-appearance of the Phantom radio team. Having already made one unsuccessful foray to try to locate them, he began to suspect he was being deliberately mis-directed by the local *maquis* in Sadoine's area. As he had been warned, inter-*maquis* rivalry was well-known and if Sadoine had established good relations with the local *Résistance*, the latter might well have been jealously keeping the signals team to themselves, particularly if supply drops of arms were a reward.

But for the moment Tonkin had other concerns. Another change of plan had been radioed from England on the 19th informing him that it was not now necessary to locate a base for Major Lepine's group. At the same time it was clear that the Germans were becoming increasingly active in the area and therefore on the same day the SAS again made a precautionary move of camp some five kilometres south, near to Pouillac. Sam Smith was to recall this first daylight move with some amusement:

> 'Our first move was actually made in French single decker buses. I can remember this distinctly because the *maquis*, to impress us, were fairly bristling with weapons. At the start of the journey, windows were opened, machine guns thrust through and teeth bared. They looked very hostile until, in the heat of the midday sun, they all dropped off to sleep!'

From the new camp Tonkin immediately took one of the jeeps out and reached the Phantom operating base near Azat-le-Ris where at last he met Captain Sadoine. The latter proved to be a 23-year-old Belgian who had escaped to England at the time of the Dunkirk evacuation, 'Sadoine' being a *nom de guerre*. A radio fanatic, he had subsequently volunteered for Phantom where his specialist knowledge would be of greater use than in the Irish Guards, his original unit. Despite his lack of operational experience, his radio skills and fluency in both French and English should have stood 'Bulbasket' in great stead.

Yet Tonkin found that Sadoine had settled down into what was a seemingly peaceful existence, with more concern being shown over finding a decent local cook than supporting the SAS team. In marked contrast, the SAS troopers who had dropped with Sadoine had been impatient to begin operations. Sergeant Eccles and Corporal Bateman, two of the old hands, had taken an early aggressive lead by going out on the night of the 13th/14th to the branch line south of Sadoine's base. There Eccles showed great initiative in laying charges on the front wheels of a locomotive in the station at Le Dorat while Corporal Bateman destroyed the points just to the south. Not content with this excellent start, the two NCOs attacked the points again two nights later after repairs had been made. While the SAS men were therefore happy to see the arrival of Tonkin, and keen to join his main party, Sadoine still displayed a strange reluctance to follow Tonkin back, claiming simply that he was not yet ready to do so, despite having procured two cars locally to provide mobility.

Though Sadoine's hesitancy was irritating to Tonkin, the latter was nevertheless not over-concerned. Like Tonkin, Sadoine held the rank of Captain and the SAS officer therefore put the signaller's reluctance down to an unwillingness to come under the orders of someone, not only from another unit, but of no more than equal rank. Moreover, Tonkin could still rely on his own two-way radio operated by Corporal Chick and supported if the need arose by Troopers Adamson and Hill who were also trained signallers. He therefore regarded Sadoine and his radio operators to 'Bulbasket' as no more than a back-up to his own facilities. So far there had been no need for such back-up and so Tonkin, for the time being, shrugged off Sadoine's attitude and returned to the SAS main camp with Sergeant Eccles and four others – the maximum he could carry in the jeep. For the moment Bateman and two other SAS troopers remained with the Phantom team.

While Tonkin was relatively untroubled by Sadoine's attitude, SAS Brigade headquarters were showing considerably more concern over the whereabouts of the Phantom team. On 22 June Sadoine received a radio message from England, clearly instructing him to join Tonkin and, when he had still not appeared the next day, Tonkin sent Lieutenant Morris over to the signallers' camp. On arrival, Morris found Sadoine effectively 'pulling rank' on him and maintaining that he was still not ready to move. Exasperated, Morris returned with Bateman and his two troopers to report the situation to Tonkin.

Another reason for Tonkin's lack of concern over Sadoine was the pressing demands of operations. On the night of 20/21 June, Lieutenants Crisp and Stephens each took a party out to attack the 'Lot 2' line, Crisp near Laverré to the south of Poitiers and Stephens at St Cyr, to the north of the city. Both successfully cut the line while Crisp also destroyed a set of points. Tonkin himself spent the night on the DZ where a Stirling of 299 Squadron was awaited. 38 Group were now coordinating their SAS supply operations out of RAF Fairford so Flying Officer Stephens had to take his aircraft there from Keevil for briefing and loading of supplies. After an uneventful flight, he successfully dropped 24 containers on the DZ at 0245 hours.

The next day Tonkin had little opportunity to catch up on his sleep. Preparations had to be quickly made to organize the *maquis* when the Germans' 277th Infantry Division was reported to be moving through the area. The aim of harassing the division was thwarted since no contact was reported, but, only five kilometres away, enemy search parties were spotted closing on the SAS position. As soon as night fell a rapid move of 12 kilometres to the north was made and camp was set up near Persac, by the River Vienne. Once settled, Tonkin had a calculated risk to take.

When Trooper O'Neill was injured in the jeep accident Corporal Allan's amputation had only temporarily eased his suffering. Despite Maurice Dieudonné having arranged treatment by a doctor in Persac, gangrene had set in and it was obvious that more intensive care was needed if O'Neill were to survive. Consequently contact was made with Doctor Pichault in Jaunay-Clan, a northern suberb of Poitiers. Pichault courageously agreed to take O'Neill in and give him continous attention, despite the grave risk to himself and his family.

To get O'Neill to the 'Pontachard' clinic, Tonkin faced a hazardous journey through the outskirts of Poitiers. With a trooper to look after the injured driver and Dieudonné as guide, Tonkin safely negotiated the Poitiers streets without meeting any German patrols and was soon heading back after depositing O'Neill safely in the doctor's care. But Tonkin and Dieudonné had ideas other than returning straight to camp. On their way in, Tonkin had cut through Poitiers on the northern fringe of the city area and passed under the main Poitiers-Tours railway line via a very narrow road, south of the bend in the River Clain and about 700 yards north of the main railway station. Both Tonkin and Dieudonné agreed that it was too good a target to miss on their return:

> 'The embankment was about 12 feet above the road. As we got up on to it, we could see two figures skulking about 200 yards away towards the station on the railway line. They had obviously heard the jeep and seen us, but they made no threatening moves (maybe hoping we'd go away?) so we got on with the job. There were four main girders and we only had enough explosive to take out two of them, so we went for the inner two (both lines), put two five-minute time pencils on them, interconnected them with primacord and took off fast. We heard the bang just as we cleared Poitiers. We took a different route home and I'm sure that we also damaged (with what little explosive was left) one rail and girder on a rail over a large ditch on the Poitiers-Châteauroux line.'

It was later reported that the damage on the bridge in Poitiers had taken two days to repair, but the two attacks led to difficulties for Tonkin. On the way back the Germans had thrown up a number of road blocks, causing enough detours and delays to result in dawn breaking while the SAS were still some way from camp. With so much enemy activity on the roads, Tonkin dared not continue in daylight so the party hid up in a wood all the next day until cover of darkness enabled them to complete their journey back to camp.

Back in camp, a result of Tonkin's enforced absence was that another resupply drop had been missed. On the night of the 22nd/23rd another Stirling of 299 Squadron had arrived over the DZ but Flying Officer Harris reluctantly abandoned the resupply drop of containers when he could spot no evidence of a ground reception party.

This proved to be the beginning of a series of missed supply drops which would prove costly for the SAS. From remaining records, it seems that not only did the RAF encounter difficulties in locating DZs but that confusion often reigned in the arrangements for such drops. On both the night of the 23rd/24th and the 24th/25th a Stirling was obliged to abandon a container resupply drop due to no evidence of a ground reception party on the DZ, yet the SAS operational record makes no mention that a drop was expected and it would therefore seem to be another example of poor planning or inadequate liaison between the SAS and RAF back in England. Indeed, on the 23rd/24th Tonkin was again committed to operations in personally attacking the railway at Fleuré, mid-way between Poitiers and Lussac, which he successfully blew. The *maquis* later reported a train halted at the spot.

Railway attacks were now being carried out repeatedly and simultaneously by small parties of the SAS roaming the countryside more or less at will in their jeeps. Lieutenant Stephens' party was still at large following their 'Lot 2' attack north of Poitiers on the 20th/21st and a team led by Sergeant Jessiman had been out by 'Lot 1' for a number of days, cutting the line in two places south-west of Eguzon during the night of the 22nd/23rd. On the 24th/25th Trooper Smith blew a rail junction near Montmorillon, not far from the bridge damaged by Stephens on the night of the main party's drop, while Sergeant Holmes led a party against 'Lot 2' south of Poitiers. After unsuccessfully waiting to attempt to derail a train, Holmes fell back on simpler methods and cut the line near Vaintray.

Tonkin again moved the main SAS camp on the 25th as a precaution against location by the enemy and established a site in the Forêt de Verrières, to the west of the Poitiers-Limoges road. Albert Dupont, the FFI's interpreter attached to Tonkin, now returned to Colonel Chêne's headquarters which had moved further south to the Château de la Combe, near Adriers. The new

SAS camp was in the opposite direction and as such caused some concern. While still within easy reach of the DZ at la Font d'Usson, the Verrières site was some 15 kilometres further north-east from the Persac camp and was only 25 kilometres from the German forces in Poitiers. Perhaps as a result, enemy jamming of Tonkin's radio transmissions was immediately encountered. With hindsight, it is tempting to suggest that the SAS were over confident, but it must be borne in mind that by now supplies were running low and access to the DZ was a priority. So too was an adequate water supply and the camp at Verrières was located on a gently sloping site which ran down into a valley where there was a stream of clear, fresh water. Tonkin was not unaware of the possible dangers, but when he attempted to look for a new DZ on the 27th he was restricted by enemy movements in the general area.

On 28 June the camp's numbers were swollen by the arrival of more SAS troopers from the now overdue 'Lot' parties. Presumed lost due to a parachute malfunction, Trooper Brown of Lieutenant Morris' party had in fact merely landed some distance away from the others. Unable to find his comrades, he had set off on his own to reach the main party but had the good fortune to be picked up by a local *maquis* group and was passed on to Colonel Chêne's headquarters where Captain Maingard of the SOE arranged for him to reach Tonkin at Verrières.

With Brown also came the 'Lot' parties of Corporal Kinnevane and Lieutenant Weaver. Both groups had been dropped blind in the early hours of 11 June and should have landed on adjoining DZs in order to attack the 'Lot 4' railway line which ran from Niort to Saumur. From the very start things had gone badly wrong for Kinnevane and his two men. Disastrously, all three had landed in the middle of the square at Airvault, a small town close to the 'Lot 4' line. Unfortunately the town suffered from a German garrison and the three SAS men came under heavy fire the moment they landed. Compelled to abandon all their explosives and equipment in order to escape, Kinnevane and one other soldier were eventually able to meet up again in the countryside thanks to assistance from the local *maquis*. But of Trooper Biffin there was no sign and it was later reported that he had been wounded and taken prisoner.

While surviving records do not make it clear, Kinnevane's companion in reaching Tonkin's main group was probably Trooper Joseph Ogg, who was certainly in one of the 'Lot' parties. Another former Auxiliary, Ogg hailed from a farming background in Morayshire, Scotland. Keen to play an active part in the war, he had first joined his local Home Guard before transferring to 101 Battalion, the Auxiliary Unit formation. There he was trained in behind-the-lines guerrilla warfare and taught to handle explosives and carry out sabotage. Despite his Auxiliary Unit service, and the possibility of claiming a reserved occupation as a farm tractor driver, Joe was impatient for a more active rôle and subsequently responded readily when called up into the Royal Artillery.

In his initial general training Ogg quickly became friends with a fellow Scot from a similar farming environment, James Robertson. Joining a field regiment in Yorkshire, the two adventurous young men still found life dull and immediately put in for a transfer to mountain artillery. To their disappointment, their request was turned down, but then, out of the blue in early 1944 came the expanding SAS's approach to former Auxiliaries. Ogg and Robertson travelled to London for tests which only 60% passed, their experience of living off the land and knowledge of explosives ensuring that the two Scots succeeded. SAS training at Darvel took them back to Scotland and from there they progressed to the parachute course at Ringway near Manchester. There fate served to part the two friends. Injuring his knee in training, Robertson had to go first to hospital and then back to Darvel without completing the course. Ogg, meanwhile, successfully finished the parachute training and when he again met up with Robertson back at Darvel, he proudly displayed the coveted and distinctive SAS parachute wings on his sleeve.[1] Towards the end of April, when the Regiment moved into the secure tented camp at RAF Fairford, Robertson had still been unable to retake the course and so was unable to take part in the parachute operations planned for the SAS. Shortly after D-Day he was therefore left behind when Ogg came to see him in high spirits to say cheerio to his friend. Without knowing too many details, he was to be parachuted into France immediately. It was to be the last the two young Scots ever saw of each other.

Lieutenant Peter Weaver had fared little better than Kinnevane when his party landed some 25 kilometres west of where they were supposed to attack 'Lot 4'. But with determination characteristic of the SAS in general, Weaver was not to be put off his task.

At 32 years of age, he was older than the majority of his contemporaries and possessed rather more experience of life than most. Born at Kalimpong in the Himalayas, his father had been a regular Indian Army officer and was killed in Mesopotamia during the First World War. Returning to England with his mother, the young Weaver had struggled at public school due to

---

[1] Upon completion of an operation behind enemy lines, SAS troops were permitted to wear their parachute wings on the left breast of their uniform, rather than on the sleeve.

dyslexia but had excelled at sport. After school, he had followed a chequered career throughout the 1930s, firstly with a paper manufacturer and then trying a variety of small businesses, none of which kept his attention for long. He sampled army life as a private soldier in the Royal Tank Regiment but eventually bought himself out in 1934. Throughout, he continued his passion for sport, captaining England at hockey and playing cricket for Hampshire. Never able to settle in a job for long, the war came as something of a relief by providing a focal point for his energies. In 1937 he had enlisted in the Territorial Royal Engineers which led to his call-up in 1939. He was then commissioned into the Dorset Regiment before being posted to another of the secret Auxiliary Units. In late 1943 he and many of his men took up the offer to volunteer for the expanding SAS and he joined B Squadron after a narrow escape during parachute training when the aircraft in which he was taking off collided with another which had just landed.

Thus it was that Weaver, with three men from his old Auxiliary Unit, landed to the west of Parthenay at 0230 hours on the morning of 11 June, almost 90 kilometres from Tonkin and the main party. Weaver himself enjoyed a good landing and quickly contacted his number two who had like-wise landed safely nearby. Numbers three and four of the group were hung up in trees, but after a half hour's struggle all were ready to set off and had hidden their parachutes in dense undergrowth. Stubbornly, Weaver had refused to go into action with the new red beret of the airborne forces in general and as he landed, he had pulled out the unique beige-coloured SAS beret and determinedly crammed it on his head. It was to stay there throughout 'Bulbasket' and in photographs taken during the operation clearly distinguishes Weaver.

His party was equipped with pistols, a one-way radio receiver and explo-sives, but no food supplies. They were told that they would have to live off the land, yet none of the party spoke any French and they had been instructed to communicate with the locals only in an emergency. Realizing they were still far from their target, they hid up throughout the next day then marched all night towards the railway. As dawn broke at 0400 hours on the 13th they heard the sound of a train, but daylight deterred them from taking imme-diate action. Again they took cover throughout the day, keeping the line under observation from a cornfield just 100 metres away while a farmer harvested all around them. Four trains passed during the day, suggesting a good chance of a derailment. As night fell and the farmer departed, the four SAS men cautiously emerged, slipped down to the line and laid their charges. Withdrawing a few hundred metres, they waited several hours but by 0300 hours no train movements had occurred and they moved back to another hide-out before dawn broke. At 1000 hours an approaching train was heard in the distance, followed shortly by an explosion. Much shouting ensued and the hiss of escaping steam from the derailed train. Satisfied, Weaver and his men then set off south-eastwards to find Tonkin.

They marched for ten nights, growing increasingly hungry. Occasionally they would halt for an hour or so and each would forage in a different direction, but with little luck. They eked out their twenty-four hour ration packs for four days but eventually there was no option but to make cautious contact with isolated farms. Not once did the local people refuse food to their nocturnal visitors. Once, moving through a wood, the SAS were startled to hear American voices and came across a major and a sergeant in American uniforms, sitting alone in a clearing and surrounded by an enormous stock of weapons and equipment, radio gear, food and money. They had been sent to supply the *Résistance*, but had yet to make contact with any local representatives. The Americans even asked if the British would like to take some of the money but Weaver reluctantly declined and the British continued on their way.

At last they reached their pre-arranged rendezvous near Montmorillon on 24 June, only to find no sign of Tonkin and the main party. Fortunately, a friendly farmer undertook to help them and alerted the local 'Gilles' *maquis* group. In no time at all a car bursting with heavily armed *maquisards* arrived and the SAS were whisked off to a nearby village where they were greeted joyously as conquering heroes. Wine flowed freely, pretty girls queued to kiss them and food appeared from every house. Weaver was worried at the lack of caution shown, but was reassured when told that all the Germans were in Poitiers. From the village the SAS were then taken to the *maquis* camp where they found the French had weapons, but little idea what to do with them. For three days Weaver and his men trained the *maquisards* until they realized that their hosts were keeping their British visitors to themselves while denying knowledge of any other soldiers. The SAS therefore had to insist upon being taken to Tonkin's camp and, though the *maquisards* reluctantly agreed, they decided to attack on the way a café used by the Germans. Packed into several cars, the *maquisards* led the way in festival spirit. When they reached the café, Weaver was greatly relieved to find it empty and they continued on to Verrières without further excitement.

Weaver and Kinnevane reached Verrières to find Tonkin still busy with dispatching sabotage teams and even the group's normally reliable radio log struggled to keep up with events. Only two days after his railway attacks on 'Lot 1' Sergeant Jessiman was reported mining the N10 road south of Vivonne and close to the 'Lot 2' line. On the night of the 28th it was the turn of Sergeant Eccles and Corporal Bateman to maintain the offensive but their target, the points in the marshalling yards at Saint Benoît, involved a calculated risk. The village lay just on the southern outskirts of Poitiers itself and, since the points were at a crucial junction leading into the city, and had already once been the subject of sabotage by the *maquis*, it was a reasonable assumption that the nearby German forces were taking measures to guard the area. Nevertheless, after their success in the station at Le Dorat, Eccles and Bateman were confident that they could evade any sentries. Sadly, their optimism was to prove unfounded.

Shortly after seven o'clock on the morning of 29 June General Curt Gallenkamp, 80th Corp's commanding General, was sleeping peacefully in his requisitioned quarters, the elegant villa 'L'Ermitage'. With the remains of a Roman aqueduct in its grounds, the house was beautifully sited overlooking the gorge at Saint Benoît through which ran the railway lines into Poitiers.

Much of the German Army's authority in the area came under Gallenkamp's control, since 80th Corps had its headquarters in Poitiers. The Corps had its origins in the 31st Corps command which had seen service in Poland, Denmark and then the Western Front in 1940. It had remained in France since then, its tactical headquarters first based at Biarritz but moved to Poitiers by the time General Gallenkamp took command in April, 1942. The Corps was responsible for security duties in an area stretching on the Atlantic coast from the Loire in the north to the Gironde in the south. Inland, the rear boundary was along the line Nantes-Niort-Saintes and this meant that, unusually, the Corps HQ in Poitiers were about 100 kilometres outside the Corps' area of responsibility. This was in order to take advantage of better communication links with OB-West (HQ Western Front) in Paris and therefore resulted in 80th Corps HQ lodging within the jurisdiction of the Poitiers *Feldkommandantur,* the sub-area HQ representing the military commander of south-western France.

The latter headquarters, commanded by *Oberst* Haugk, were responsible for policing the Poitiers region, chiefly involving anti-*maquis* duties. These had not been as exacting as could be expected in more mountainous districts, where the terrain lent itself more easily to guerrilla warfare, but nevertheless sabotage and attacks had been steadily increasing. The local *Résistance* forces had already co-operated for some years with the SOE's agents who, in turn, arranged for weapons and explosives to be dropped. With these arms the *maquis* bands, particularly those of the communist FTP, had stepped up their offensive operations in the Vienne throughout the spring of 1944 to the extent that the occupying forces rarely ventured out of the major towns unless in considerable strength. Remaining records testify to the effectiveness of the *maquis'* operations with evidence that 80th Corps' medical officers no longer dared to make fishing trips outside Poitiers by June, 1944.

In addition to 80th Corps' headquarters, Poitiers was also the base for two reserve security divisions, the 708th and the 158th, both largely up to strength but with around 15% of foreign 'volunteers'. According to local French sources, these included Cossacks of Vlassov's army which had fought alongside the Germans on the Russian front, and Indians of the 950th Indian Regiment. Only 40% could be said to be fully trained, the balance being made up of young recruits and rear echelon non-combatant troops. In total, therefore, the Poitiers area boasted some 60,000 enemy troops. From these, and local *Milice* forces, the enemy had created '*Unité 602*' and '*Unité 608*', two mobile, fast-reaction 'repression columns', also known as '*Sections Rapides*', which were to encounter numerous actions against the *maquis* to the east and south of Poitiers. Normally such actions were at the request of the *Sicherheitsdienst* (SD), the feared Security Police of the SS, whose headquarters were at 13 rue des Ecossais in Poitiers. If an additional hard core of troops were required for difficult operations, call could also be made on one of the German Reich's most fanatical fighting forces, the *Waffen* (Fighting) SS. The 17th SS *Panzergrenadier* (Infantry) Division, the *Götz von Berlichingen*, had been based to the north-east of Poitiers at Châtellerault and Bonneuil-Matours and, while the Division's main fighting units had immediately headed north after D-Day for the Normandy beachhead, the recruits' depot remained in Bonneuil-Matours. If needed, 200 to 300 SS troops could therefore be depended upon.

As senior German officer in the area, the 54-year-old Gallenkamp was an experienced and respected officer of the regular *Wehrmacht*. Many of 80th Corps' personnel came from the Württemburg region of Germany, among them its Chief of Staff, the 41-year-old *Oberst* Herbert Koestlin and *Hauptmann* Dr Erich Schönig, the headquarters' Senior Intelligence Officer. This helped to knit the officers together as a team and, while the Corps lacked truly first class fighting formations, its headquarters staff would seem to have been as established and capable as the General could have wished.

On the morning of 29 June, however, General Gallenkamp's slumbers and the complacency of his headquarters were rudely disrupted by two large explosions. Dressing quickly and expecting to learn of yet another *maquis* attack, Gallenkamp was startled to hear that the explosions were the work of British 'commandos' in nearby marshalling yards. Better news was that those responsible had been captured.

Following normal operating procedures, when Eccles and Bateman had been taken to St Benoît by their driver, the trooper stood off to guard the jeep while the two NCOs approached the line. There they obviously succeeded in laying charges on the main points since loud explosions shattered the early morning calm. Yet neither of the two returned and the jeep driver left on guard had no option but to return to Verrières, expressing hope that the two had been taken prisoner due to the absence of any gunfire.

The trooper's hope was valid. Soon after placing their charges on the line, Eccles and Bateman had run into the sentries of the 80th Corps Signals Detachment, based in the village. Caught by surprise, they could only raise their hands in surrender and were quickly taken to 80th Corps headquarters. While the capture was reported to General Gallenkamp, *Hauptmann* Schönig, of the Corps' Intelligence section, began questioning the two SAS men. Schönig was later to describe the occasion:

'These men were brought before me for interrogation. They were said to be Englishmen. As I myself do not speak English, the interrogation was carried out by my interpreter, *Sonderführer* Hönigschmidt. The men were without headgear, they did not wear any badges of rank or any other military insignia, but they had a kind of paybook as identification. The colour of the overalls was, as far as I remember, grey-green. Below the overalls the men wore khaki coloured shirts and khaki coloured trousers. The interrogation lasted only a short while, as the parachutists refused to make other statements beyond their name, rank and unit. To support their refusal, they referred to the Geneva Convention which did not permit them to make a further statement. I therefore had the interrogation broken off and ordered cigarettes and coffee to be offered to them. The only result of the interrogation was that these men were SAS men. Their mission was to blow up the railway line.'

Schönig reported the result of the interrogation both to *Oberst* Koestlin and to General Gallenkamp while the the prisoners were taken from Corps headquarters and secured in the cells of the Poitiers *Feldkommandantur*. The following day, 30 June, *Sonderführer* Hönigschmidt visited the *Feldkommandantur* to attempt a second interrogation but returned without success. As experienced veterans, the two NCOs knew that their silence should buy their comrades time to move camp. They would have been aware that Tonkin had already tried once to leave Verrières on the 27th and it was therefore only likely to be a short matter of time before the main party moved on.

With the permission of Koestlin, 80th Corps now handed over the questionning of the two prisoners to the SD, the SS Security Police. The SD were interested in the matter since it was a case of sabotage and it was Schönig who notified them of the situation and of his Chief of Staff's agreement that the SD could take over the interrogations. For Eccles and Bateman the ordeal was about to begin.

4

VERRIÈRES

By the end of June Tonkin and his men had been in France for up to three weeks. At night they reconnoitred the area or sent out small teams to sabotage rail targets, often 35 kilometres or more away.

Of the officers, Twm Stephens had scored an early personal success by his pin-pointing of the petrol trains at Châtellerault and he had then continued to operate aggressively against railway targets. Operating from the camp near Nérignac, he had carried out two such attacks in a single sortie which lasted some ten days, his party's return not having been made any easier by the main group's move to Verrières on the 25th during his absence. Reported overdue to England, Stephens nevertheless caught up and found the new camp on 1 July.

The taciturn South African Lieutenant Morris, who had carried out one of the successful 'Lot' railway attacks, quickly joined up with the main party and then proved a major asset in another field. Faced with an overwhelming amount of radio traffic, John Tonkin had found Morris the best administrator and organizer for managing the radio work.

Lieutenant Peter Weaver, dropped way off target, had been delayed in joining the main party but had nevertheless derailed at least one train on the way and had done wonders for the morale and fighting enthusiasm of the *maquis* group he had stumbled acoss.

Last, but not least, Lieutenant Richard Crisp, the young officer known for his quiet concern and sensitivity, had established his reputation as the group's road-mining expert. He had developed a technique of spreading dirt across the road at intervals, compelling the enemy to stop and sweep constantly after the first explosion. If the location were suitable, a long burst of Vickers 'K' machine-gun fire from a jeep added to the enemy convoy's discomfort before Crisp and his men withdrew.

Tonkin's NCOs were as active as their officers, the Sergeants and Corporals all being relied upon to lead sabotage parties just as effectively. But for the remainder of the men, many of whom did not go out on the sabotage operations, the greatest problem was the boredom of life in the camps. With only four jeeps, no more than sixteen or so men could be out on operations at any one time and although Tonkin had already requested five more vehicles to be dropped, Brigade had not responded. Tonkin was also later to acknowledge that he had been slow to appreciate the initiative and ability of the ordinary troopers, relying too frequently on the efforts of the officers and NCOs only. The others therefore had little to occupy their energies. They ate their own tinned steak and kidney puddings which, despite their cook's claims, did not taste different if cooked on their end, rather than on their side. Variety only came with local food supplied via the *maquis*.

So generally the men relaxed around the camp area for much of their time, chatting to their French helpers in fragmented English or French and trading soap for local tobacco. The latter, rolled in army issue toilet paper, provided a steady, if foul-tasting, supply of cigarettes. Trooper John Fielding found that regular shaving and cleaning his teeth helped maintain his morale, he and Sam Smith having gone equipped with a tube of toothpaste and a shaving stick. The war and the invasion at times seemed a million miles away, but it was thought that it would only be a few weeks before the advancing allied armies overran them. One of the few reliefs to boredom came when the BBC broadcast their daily coded messages to the party. As the preceding jingle of a few bars of 'Sur Le Pont d'Avignon' came over the airwaves, it became standard practice for everyone to leap to their feet and jive to the tune, waggling one finger in the air as they did so.

John Tonkin himself went out repeatedly to attack the railways, but as a result was becoming very tired. The size of the group required him to spend most of the daylight hours in camp, keeping a grip on the logistical and re-supply demands. At night long hours were spent on the DZs, often fruitlessly due to a combination of difficulties. Consequently the SAS missed several of their supply drops and this meant that the jeeps were always short of petrol and even explosives stocks ran low.

Of even greater concern to Tonkin was the ever-present possibility of discovery by the enemy. He was always aware of the dangers of remaining too long in one place, where informers or German radio direction-finding might pinpoint the camp. But there was also a need to remain within easy reach of suitable DZs for supply drops and to find camp sites with an adequate water supply. The summer of 1944 proved to be one of the driest for many years, with drought conditions throughout the region. For anything up to seventy men, a constant supply of fresh water was therefore a major concern.

The Verrières camp thus held a number of attractions. Reasonably close to the DZ at la Font d'Usson, the forest of young trees also had a pleasant stream running through it, guaranteeing the all-important water supply. But the SAS had been there since 25 June and Tonkin was beginning to feel uneasy. There was still no sign or word of Eccles and Bateman and it therefore had to be acknowledged there was the possibility they had been captured and made to reveal the camp's whereabouts. There was also worse news, revealed by Jean Dieudonné when Tonkin returned from an urgently requested call to Maingard's headquarters on 1 July. Apparently news of the SAS camp had reached local people in the village of Verrières and a number of young women, looking for a hint of adventure, had sought out the camp in the forest to try to get to know the brave young Englishmen who had come to fight for them. Angrily, Dieudonné had mounted a *maquis* guard and forbade any visitors. Undeterred, however, two or three of the SAS troopers had taken advantage of Tonkin's absence to stroll into the village for a drink in the bar there, hoping to pursue friendships with the local girls. Dieudonné was furious and wasted no time in warning Tonkin that news of the SAS would inevitably soon reach the Germans.

Other events added to Tonkin's unease. Firstly, a man from a nearby hamlet came to warn the *maquis* of a suspect car seen several times touring the area of the forest and Verrières village. It was thought that this might be a radio-direction finding vehicle, although no mention was made of the aerials or antennae which would have been necessary for this purpose. Secondly, a downed American pilot was brought into the camp by the *maquis* on 1 July. Introducing himself as Lieutenant Lincoln Bundy of the 486th Squadron, 352nd Fighter Group, the flyer had a ready story of how his Mustang fighter had been shot down by *flak*. He had then been picked up by the *Résistance* and passed from *maquis* to *maquis* until he had reached Verrières, but the SAS were suspicious of the circumstances and, fearing a German 'plant', immediately radioed to London to check the American's identity.

To guard against what was now deemed a probability that the Germans knew something of the activity in the forest, a decision was made to move and early on 2 July a new base was set up just a few kilometres to the south, in the Bois des Cartes.

The reason for not moving further from Verrières was that Tonkin was expecting a critical re-supply drop on the night of 3/4 July, including another

Eureka set, promised in a radio message from England on the 30th. He did not therefore wish to move too far from the DZ at la Font d'Usson. But even the new camp did little to make the SAS feel safer. During the day of the 2nd a German aircraft dropped leaflets over the area, urging the *maquis* fighters to give themselves up to the German authorities in Poitiers, with a promise that no harm would come to them. While the *maquis* knew better than to accept this promise and laughed off the invitation, Tonkin and Dieudonné were nevertheless concerned that the Germans were showing so much interest in the area. Worse still was the all-consuming issue of water supply. One of the attractions of the Bois des Cartes had been the discovery of an old well among the trees, but when the SAS set up camp there, the well dried up after the first few buckets were drawn.

Reviewing their options, Tonkin and Dieudonné took into account that it was now over two days since Eccles and Bateman had disappeared and there had as yet been no direct German reaction. It was a risk, but the decision was made to return temporarily to Verrières and its abundant supply of fresh water until Tonkin found another site. At most, their return was expected to last no more than a day.

But Dieudonné had been right to fear that the Germans knew about Verrières. Even as the SAS moved back to the forest, German troops in Poitiers were mobilizing quickly with the express purpose of dealing with 'Bulbasket'.

The SS Security Police, the SD, already had information that the SAS camp was somewhere in the Forêt de Verrières and on 1 July had sent their agents to the area to pinpoint the camp's location. Almost certainly, these were the two men who ran into one of the SAS sentries, Trooper John Fielding, on the edge of the forest:

> 'I was on guard at the junction of the road and the track leading into the forest during daylight, presumably some time during the middle of the day, when I saw a motorcycle and side car being pushed down the incline towards me, along the road, by two *maquis* with black berets. They arrived at the track and I laid low for a few minutes. I then showed myself and started talking to them. They explained to me that they had got a puncture in the wheel of the side car and after consideration I then took them up the track to the base where John Tonkin saw them and the necessary repairs were carried out. They spent some time at the base.'

When questioned by Dieudonné and his men, the visitors announced themselves to be of another *maquis* group and answered all the testing questions put to them. They were permitted to leave.

If these two men were in reality the SD's agents, then it was they who quickly reported back to Poitiers. *SS-Obersturmführer* Hoffmann, the SD's acting second in command and responsible for operations, immediately began to gather a force to mount an attack.

Hoffmann did not have much to call on by way of fighting men but nonetheless managed to assemble a scratch force of about four hundred troops. The main component was the 17th SS *Panzergrenadier* Division's holding battalion, based at Bonneuil-Matours, while other troops came from the Poitiers *Feldkommandantur*, a number of radio units and a Reconnaissance Bicycle Squadron of the 158th Security Division. The squadron, under the command of *Oberleutnant* Vogt, was attached temporarily to 80th Corps HQ to provide resources for anti-*maquis* operations such as the SD now planned at Verrières. Together, Hoffmann of the SD, *Oberst* Koestlin of 80th Corps and *Oberleutnant* Vogt of the Bicycle Squadron made their plans for an assault on Verrières.

In the forest John Tonkin was still anxious to find another camp location as soon as possible. On the evening of the 2nd he therefore went out searching for a suitable site but soon after he returned in the early morning, disaster struck. Hoffmann's force had stealthily crept forward under cover of darkness to ring the area and, either by fortune or because the Germans cannily permitted it, Tonkin had probably passed right through the enemy's cordon without detecting it.

In the quiet of the forest camp forty of the SAS party, the American flyer Bundy and nine of the 'Amilcar' *maquisards* slept unsuspectingly. In the early hours of the morning Dieudonné had been briefly awoken by the sound of vehicle engines, but thinking it was a replenishment party returning, and being so tired, he immediately fell asleep again. Some of his men were soon to find the true significance of the noises.

Denis Chansigaud recalls that Maurice Salmoni, known as 'Pierrot Le Corse', left the camp at around six o'clock that morning to return a wheelbarrow which he had borrowed from a nearby village. It is thought that he was therefore the first to be captured by the Germans, taken by surprise and without the enemy having to open fire. There is local conjecture that Salmoni was also forced to confirm the camp's precise location. Whatever the circumstances, the Germans' element of surprise was not to last much longer. An hour later at the most, two more of Dieudonné's men, Pierre Lecellier and Marcel Weber, sprang the trap.

The two *maquisards* had been part of a group which had gone into

65

Verrières the previous evening to obtain supplies. Lecellier and Weber were friendly with a couple of local girls and were given the opportunity of spending the night in the village. They readily accepted and warned their returning comrades to expect their return to camp at around seven o' clock the following morning. Marcel Weber would never forget that morning of Monday, 3 July, 1944:

'Towards 7 o'clock in the morning, coming from Verrières with my comrade, Pierre Lecellier, we arrived within sight of the village close to our camp. We were in civilian clothes . . . suddenly, forty metres ahead and on the right, I noticed something strange. The bushes themselves seemed to move. I stopped and at that moment a German soldier, camouflaged with foliage, stood up and shouted to us in German, 'Surrender, you are surrounded'. Quickly and together, we drew our weapons, but at the same moment behind us six other German soldiers showed themselves. They had let us go by them and they shouted at us to stop or they would open fire.

'Pierre ran towards the village and in among the houses there. From then on I didn't see him again. I turned back and, with the Germans firing at me, went round the village. There were Germans in the houses in the village and they fired on me from the windows. I ran down a street and into the middle of a group of them. One grabbed me by the neck but I struggled free by elbowing him in the stomach. He let me go and with some difficulty I ran off through the shrubbery opposite. The Germans continued to shoot at me and now that I was discovered I made towards the camp, zig-zagging as I ran. I felt a strong burning sensation in my right thigh and soon the sensation of blood flowing – I had just been 'winged' by a bullet. I continued despite the pain and reached the camp where I found my comrades standing ready with their weapons, having been alerted by the firing of the Germans. I ran through the middle of them and shouted 'Look out! The Germans are coming! I've just lost Pierre and I'm wounded.' I went on and lay down among a group of the SAS. A lieutenant, with the aid of the medical orderly, made me a wound dressing.'

The SAS had been caught completely by surprise as John Tonkin related:

'My memory says we were attacked at dawn, but my report says 7.00 am. I don't know what time dawn was. What is for sure is that

I was asleep in my sleeping bag when the first shells and mortars landed.

'Of course, as soon as the first explosions occurred, everyone was alert. There was Schmeisser fire coming from the open fields to the north of us. I had better explain that we were camped on the northern edge of the forest (too grand a name for the thin small tree cover that was there) above a little valley that had permanent water. The site was chosen because it also had access for vehicles from four directions roughly at 90 degrees.

'I think it was Peter Weaver and I plus Dieudonné who went to the northern edge of the forest. I could see a considerable number of German troops working their way towards us along the hedgerows, but still some 200 yards away. I was pretty certain they were trying to drive us into a trap. We went back to the men, who were being organized by Lieutenants Stephens and Crisp into small groups led by an officer or an NCO. I told them all to follow our rehearsed procedure of scattering *into* the forest to the west, in ones and twos (it was a very large area) and to conceal themselves. It was pointless to try to fight our way out as a group; I *can* remember considering using the Vickers 'K' on the three jeeps and then deciding that scattering quietly was our best bet.'

Sleeping just a few metres from the SAS party, the *maquis* group were likewise caught unprepared, though some of them had woken to the rattle of machine-gun fire as Lecellier and Weber stumbled into the Germans. Almost immediately, however, mortar bombs crashed down into the forest as the Germans attacked before their element of surprise was completely lost.

Grabbing their weapons, the *maquis* crouched in the undergrowth but could initially see nothing out of the ordinary. Then, only about 15 metres away, the forest growth itself seemed to move and the Frenchmen realized they were looking at a dozen or so German troops moving stealthily forward, their camouflage-pattern uniforms covered with ferns and small branches. The *maquis* opened fire and the Germans went to ground, immediately returning a deadly fusillade in the general direction of the French. The latter slipped away and regrouped with their leader Dieudonné in time to confront another party of Germans. This time the French threw grenades before again melting away into the woods towards the stream. As they did so, Marcel Weber dashed through them, dragging his wounded leg but still moving rapidly nevertheless. Behind him came Corporal Allan, the SAS group's medical orderly, clearly identifiable by his red cross arm band and apparently intent on catching and treating Weber.

The *maquisards* now looked to Dieudonné for their orders and joined the SAS group who, assembled into some form of order, were awaiting Tonkin's commands. But tragically, at that very moment, one of the SAS troopers suddenly dashed through the assembled group in headlong flight, half naked and shouting, 'They're coming, they're coming!' In an instant the man's panic was transmitted to the others and the majority broke, running after him. Aghast, Tonkin realized he must act quickly:

'A large body of both *Résistance* and S.A.S. went *down* the slope into the valley. That was the worst thing to do, so I shouted for Weaver, Crisp and Stephens (I think) to go after them. That was the last I saw of them. Of the remainder, Sergeant Johnny Holmes and Corporal Rideout each stood firm with two men, as did McNair. Corporal Allan was tending a trooper wounded by a mortar splinter. I cannot remember whether it was then or later that we put some time pencils in some of the canisters of explosives. Then we all went off westwards *into* the forest. We had not gone far when I remembered that I hadn't seen Corporal Chick (our R/T operator) take the main Sabu 4 code book, and the transmitter was still there unharmed. I told the others to push on and went back. Dieudonné said he would come with me but I said one was better and he kept going. I couldn't find the book. As I turned to leave I could see that the Germans had entered the forest in two prongs either side of me and I was cut off because the only other way was down into the valley, which was overlooked and open. So I sat down in some rough ground a little way down the slope and about 50 yards from the camp. The cover was very thin, so, being in my camouflaged jumping jacket, I sat down with my back to a rock, my face in front of some white lichen and kept *very* still, and only just in time, for a German, armed with a Schmeisser, came into full view on the top edge of the slope, not more than forty yards away, and looking straight over the top of me at the far side. There was heavy machine-gun and Schmeisser fire the other side of the valley. The nearby German then moved back to the camp site and joined the others that I could hear there, so I moved quietly along the slope to the west, *into* the forest. My impression for all these years is that I was by that rock for several hours, but it could only have been ten minutes or so.'

Peter Weaver had watched helplessly as his section joined the main body of men in running downhill towards the eastern boundary of the forest. At Tonkin's order, and in company with Stephens and Crisp, he then set off after them and caught up as they reached the edge of the woods. As they cautiously moved out from the cover of the trees, heavy automatic fire opened up from across the open fields ahead and there was no option but to turn back into the tree line. Crossing the small valley of the stream, the men stumbled along the southern bank, still reluctant to scatter and preferring to seek safety in numbers. After only a short distance they reached the Verrières road and made a rush across it, tensing for the enemy fire which they expected would be covering the spot. But as luck would have it, they had reached the road where it twisted and dipped slightly to cross the stream. The Germans had indeed covered both ends of the road with heavy machine guns but the SAS unwittingly crossed in the enemy's only blind spot. For the moment they were safe.

At the far side of the road the men doubled back among the trees and again headed eastwards, towards Verrières. Once more they reached the edge of the woods but again the enemy were waiting for them with blistering fire power. Back they turned again, now beginning to sense that the Germans had prepared their trap well. On their left lay the southern edge of the trees and corn fields, but any move from the woods brought down devastating fire. The main body of the forest now lay ahead and westwards, but the Germans seemed to be lying in wait there too. Again the stream was crossed but the enemy was clearly ahead. It was realized that only small groups might stand a chance of slipping through the net and Lieutenant Crisp turned back to cross the road again with one party. Their previous good fortune now became apparent, for as they dashed out of the trees they were in the line of fire of the enemy machine-gun posts and Crisp fell wounded with a bullet in his thigh. Watching this failure, Lieutenants Stephens and Weaver led another group back to the south-eastern edge. Still the enemy's fire waited for them to emerge from the woods and, feeling there was little that could now be done to escape, Weaver advised splitting up.

In a crouching run, he tried to head westwards for the depths of the forest but, soon after he set off, he came upon a line of Germans sweeping through the trees towards him. With no other choice, he turned out of the woods and crawled away into the corn field. The enemy opened fire and bullets ripped through the corn just above his head. Behind him, another small party was flushed out of the woods and started across the field but were halted as mortar shells crashed down amongst them, badly wounding Trooper Pascoe. Taking advantage of this diversion, Weaver managed to cross the remainder of the field and dashed into the cover of some trees at the far side, albeit with the Germans' fire still in hot pursuit. Jumping a stile, he came across a small water course and paused for a second to slake his thirst. Refreshed, he then chose a thick thorn bush and scrambled into the centre. Pistol in hand, he lay there until night fell and it began to rain. Emerging from his cover, he crawled across a field and suddenly found himself confronted by a large dog. Making off as fast as he could, Weaver again found cover and, exhausted, fell asleep.

Clearly there had been almost total confusion when the majority of the men stampeded down the hill to where the Germans were waiting for them. Only those who made a dash for safety uphill, away from the stream in the same manner as Tonkin, also escaped. Tonkin counted himself fortunate to have got away:

> 'There were still bursts of firing for quite a time, but I think that was probably the Germans trying to flush us out without knowing where we were. I think that all who were caught or killed were in the initial large mob who went down into the valley. We will never know for sure, but the trees on the edge of the forest just on the southern side of the valley were heavily cut by machine-gun fire, and it is about where they would have come out had they stayed as a mob. Some of our survivors and the villagers later told us that they thought the Germans had laid a fire trap on the south side. It would have been the thing to have done. But they didn't get it all their own way. The villagers reported some twenty Germans dead and some wounded.'

Denis Chansigaud, with Dieudonné and several other *maquis*, had followed the main SAS party and had dashed across the road behind the soldiers. Despite coming out into the open, no shots had come their way and the Frenchmen began to think the worst was behind them – 'We thought ourselves safe as we were already 500 or 600 metres from the camp,' recalled Chansigaud. But they were wrong. In the woods on the south side of the road the *maquis* joined Lieutenant Stephens and several SAS troopers on the edge of the corn field, but they had ventured no further than 20 metres from the tree line before a withering fire opened up. As they turned back for the woods, Stephens was hit and, wounded, he dropped down at the edge of the trees, urging the others to flee. The Germans again seemed to be everywhere and Dieudonné went on ahead to try to find a way out, pledging to return to his men who bandaged Stephens' wound while they waited. Dieudonné was to find his return blocked, however, so his men, now just some four or five in number, attempted to climb into a large tree to avoid the murderous fire all round. Only Pierre Crest made it and they left him there, safely hidden in the topmost branches.

The rest split up, Chansigaud taking one direction while his friend, Choisy, took the opposite – to his death with a bullet in the head. Chansigaud eventually reached the road again at La Couarde, where he hid himself at its edge as the German soldiers milled about in the road. Lieutenant Twm Stephens was discovered in the bushes and raised his arms in surrender. But a German took Stephens' rifle and with its butt viciously clubbed the already wounded officer, bludgeoning him to the ground and leaving the battered body motionless in the road. Dozens of the enemy were now assembling immediately in front of Chansigaud, congratulating themselves loudly on the success of their attack. There were several British prisoners, heavily guarded, and enemy vehicles passed continuously along the road. A large black Citroën and a half-track pulled up and several civilians and soldiers got out. They went into the trees some 15 metres from Chansigaud and he heard bursts of machine-gun fire, followed by a number of single shots. He was later to learn that this gunfire signalled the summary execution of his *maquis* comrades who had been captured. The new arrivals reappeared from the woods and passed just two metres from the young Frenchman's hiding place before climbing back into their vehicles and driving off.

Chansigaud endured hours more cramped waiting while the German soldiers then settled down to eat, throwing the debris of their meal into the bushes at his side. At last they moved off and after a careful wait, Chansigaud edged out of his cover and set off across the fields for the village. On reaching Verrières, he ran on through the village, the local people shouting to him to keep going as the Germans were still about. He went on across the fields, not knowing and not caring in which direction. Reaching a lake, he submerged himself in its waters and waited until nightfall before daring to go on. Eventually he saw a light in a farm and knocked at the door to ask his whereabouts. He was near Mazerolles and the sympathetic farmer fed him and hid him in a barn overnight.

Marcel Weber, wounded but driven by adrenalin, had been equally fortunate:

'Bullets were flying everywhere and branches were literally snapped above our heads, the firing became more and more rapid and accurate. My dressing was only half applied but I took my trousers in my left hand, my pistol in my right and crawled away as well as I could with my useless leg. I used the lie of the land as cover and with my unfinished dressing trailing behind me, I managed to get to my feet again and made off into the wood which gives onto a little road behind Dienné. I had just torn off the remainder of the bandage behind a tree when again the Germans opened up on me with a machine gun, from some 30 metres away. I went on into the forest and reached the Verrières road. I again stopped behind a tree in order to watch the road before crossing it. It was as well I did, because I noticed in the ditches on each side of the road two machine-gun posts. Their crews had already heard me coming and opened up in my direction, but despite their fire, I crossed the road in three or four bounds and entered the woods opposite, thinking myself saved at last. I walked along a little and looked at my wound. My shoe was full of blood from it and my trousers were stained red and hard as leather. I remade the dressing with a handkerchief and then went on until I reached the edge of the wood. Suddenly a burst of firing surprised me and ducking behind a tree I could see a machine gun which was shooting at me. With just my revolver I could do nothing as it was out of range. I turned back and a little further on I once more tried leaving the wood through a field of corn. I was again engaged with automatic gunfire, but I zig-zagged away, distancing myself from the forest as fast as I could and crawling when the bullets came too close. The Germans never stopped firing and several bullets ripped through my trousers, but the ground sloped and after some 200 metres I was out of the line of fire and the Germans could no longer see me.

'To my right was a farm, but while I needed rest and treatment, I knew that the Germans would burn the farm and shoot its inhabitants if they saw me enter. Therefore I went on for at least another 500 metres in the field before re-entering the forest. My foot was bathed in blood and I was soaked with sweat. I crossed a stream and then a clearing before, exhausted, I lay down behind a large rock. My head was spinning with the loss of blood and I lost consciousness. I came to, trembling and feverish and could not remember how long I had been there; my revolver was covered with blood. I set off again but had scarcely gone a hundred metres when I was greeted by a burst of machine-gun fire and a shower of grenades. The Germans were still there, there were so many of them that they seemed to fill the whole forest. I felt hopeless, demoralized. I thought of killing myself to avoid being captured and tortured. I made one last attempt to get out of the forest by fleeing down a path without even trying to hide since the Germans were everywhere. After 500 or 600 metres I found myself out of the forest, but was wary because the path twisted endlessly alongside the forest and I risked bumping into the enemy again. But I met no one and, after having run another 300 or 400 metres, I noticed a house close by on my right. I approached it carefully and asked a woman there if any Germans were about. She replied, 'No', but I did not want to go into the house so I just asked her where I was in order to get my bearings. I also told her that I was wounded and asked her for a towel. She saw my leg covered in blood and quickly went off to find the towel. She came back with two other women and, on seeing all the blood, one of them fainted. The two others looked after me and then I went on as quickly as possible.

'After running for about a kilometre across the field I spotted a car and signalled to the driver. He stopped, picked me up and turned round to take me home with him. He told me it was half past nine.'

Despite the danger, the car driver and his family hid Weber in an old ruined house as rain began to fall. Throughout the remainder of the day Weber hid there but by night time his helpers had been unable to bring a doctor to him and he had no alternative but to spend the night there with only a nest of noisy owls to keep him company. The next day he was cared for by the two women he had met the day before, who also brought him food. He could hear the noise of aircraft wheeling above the forest and was told that a number of his comrades had been shot and a wounded English officer 'finished off'. Among the bodies of those shot was his good friend, Pierre Lecellier, and Weber could not hold back his tears at the news. He stayed in the ruined house for all of Tuesday until, on the Wednesday morning, 5 July, four *maquisards* came to pick him up. They took him to a farm near Persac where the Dupuis family hid him until his wound healed. Even then his difficulties were not finally over. On 4 August the Germans suddenly swept into Persac and rounded up all the male inhabitants. As Weber was herded into the village square, he appreciated his leg wound could give him away and he therefore again took his chances and made a break for it. Behind him the Germans opened fire and Weber was slammed to the ground as the machine-gun bullets found him. The Germans did not give any attention to the body, but Weber's extraordinary luck had held. His wounds were no more than two bullets to the shoulder and, after the Germans left, he was once again cared for by the people of Persac, and survived.

On 3 July Jean Dieudonné was one of the few who had managed to cross the corn field safely and he had spent the rest of the morning taking refuge in a cabbage field. Realizing that the SAS might still need help, he obtained a bicycle and set off to reach the 'Vauquois' *maquis* group of Capitaine Robichon who, having heard the noise of the battle, had dispersed his own men into the countryside and told them to hide their arms. Dieudonné therefore went on to Colonel Chêne's headquarters, where he was given fifty men under the command of a former Foreign Legion officer. They set off back towards Verrières, but, upon arriving at the village around two o'clock in the afternoon, they found that the Germans already had the SAS troops in the bag and were assembling the men of Verrières in the village square. In the face of a much stronger enemy, and wanting to avoid civilian casualties, the *maquis* stood off and could only await the departure of the Germans.

The Germans had finally left the forest around midday on the 3rd and had then driven into Verrières. They assembled the men of the village in the square and few doubted that reprisals would soon follow. But instead the Germans suddenly seemed to change their minds. They told the villagers that there were some bodies to be retrieved but it was forbidden to place them in coffins, they could only be wrapped in sheets. Ignoring the order, the Verrières municipality immediately ordered coffins to be made as the Germans began to pull out of the village square.

A reason for the hurried departure of the Germans was subsequently suggested by Robert Artaud, commander of the 'Amilcar' *maquis*. A messenger had been sent by motorcycle from Colonel Chêne's headquarters to inform the 'Amilcar' group that the SAS party and their own detachment had been attacked somewhere in the Forêt de Verrières. Lacking sufficient vehicles, but having to react quickly, Artaud could only muster two lorries and forty five men and they set off for a journey of some 30 kilometres. One kilometre from Verrières Artaud and his men split up into small groups to slip into the village. They arrived just after the Germans had left and found all the men of the village still assembled in the village square. It was Artaud's belief that the change of plan of the Germans was due to the fact that the two lorries he had with him had both lost their exhausts. They could be heard from six kilometres away and sounded like a convoy of at least forty lorries! Artaud was therefore convinced that the Germans had heard what they took to be the approach of a large force of *maquis* and had chosen to avoid another fight.

After the arrival of Artaud, and with nothing further to be done in the village, Dieudonné headed for 'La Roche' farm, home of Monsieur Bonnet ('Baptiste') and the pre-determined rendezvous point in case of problems. It was there in the evening that Dieudonné suddenly passed out for a short while, probably from delayed action shock. The next day other survivors of the attack began to trickle into 'La Roche', among them Trooper McNair with John Tonkin. The latter told Dieudonné how he had lain hidden in the camp while the Germans had eaten their food supplies, even throwing their egg shells and empty cheese boxes over him. After the enemy had gone, he had then wandered aimlessly throughout the afternoon and the rest of the day had been no more than a blur.

Many years after the war Tonkin learned that he had walked into the village of Verrières, dazed with shock, to find that the Germans had gone, taking all but one of their SAS prisoners. Lieutenant Twm Stephens' body had been left with those of the executed *maquisards* and Tonkin was taken to them by the Mayor. Scarcely speaking, Tonkin identified Stephens' body and gave the French the dead officer's service number and rank.[1] He also left a 1st SAS shoulder flash and winged dagger cap badge to put on the burial cross. Tonkin then stumbled out of the village into the gathering darkness where he came across another survivor, Trooper McNair:

'The next I remember is the trooper I mentioned above coming up to me in the late evening and telling me that he had come to find me and that he:
- had located some survivors and directed them to our emergency R.V.;
- had left messages for the parties that were out, in our message hiding places;
- had sent word via the Mayor of Verrières to another *Résistance* group as to what had happened.

'McNair then suggested that we both get sleep. We went to a farm. Again typical of the country French, the farmer and his wife took one look at the two of us, exhausted as we were, fed us with a hot rich soup and then insisted we have their only bed – an enormous feather one – whilst they kept guard. They knew what had happened and knew they would die if the Germans found us there'.

---

[1] Several other accounts of Stephens' death have perpetuated a misunderstanding which arose at this point. Since Tonkin came across Stephens' body in the village, and it was known that the local people had been assembled in the square by the Germans, it was thought by the SAS that Stephens had been publicly beaten to death before the villagers. The author has confirmed, through Denis Chansigaud, that Stephens was definitely killed on the edge of the forest. The inhabitants of Verrières also confirm that they were not witness to any killing in the village square.

When Denis Chansigaud arrived at 'La Roche' on the 4th he found most of the other evaders already gathered and joined Dieudonné and Tonkin who were reviewing the tragic circumstances of the previous day. At one point Tonkin considered withdrawing south towards Spain in order to return to England, but rejected this option as he gradually came to terms with the situation. Peter Weaver then walked in, the hiding place where he had spent the previous night having proved, by daylight, to have been almost next door to 'La Roche'. He was greeted with a heartfelt 'Thank God you got through' from Tonkin. Chansigaud was detailed to look for one of the SAS troopers thought to be still hiding in the middle of a small juniper wood. Several times he walked through the wood whistling the British national anthem but there was no response and he was on the point of leaving when the SAS trooper stepped out of a clump of brushwood, having recognized the Frenchman. Together they returned to 'La Roche'.

News of the disaster spread rapidly throughout the towns and villages of the Vienne. Inevitably the story became distorted, to the extent that all the SAS were reported to have been killed, along with all the *maquisards*, including some who had not even been there. In Montmorillon the local *Gendarmerie* broke the news to Monsieur and Madame Dupont that their son, Albert, had been killed in the fighting. Only a short while later, Raymond Jovelin, a friend of Albert's who also served Colonel Chêne's headquarters, called in to see the Duponts and casually mentioned he had seen Albert that same morning. Madame Dupont took a great deal of persuading that Jovelin was not mistaken. Albert had not been at Verrières and contrary to the *Gendarmerie's* report, was alive and well.

But the Germans could nevertheless claim success. Stephens had been killed, and thirty SAS men, three of whom were badly wounded, had been captured, along with the medical orderly, Corporal Allan and USAAF Lieutenant Bundy. Only four *maquisards* – Dieudonné, Chansigaud, Weber and Crest – had escaped, the latter with two bullet wounds in his arm. Seven of their comrades had been shot just inside the forest at La Couarde. While the other bodies were returned to their home villages for burial, Salmoni, the Corsican, was laid to rest in the local graveyard in Verrières, as was Lieutenant Twm Stephens. Touchingly, the villagers insisted that the body of the young Welshman should lie alongside the dead of the village and he was thus interred in the tomb of two local families. Within the chapel-like vault his military cross was placed to one side, displaying the SAS insignia given by John Tonkin.

Meanwhile, flushed with success, the Germans were eager to glean as much additional information as possible from their prisoners. From Verrières all the captured SAS men and equipment had been taken directly to the *Feldkommandantur,* the *Wehrmacht's* sub-area headquarters in Poitiers in the rue Boncenne and rue Saint-Louis where the prisoners, including those who were wounded, were secured in the military prison. There, in an effort to learn more about the SAS operations, the cells were first bugged by Major Bongartz's Signals Detachment and the prisoners were then left in groups of six to eight to encourage conversation. The results, both of this exercise and interrogations by the SD, were disappointing and left the Germans with little additional information. No details were obtained regarding the home aerodrome, the flight from England, types of aircraft used, the organization of the unit and so on. The prisoners only stated that they had landed with orders to carry out sabotage against traffic targets which were essential to the German Army in the area behind the lines. A further disappointment for the Germans came shortly afterwards when Tonkin's time pencils detonated the captured explosives and destroyed some of the SAS's equipment seized at Verrières.

On the afternoon after completion of the operation *Oberst* Koestlin, 80th Corps' Chief of Staff, lost no time in driving to the SD's offices in order to inspect the booty which had been brought in and to speak to the officers of the SD concerning its distribution. The three jeeps taken were clearly regarded as the most valuable spoils and 80th Corps' headquarters wished in particular to lay claim to one of these vehicles for themselves on account of the participation of their troops in the operation. After some discussion, the SD agreed to share out the jeeps equitably, one being kept by the Bicycle Squadron, one by the SD and one was presented to Koestlin as he had wished. 80th Corps also received a machine gun and a carbine rifle.

While the Germans haggled over their spoils, three of the SAS were so badly wounded as to be clearly in need of medical attention. The SD called for a doctor to look at Troopers Ogg, Pascoe and Williams, but for some reason the *Feldkommandantur's* own medical officer, *Hauptmann* Dr Paul Tönshof, was unavailable. Instead one of 80th Corps' own medical officers, *Hauptmann* Dr Georg Hesterberg, was summoned.

At 49 years of age, Hesterberg was an unusual mixture of able physician, academic and experienced soldier. Having seen service in the First World War as an artillery gunner, he resumed civilian life and qualified as a Doctor of Economics. A complete change of career, relatively late in life, had then seen him take up medical studies at the University of Berlin in the 1930s. Qualification as a Doctor of Medicine had come just in time for his return to the German Army as a medical officer and as such he had served in Spain and later with a *Panzer* division before his transfer to 80th Corps in Poitiers. Here Hesterberg was able to pursue a relatively settled existence, looking after some 3,500 troops from the Corps' various headquarters units. He had also set up a small clinic for the treatment of those local French people needy enough not to balk at the offer of medical treatment from their occupying power. Looking forward to his expected promotion to Major in July, Hesterberg tried not to worry too much about his wife and 18-year-old daughter, a dental student, back in Berlin. Already, in November, 1943, an allied air raid had completely destroyed their home and all possessions and he fretted over the continued safety of his family. But, when called to the *Feldkommandantur's* prison, Hesterberg was to find that his other worries paled into insignificance. Confronting him was a dilemma well beyond the bounds of even his own considerable experience of life.

Hesterberg was met at the *Kommandantur* by plain-clothed members of the SD and was led into a large room on the ground floor where he found seven or so wounded British troops, one of whom (presumably Trooper Ogg) was lying on the floor with an exposed leg showing bullet wounds. All wore khaki uniform with a red strip by the shoulder and none had headgear. After only a brief inspection of their wounds, Hesterberg was in no doubt that three of the wounded were not fit to be kept in prison. Upon his advice, the SD therefore arranged the transfer that same evening of Ogg, Pascoe and Williams to the Hôtel-Dieu, Poitiers' main hospital situated in an imposing period building in the heart of the old town. Hesterberg's main concern was to have the Hôtel-Dieu x-ray Ogg's leg wound which he assumed had resulted in a bone fracture. Before leaving the *Kommandantur*, Hesterberg was able to advise Corporal Allan, the RAMC orderly, about looking after the others with more minor wounds.

At the Hôtel-Dieu the arrival of the wounded British prisoners certainly caused a stir, but was nevertheless routinely recorded. Monsieur Georges Polet, Director of the Hôtel-Dieu and also of two other hospitals in Poitiers, was later able to quote from this meticulous record which also included the initial diagnosis made by a surgeon:

'WILLIAMS, John, Reginald, born 22nd April, 1921, Worcester, Kidderminster. Wound in the back, haemothorax, in the back of the chest.
Date of admittance: 3rd July. Date of release: 8th July. Duration of stay: 5 days. Brought and taken away by the *Kommandantur*.
OGG, Joseph, born 2nd December 1922, Scotland,

1. Lt-Col. Paddy Mayne, C.O. of 1st SAS Regt. (*Royal Ulster Rifles Assoc.*)

2. Trooper Sam Smith. (*Mrs E. Smith via J.L. Fielding*)

3. Trooper John Fielding. (*J.L. Fielding*)

4. Capt. John Tonkin. (*J.E. Tonkin via J.L. Fielding*)

5. Lt Richard Crisp. (*Miss I. Crisp*)

6. Col. Félix Chêne, 'Bernard', head of the Vienne FFI. (*R. Picard*)

7. A Short Stirling IV of 620 Squadron, RAF Fairford. This type was to conduct most of the parachute drops of men and supplies for 'Bulbasket'.
(*N. Chaffey*)

8. Mosquito FB VI MM403 of 464 RAAF Sqn. which participated in the attack on Châtellerault, 11.6.44.
(*Australian War Memorial*)

9. A jeep at point of release from a Handley Page Halifax bomber. (*D. Ellis*)

10. (L to R) Raymond Jovelin, Lt Crisp, Camille Olivet, Col. Chêne, Capt. Robert Artaud ('Amilcar'), Albert Dupont and (sitting) Lt Stephens. Taken at 'Sazas', south of Montmorillon around 10.6.44. (*J.E. Tonkin via A. Dupont*)

11. Lt. Stephens (centre) dressed for his petrol trains reconnaissance of 10.6.44 with Tonkin (left) and Crisp. (*J.E. Tonkin via J.L. Fielding*)

12. W/C 'Black' Smith of 487 RNZAF Sqn. (*Grp Capt. I.S. Smith*)

13. AVM Basil Embry (left) with Grp. Capt. Peter Wykeham-Barnes. (*Author's Collection*)

14. W/C Bob Iredale (centre, hands in pockets) and crews of 464 RAAF Sqn. (*W/C R. Iredale*)

15. The 'Bulbasket' camp south of Montmorillon after the main party's arrival, around 12.6.44. (*J.E. Tonkin via J.L. Fielding*)

16. Sgt Bob Holmes (front left) and three troopers in front of a camouflaged jeep at Verrières. (*J.E. Tonkin via A. Dupont*)

17. (L to R) Jacques Hirsch (SOE), Col. Blondel (FFI), Capt. Maingard (SOE) and John Tonkin near Col. Chêne's FFI HQ, 1.7.44. (*A. Dupont*)

18. This photograph is believed to be of Trooper George Biffin wh▮ disappeared without trace. (*D. Braddick/P. & M. Ashley*)

19. Capitaine Robert Artaud, 'Amilcar' of the FTP *maquis*. (*J. Blanchard*)

20. Jean Dieudonné, 'Maurice', of the 'Amilcar' FTP *maquis*. (*M Fuzeau*)

21. Camille Olivet, 'La Chouette', of the FTP *maquis*. (*D Chansigaud*)

22. Peter Banks, Mustang escort pilot to the Mosquitos attacking the barracks at Bonneuil-Matours on 14.7.44. (*P.M. Banks*)

24. Captain Sadoine, alias Octave Dupont, C.O. of the Phantom signals team attached to 'Bulbasket'. (*J. Blanchard*)

23. Trooper Alan Ashley. (*P. & M. Ashley*)

25. F/L Hester makes a low pass over the burning Château du Fou in his Mosquito of the RAF's Film Production Unit, 2.8.44. (*Imperial War Museum*)

26. The Château du Fou, partly restored and in use as a residence and equestrian centre 50 years after the attack. (*Author*)

Enzipartshire [*sic*][1]. Foreign body (confirmed as a bullet) in the 'plateau tibial'.

Date of admittance: 3rd July. Date of release: 8th July. Duration of stay: 5 days. Brought and taken away by *Kommandantur*.

PASCOE, Henry, James, born 22nd February 1916, Wellington, Sommerset. Vertebral fracture, contusion wounds in the lumbar region.

Date of admittance: 3rd July. Date of release: 8th July. Duration of stay: 5 days. Brought and taken away by *Kommandantur*.'

André Clert, a young interne at the Hôtel-Dieu, had helped the surgeon to dress the troopers' wounds. He did not remember Williams very well, since he was the least seriously wounded and needed only minor bandaging, but the more serious wounds of Ogg and particularly Pascoe, made a profound impression on Clert:

'I remember Ogg well. The evening he was admitted to hospital he was x-rayed and we found a bullet in the knee.

'As far as Pascoe was concerned, we cleaned his wound on his admittance to hospital. The wound was too severe to do anything else just then. This wound had been caused by a bullet or fragment which had struck the bone on a tangent and the lips of the wound were spread wide. There might have been a small fracture of one of the vertebrae on the spinal column.'

While the three seriously wounded men were benefiting from proper medical attention, a report of the successful operation at Verrières was telephoned to 1st Army HQ in the regular report by 80th Corps' Intelligence branch on the evening of 3 July. The report briefly gave the number of prisoners and the amount of captured material and was made by Hauptmann Dr Erich Schönig[2], the Corps headquarters' Senior Intelligence Officer. Schönig was immediately asked over the telephone by Major Hay, his equivalent at 1st

---

[1] 'Enzipartshire' was thought at the time to have been a confused spelling of Perthshire. In reality, Ogg came from Alves in Morayshire.

[2] Several of the SD and army Intelligence community in Poitiers had gained academic doctorates, e.g. Dr Karl Herold and Dr Walter Linn of the SD and Dr Egon Deter of 80th Corps' Intelligence branch. These qualifications should not be confused with the medical doctorates of Dr Georg Hesterberg and Dr Paul Tönshof. Hauptmann Dr Erich Schönig's qualification related to his pre-war profession of dentist.

Army headquarters, what 80th Corps considered doing and whether Hitler's *Kommandobefehl* was not known to them. Schönig confirmed his understanding of the *Kommandobefehl*, but told Hay that 80th Corps would be leaving the prisoners to the SD so that they could be taken away. Apparently Hay was sympathetic to the position in which the 80th Corps officers now found themselves and made no attempt to increase the pressure already building up, commenting merely that the affair was *'Heisses Eisen'* – a tricky business. Hay's reluctance to involve himself further would serve him well in the future.

The *Kommandobefehl* – 'Commando Order' to which Major Hay had referred was a personal edict, issued by Hitler on 18 October, 1942, which was to bring great shame on the name of Germany's armed forces. Infuriated by the growing number of Commando-type operations against the occupied continent, and in particular by a recent raid on the Channel Island of Sark, the German Führer had retaliated with this order which, among its general spite, included:

> '... in the future, Germany, in the face of these sabotage troops of the British and their accomplices, will resort to the same procedure, that is, that they will be ruthlessly mowed down by the German troops in combat, wherever they may appear ...
>
> '... From now on all enemies on so-called Commando missions in Europe or Africa, challenged by German troops, even if they are to all appearances soldiers in uniform or demolition troops, whether armed or unarmed, in battle or in flight, are to be slaughtered to the last man. It does not make any difference whether they are dropped by parachute. Even if these individuals, when found, should apparently be prepared to give themselves up, no pardon is to be granted them on principle ...
>
> '... If individual members of such Commandos, such as agents, saboteurs, etc., fall into the hands of the military forces by some other means, through the police in occupied territories, for instance, they are to be handed over immediately to the SD. Any imprisonment under military guard, in Prisoner of War stockades, for instance, etc., is strictly prohibited, even if this is only intended for a short time ...
>
> '... I will hold responsible, under Military Law, for failing to carry out this order, all commanders and officers who either have neglected their duty of instructing the troops about this order, or asked against this order when it was to be executed.'

The order claimed that Commando troops fell outside the protection of the Geneva Conventions and there was little doubt that any German officer refusing to implement the order could expect similarly brutal treatment to that designed for the Commandos.

On the 4th Schönig therefore quickly passed on to Koestlin his conversation of the previous evening with Major Hay at 1st Army. Koestlin immediately recognized the gravity of the matter and consulted 80th Corps' commanding officer, General Curt Gallenkamp. Gallenkamp and Koestlin should have been able to expect that, in accordance with the *Kommandobefehl*, the SD would claim the prisoners for themselves, in the same way as they had appropriated the booty. But, from their knowledge of the individuals of the SD headquarters in Poitiers, the two *Wehrmacht* officers expected that the energetic *SS-Obersturmführer*[1] Hoffmann would demand that the *Kommandobefehl* be carried out by the SD, but that the hesitant *SS-Sturmbannführer* Dr Karl Herold, who only gave the appearance of being energetic, would perhaps decline the responsibility for the prisoners' fate. Koestlin therefore requested that Herold, the SD commander, should visit him and he informed the SD's headquarters that 80th Corps intended to hand the prisoners over to the SD.

Herold was taking a medicinal cure at Niort when news reached him of Koestlin's request for a meeting. He nevertheless quickly returned to Poitiers and immediately went to 80th Corps' headquarters along with his assistant, *SS-Haupsturmführer* Dr Walter Linn, the officer responsible for SD activities in the remainder of the Vienne region beyond the Poitiers district. The two secret police officers, despite an age disparity, could have come from the same mould. Of similar height and heavy build, their close-cropped hair and piercing blue eyes were enough to chill the blood of many local Frenchmen, Linn's Teutonic background being further emphasised by the two parallel duelling scars he bore across one cheek. With his experience as a pre-war lawyer in Munich, and a good working knowledge of French, Linn was a much more daunting opponent for the *maquis* than his chief. At 50 years of age, Herold was almost twice as old as Linn, had very little command of the local language and seemed to prefer a good cigar to dealing with the problems around him.

When Herold and Linn arrived at 80th Corps headquarters, accompanied by Hoffmann, Koestlin saw them on his own and put the suggestion to them

1 As the SD was the Security Police of the SS, its personnel bore SS ranks. See Glossary for explanation of ranks.

to take over the prisoners and to deal with them according to the *Kommandobefehl*. As expected, however, Herold declined, protesting that the Poitiers SD itself was in a difficult position. The SS officer later repeated his arguments to Schönig who recalled:

> 'As I found out during my personal interviews with Hoffmann and Linn, the *Kommandobefehl* was known to the SD too. The SD, however, declined to carry out the order, since for operations they only had use of about fifteen to twenty men who, incidentally, were in action day and night owing to the fact that the sabotage cases were increasing more and more.
>
> 'For that reason the SD commander of Poitiers, *SS-Sturmbannführer* Herold, who at that time was a patient in the hospital of Niort, specially drove to see the Chief of Staff in order to decline categorically to the Chief, in the presence of Hoffmann and Linn, to have the *Kommandobefehl* carried out by the SD. This occurred at a conference at which I was not present, about which, however, I was informed immediately afterwards by Herold himself.'

Herold himself was to later recall his meeting with Koestlin:

> 'He told me about the case and said he would hand over the Englishmen to me. I said I would not take them. Koestlin reminded me of the *Kommandobefehl*. I replied, 'Yes, but I also know how the order came into being.' Koestlin said that if I did not carry out the *Kommandobefehl* I might go before a court martial. I said, 'Yes, but I shall not let it get that far.' I said I would go to the highest military authority and ask for a written decision. I thought I might have to go to Paris OB-West. Koestlin was silent for a few minutes and said 'I did not expect this of you, the matter is closed.'

Having confirmed Herold's reluctance to take over responsibility for the prisoners, Koestlin ended the short meeting, claiming later that he did so as he did not wish to give Herold the idea of dealing with the prisoners by using troops loaned by 80th Corps. Koestlin also later argued that he thereby achieved his intention of keeping the prisoners in the hands of the *Wehrmacht*, in order to maintain a free hand and to gain further time. Confusingly, however, Koestlin was also to say later that he had thought at the time that if an execution became inevitable, it would be preferable to have the task carried out properly by soldiers. This supposed motive is clearly somewhat at odds with Koestlin's wish to avoid Herold using *Wehrmacht* troops for a firing squad. Whatever Koestlin's somewhat contradictory aims were, the SD was successful in leaving the dilemma entirely with 80th Corps.

Koestlin meanwhile attempted to keep as many options open as possible, but a blow to any possibility of safeguarding the fate of the prisoners came on the 4th when 80th Corps received an official German Army news communiqué, transmitted to the world's press. The statement boasted of the successful capture of the SAS and went as far as to claim that the troopers had already been 'liquidated'. *Hauptmann* Schönig realized immediately that this announcement gave 80th Corps little room to manoeuvre:

> 'On the next day after the operation I recollect exactly that I read
> the *Wehrmacht* communiqué concerning the success in the Corps
> area. I also know, however, that I talked about it to my clerk Maunz
> or *Leutnant* Felden, since the number of the prisoners given was too
> high and because I was annoyed at the expression 'liquidated.'

Two other communications received the same day increased the mounting pressure on 80th Corps. In the afternoon teleprints from both OB-West High Command and 1st Army enquired what had happened to the prisoners. In reply to 1st Army, Koestlin gave Schönig instructions to report that interrogations were still continuing and that their completion would be notified to 1st Army at the proper time. The OB-West signal could not be brushed off so lightly. Koestlin recalled its contents to have been:

> 'Report must be made at once to OB-West about the whereabouts
> of the prisoners as well as certificate of the destruction of this
> teleprinted message.'

The reference to destroying the message was a clear indication of the High Command's sensitivity over the subject and therefore, at the insistence of Koestlin, Schönig immediately went to Gallenkamp with the teleprinted message. The General was very perturbed and agitated, giving Schönig to understand that he found himself in a most difficult position. On account of this teleprinted message, said Gallenkamp, a Court Martial or a concentration camp might lie ahead of him. The General ordered a 'stalling' reply to be composed by Koestlin, signed it himself and sent it off to OB-West.

The next morning, at a critical moment in deciding the fate of the SAS prisoners, one of the major players left the stage. At 0800 hours on the 5th

General Gallenkamp left Poitiers for a tour of inspection of the forward areas of his 708th Division, around the Garonne river estuary on the Atlantic coast. No record or testimony remains as to whether the trip had already been arranged, but the timing could not have been more convenient if Gallenkamp had wanted to distance himself from deciding the fate of the prisoners. For his Chief of Staff, Koestlin, the General's departure could not have come at a worse time. Koestlin was later to claim that he had kept his commanding officer informed of circumstances by telephone and that, by the same medium, the General had eventually sealed the prisoners' fate. In reality, however, it would seem that no such communication took place and, in Gallenkamp's absence, Koestlin found he was left with the terrible onus of responsibility for the prisoners.

Desperately the Chief of Staff spent the remainder of the 5th looking for a way out. Help from higher echelons of the *Wehrmacht* was clearly out of the question since 1st Army, which ought to have been interested in the interrogation of the prisoners, categorically declined to take them. Therefore Koestlin next explored the possibility of handing the prisoners over to the air force, as the SAS were airborne troops. This line of thought was taken up by Schönig who promptly made efforts to contact the closest *Luftwaffe* units:

> 'I discussed with the Chief of Staff whether the prisoners could not be transferred to the airfield at Tours. This also failed since I was informed in reply to my inquiry over the telephone that the airfield was completely destroyed and that only a small group was left which was too weak to guard the prisoners. Besides, they replied that there was no accommodation for the prisoners and that evacuation from there would not be possible on account of the destroyed railway lines. As a further airfield, Cognac could have been considered. Cognac, however, was too far away and besides, the way there lay through an area rendered unsafe by *maquis*. A convoy there would not have been possible without a strong guard. A motorized convoy of this strength, however, was not available from 80th Corps.'

In attempting to pass on responsibility for the prisoners, Koestlin later explained his motives thus:

> 'The further attempt to hand over the prisoners as Air Force personnel to our own Air Force was, for my part, merely a struggle to gain time in order to postpone the decision concerning the

prisoners' fate with the but slight hope that greater decisions, for example contact with the enemy, might put the existence of the Commando group into the background or perhaps even allow it to be forgotten at superior headquarters. Had the transfer to the *Luftwaffe* been successful, it could have been rescinded as an erroneous conception of Corps HQ had superior formations interfered. By this, once again time would have been gained.'

But all the efforts of the Chief of Staff failed. Not surprisingly, no other branch of the German armed forces was keen to take on prisoners with a death sentence already hanging over them. Koestlin was left to conclude:

'The next idea to hand over the Commando group as Prisoners of War from the front could not be carried out since:-
a) there was as yet no contact with the enemy on the Corps front;
b) there was no PoW camp in the Corps area in which the prisoners could have disappeared under Corps direction;
c) had they been transferred to a PoW camp in the area of OB-West, it would not have preserved them from the fate of shooting, since the prisoners' origin was already known on account of the first report of the Corps HQ.'

Clutching at straws, Koestlin finally hoped there might yet be some legal loophole under military law to relieve him of his responsibility. He therefore requested to see the *Kriegsrichter*, the military court judge of the *Feldkommandantur,* and outlined to him a supposedly theoretical scenario where a Commando group had been captured and where it was proved that the Commandos had helped in the organization and activity of the *maquis* and had participated in sabotage behind the lines. Was a Court Martial sentence necessary or possible in view of the existence of the *Kommandobefehl*? The judge answered immediately and without hesitation – on account of the *Kommandobefehl* no military court process was necessary. If Koestlin's claimed motives are to be believed, this pronouncement dashed the the Chief of Staff's last hopes of avoiding sending the prisoners to their deaths.

Having exhausted all other options, Koestlin called for *Oberleutnant* Vogt on the evening of the 5th. It was Vogt who had led the Bicycle Squadron in the successful operation at Verrières, yet it is difficult to imagine an officer less suited for Koestlin's task since Vogt was a pre-war protestant clergyman from Tuebingen in Württemburg. Despite such a background, it was now to

Vogt that Koestlin personally gave the order to execute the prisoners. The next day Vogt was to select the place of execution and dig the required graves. The day after that, the 7th, he was to carry out the execution at dawn. What the former clergyman made of his orders is not known, but no record exists of a refusal to undertake the duty.

The execution itself was to be performed by a firing squad of Vogt's men. *Hauptmann* Schönig was to be present and an interpreter was assigned to assist the proceedings. It became the responsibility of Schönig to provide the latter and he briefed *Sonderführer* Hönigschmidt on the distasteful task ahead. To his credit, Hönigschmidt immediately protested, expressing his personal repugnance at the execution. He asked to be allowed to speak to Koestlin on the issue and was granted permission to do so. After only a short while, Hönigschmidt returned from the Chief of Staff. Much depressed, he told Schönig that his representations had not met with any success. The Chief of Staff considered that he was bound by the *Kommandobefehl* and could therefore not allow his mind to be changed.

One final initiative by Schönig casts some doubt on Koestlin's expressed claim to have been bound by orders. The Intelligence Officer did not feel that Lieutenant Bundy, the American pilot captured with the SAS, should fall under the *Kommandobefehl* and Schönig therefore presented his point to Koestlin. Where he might here have exercised a lenient stance, with little fear of later challenge, Koestlin instead replied that the American officer had acted in a common cause with the SAS and the *maquis*. It was therefore the Chief of Staff's opinion that Bundy *did* come under the *Kommandobefehl*. The fate of all the prisoners was firmly sealed.

Oberleutnant Dr Egon Deter was the 35-year-old assistant to Schönig in 80th Corps' Intelligence duties. With an impressive record of front-line service, Deter had only turned to Intelligence work after being wounded while a company commander on the eastern front in 1942. He had first met Schönig while re-training and in August, 1943, was posted to 80th Corps HQ where he later became the deputy Intelligence Officer. Since his arrival in Poitiers his duties had normally been agreeable but on the night of 6 July Deter was troubled to learn he was ordered to join *Hauptmann* Schönig and *Sonderführer* Hönigschmidt in a journey to the Poitiers *Feldkommandantur*.

At the *Feldkommandantur* the three officers arrived in time to watch the SAS prisoners and Lieutenant Bundy being ordered into five trucks. In their car, they then followed the prisoners' convoy in a south westerly direction out of Poitiers. After some thirty kilometres the vehicles turned off the long straight N10 road into the Bois de Guron, part of the Forêt de Saint-Sauvant and 5 kilometres east of the village of Saint-Sauvant. Deter recalled that they stopped in a forest ride, a location chosen the day before by *Oberleutnant* Vogt.[1]

First to dismount from the trucks was the firing party which immediately took up position, two riflemen to each prisoner. The prisoners themselves were then ordered out of the trucks and were ushered to the opposite side of the ride from the firing squad. The three wounded troopers, Pascoe, Ogg and Williams, had been left in Poitiers, but the remainder of those captured at Verrières had been joined by two others, Sergeant Eccles and Corporal Bateman. The two NCOs had been held by the Germans since their capture at St Benoît on 28/29 June and had now been permitted to join their comrades only to share the same fate. Deter noticed that Hönigschmidt talked to one of the prisoners, but could not understand the conversation. Later Hönigschmidt told him that the exchange had concerned sparing one of the prisoners and it was Deter's vague recollection some years later that Corporal Allan, the RAMC medical orderly, was involved. Whether this was a case being made for Allan, as a medical orderly, to be spared, or Allan himself perhaps making a special case on behalf of the American airman Bundy will never be known.

As dawn broke on Friday, 7 July Schönig called for Lieutenant Richard Crisp, just 20 years old but the senior ranking prisoner. Limping from a leg wound received when he had been captured, Crisp might have escaped at Verrières had he not remained to look after one of the seriously wounded men, a gesture typical of the young officer. Now, the condemned troopers could have no better leader for their final moments. Turning to Hönigschmidt, Schönig asked the interpreter to translate the order of execution to Crisp and to also convey his own sense of personal shame, as a German officer, in having to carry out the *Kommandobefehl*. Hönigschmidt did so as Schönig struggled to look the young Englishman in the eye.

Returning to the men, Crisp conveyed the confirmation of their death sentence, a fate no doubt anticipated following the unexplained journey through the night to the isolated forest. The prisoners were allowed to smoke a final cigarette and take their leave of one another. As final handshakes and embraces were exchanged, Vogt called his firing squad to order.

It is difficult to even begin to imagine the thoughts of the thirty British and

1 The choice of this area was unusual in that the Germans knew it to harbour *maquis* forces. On 27 June, 1944, the FTP *maquis* 'Noel' had been awaiting a parachuted supply drop in the south of the Saint-Sauvant forest when a German repression column had attacked. Twenty seven Germans were reported killed in the engagement, but the *maquis* lost thirty-two men, including their leader, 'Papineau'.

one American as they then turned to face their executioners. It was reported that some chose to throw their watches, photographs and other personal effects to soldiers of the firing squad for safe-keeping.[1] Not wishing to watch the proceedings any further, Deter left Schönig to witness the final act and walked back to the car. As he reached it, a salvo of firing shattered the early morning air, followed shortly by a number of single pistol shots as *coups de grâce* were swiftly administered.

Schönig spent a few minutes grimly collecting identity discs from the bodies before he returned to his car and, with Deter and Hönigschmidt, returned immediately to Poitiers. Behind them Vogt's men were left to bury the bodies in three mass graves which had previously been prepared just inside the trees at the edge of the ride, out of sight of the place of execution. Reporting to Koestlin back in Poitiers, Schönig, who had stood about ten metres to one side, described the the prisoners' last moments:

> 'The execution was accomplished militarily and with dignity. The parachutists died in an exemplary, brave and calm manner, after the decision of the execution had been made known to them in the English language by an interpreter . . . .the prisoners – they were not chained - stood in a line. They linked arms . . . The fire order was given by *Oberleutnant* Vogt.'

Conveniently, General Gallenkamp had returned to Poitiers on the afternoon of 7 July, only a few hours after the execution had taken place. Almost immediately, *Hauptmann* Schönig reported to him on the first floor of his residence 'L'Ermitage' and described the morning's events. In contrast to the subsequent claim of Koestlin that Gallenkamp had been kept informed of the situation during his absence, and indeed had ordered the shootings, the General expressed astonishment at Schönig's news, stating that the *Feldkommandantur* should have been responsible for the custody and care of the prisoners and the SD for their interrogation and subsequent execution. Gallenkamp was also later to maintain, with the aid of a diary which he had kept throughout the war, that he would certainly have vetoed use of the Bicycle Squadron as the firing squad. This was due firstly to their commanding officer being a clergyman who should not have been faced with

---

1 Some doubt must be cast on this description of the execution, which comes from German sources. The bodies of the SAS were found with their hands tied behind their backs. In such circumstances, it is difficult to see how they could have thrown their personal belongings towards the firing squad.

such a conflict of conscience, and secondly it was composed to a large extent of men of the 78th Infantry Division, of which Gallenkamp had been in command for two years. Nor did the Corps Commander approve of the shooting of the prisoners in the same forest in which, only a short while before, other *maquisards* had been killed and buried.

The General then questioned his Intelligence Officer on the reaction of the SAS to their death sentence. He was told that at least some of the British seemed to regard their execution as no more than they expected, and that they had been warned of such a possibility before leaving England. Several had handed over their rings, photographs and other personal effects and Schönig showed Gallenkamp at least one of the photographs, prompting a discussion as to what should be done with the items and whether, in the circumstances, they could be returned to next of kin. Finally, Gallenkamp asked about the execution itself:

'To my question as to how the Englishmen had accepted the announcement of their execution by shooting, Schönig reported that their bearing had been impeccable. He finished his report with the following words: 'General, you may be assured that this was the most terrible day and the hardest hour of my life!' and his eyes filled with tears.'

If Schönig then thought that his part in the affair was over, he was very much mistaken. When he later met Koestlin to present his normal daily report he found General Gallenkamp also present. According to Schönig, Koestlin came straight to the point and said that now the other SAS prisoners were dead, the three wounded must be disposed of in order to avoid them acting as witnesses to what had taken place. He ordered Schönig to again use Hesterberg and to instruct the doctor to kill the wounded by lethal injections. Despite the presence of the General, Schönig protested:

'I replied to the Chief of Staff that this was terrible and in contradiction to soldierly and humane feelings. He repeated his reasons and said that he assumed the responsibility for it.'

Reluctantly, Schönig returned to his office and asked Hesterberg to come to see him. On the doctor's arrival, he passed on the order of the Chief of Staff and tried to explain it by saying that the SAS men had fought bravely and that they therefore deserved assistance; they should not be left to suffer any longer. Although orders existed for their execution, Schönig wanted to avoid shooting the troopers in their beds and he suggested to Hesterberg that a fatal injection or anaesthetic would be more humane. Schönig left no doubt as to what the wounded could expect if Hesterberg did not put them out of their suffering and informed the doctor, 'The others are gone already.' According to Schönig, Hesterberg voiced his displeasure, but then shrugged his shoulders and grudgingly consented to carry out the task.

When Hesterberg reported to the *Feldkommandantur's* prison, he learned that the three SAS wounded had been brought back from the Hôtel-Dieu hospital following a daring *coup de main* which had seen the *maquis* rescue two of their own wounded on the morning of 8 July.

The two Frenchmen spirited away were members of the 'Lagardère' *maquis* who had been wounded and captured by the Germans in an action at Bonneuil-Matours on 11 June. One of the two prisoners, Henri Baudinière, was the brother of the leader of the 'Lagardère', Capitaine André Baudinière and, as such, could expect the group's full efforts to effect his rescue. Despite their wounds, the captured *maquisards* had been brutally interrogated at length by the Poitiers SD before they had been allowed treatment at the Hôtel-Dieu under close guard. It was there that André seized his chance, realizing that his brother could be executed at any moment. Lieutenant 'Thomas' and two other *maquisards* simply drove into the hospital's courtyard at 8 am and, while one man kept guard over the getaway vehicle, the two others entered the building armed with sub-machine guns. The enemy's guards were surprised and held at gunpoint while the two wounded men were found and helped from their beds. Moments later, and without a single shot having been fired to raise the alarm, the *maquisards* were speeding from the city in triumph.

Behind them a sad irony was revealed. Without the 'Lagardère' *maquis* knowing, the three SAS wounded had been in the very same ward as the *maquisards*, and could easily have been rescued at the same time had the situation been realized and adequate transport provided. The SD had therefore taken swift advantage of their good fortune and hastened to the hospital the same evening in order to return the three British to the security of the *Feldkommandantur*. Interne André Clert was to recall the circumstances in which the Germans reclaimed the three troopers from the hospital:

'I seem to remember that the German who was there, the Gestapo,[1] told us to get some stretcher bearers and some stretchers, so we had

1 A common misconception – it was not the Gestapo who were involved but the SD, the SS Security Police.

the wounded men dressed and placed them on stretchers. I believe that the Germans themselves had stretchers in their vehicles, but I cannot be sure of that. I seem to remember that they were taken away lying down. At that time they were taking a number of their sick to Tours; but I do not know whether these men went to Tours. They were moved, since in the same room where they were there were *maquisards*. In the morning a car had come full of armed men and the two *maquisards* who were in the same room as the others were kidnapped by armed men who were *Résistance*. That evening several Germans in civilian clothes whom we knew quite well, since they often came to see their own sick, asked for me and asked me if these sick men could be transported. I told him no; but they ignored my answer and they told me, 'This morning you let the *maquisards* go, tonight you might let the Englishmen go; so we might as well take them away with us now.' I knew one of them; he is dead. He was killed. He was the only one whose name I knew, since he was a Frenchman from the district; he was not a German.'

When they were taken away, Clert believed that the three were better than when they had been first admitted, though Ogg was giving cause for concern since his knee wound was inflamed and he was running a temperature. Pascoe also still required a lot of care, though he could be moved if proper precautions were taken. He could not be allowed, for instance, to sit up. Clert's opinion was that both Ogg and Pascoe would have still needed a lot of care and regular dressing of their wounds to prevent suppuration.

By the time of Hesterberg's second visit to the *Kommandantur,* however, such care had clearly not been forthcoming. The wounded troopers were lying on wooden board beds, without sheets but with blankets. The latter gave off a foul smell and the doctor guessed at the reason when he noted there were no chamber pots in the cells. The wounds were not dressed and discharge from them had further fouled the blankets.

'My second visit was after *Oberst* Koestlin's instructions to kill them had been passed on to me by *Hauptmann* Dr Schönig. This occurred several days after the SD had brought the wounded back back from the Hôtel-Dieu to the prison.

'Contrary to the instructions to kill them, I did everything possible for their wounds and gave injections to ease their pain. I never had any intention to kill the men and I believed that Dr Tönshof, in his capacity of prison doctor, would have them removed to an army hospital. I therefore instructed the NCO in charge, *Oberfeldwebel* Allendorf, to call in Dr Tönshof at once. Because of Dr Tönshof's resonsibilities at the Hôtel-Dieu, he knew the wounded had been returned to the prison.'

Hesterberg was to claim that he had then only applied sulfonamide and given morphine injections to all three before leaving and that, on his return to Corps headquarters, he had managed to avoid directly answering Schönig's questions as to what action he had taken.

Seemingly, Hesterberg's evasiveness did not fool Schönig, since, sometime around 13 July, Hesterberg was again asked to visit the prison. The Corps doctor was reluctant and could not understand why Dr Tönshof was still not available for the job. Indeed, Hesterberg had recently mentioned his calls to the prison to his own immediate superior, Major Weber, and had been told in no uncertain terms that the prison was not his responsibility and that he should 'keep his nose out'. Schönig, however, was insistent upon a third call by Hesterberg to the *Feldkommandantur* and on arrival he was again met and shown to the prisoners by *Oberfeldwebel* Allendorf. The condition of the three men shocked Hesterberg and he took the time to inspect their wounds carefully.

Trooper Ogg had a bullet wound and possible fracture of the tibia below the knee which had become gangrenous. Williams had a gunshot wound in the back which, although originally the least grave of the troopers' injuries, was also by now severely infected and it was not clear whether the bullet was still in the wound or not. Pascoe, plainly the most seriously ill, had a deep, wide wound at the bottom of his back. All three men were now suffering from serious septicaemia, their bandages were dirty and soaked in wound matter and Hesterberg could not believe Allendorf's assertion that Dr Tönshof had seen the prisoners:

> 'On my third visit, I found that the wounded had not been attended to by Dr Tönshof as was his duty – they were in a neglected and moribund condition. I treated their wounds again and gave instructions to ease their pain. Such were for a twilight sleep to ease pain and could in no way cause death.'

Hesterberg returned straight to Schönig's office where the latter listened gravely to the doctor's report of his prison visit. Hesterberg was to claim later that, at this meeting, he made it clear to Schönig that the wounded men would be dead in a matter of days. Two to three days later he was told that his prediction had proved correct and that the three had died. But Schönig again had a different story to tell:

> 'After a few days – three or at most four days may have passed since the transfer to the prison – Hesterberg came to see me again in order to inform me that he had given the injections to the men. He requested me to inform him in case a prison report on deaths which had occurred should reach me.
>
> 'The day after Hesterberg had informed me that he had given the injections, *Hauptmann* Maurer of the *Feldkommandantur* came to me in the morning and informed me of the decease of the wounded Englishmen. He was agitated, and gave me to understand that the prisoners had died an unnatural death. A discussion over this question did not take place between us both. I recollect that Maurer gave expression to his annoyance at the difficulties which would arise for him through the burial. The interment of the dead men was brought about by the *Feldkommandantur*. I reported to *Oberst* Koestlin about the visit of *Hauptmann* Maurer.'

Schönig's version of the events thus presents compelling evidence that, on his third visit, Hesterberg had followed his orders and that Troopers Ogg, Pascoe and Williams were murdered in their prison beds by lethal injections on or around 13 July, 1944. Their bodies were disposed of secretly and no record was kept of either the means or location.

5

REVENGE FROM THE AIR

While the Germans in Poitiers agonized over their duty to the *Führer*, the SAS had gradually regrouped in the countryside near Verrières. On 4 July the eight survivors[1] from the Verrières attack were joined at 'La Roche' by the three troopers who had been away on the operation to attack 'Lot 2'. It had been Trooper Sam Smith who, bored with the inactivity suffered by most of the ordinary troopers, had personally approached Tonkin and asked permission to carry out an attack. Appreciating Smith's frustration, Tonkin agreed, but warned him that a railway attack might be difficult due to the sentries which were now frequently encountered on the lines. Undaunted, Smith, joined by Robert Smith and John Fielding, set out after dark on the evening of 1 July. A driver was to drop them near the line, but then had to return to Verrières to help with other operations. As his first taste of action, the operation is clearly recalled by John Fielding and provides an appreciation of a typical railway sabotage operation:

'My guess is that we were dropped from the jeep somewhere near Gençay. I recall that the driver of the jeep reported to Sam that he was lost and after a time Sam got fed up and told him to stop and leave us at a junction. This he did and when we had got out of the jeep we got out our maps and tried to orientate Sam with the signpost, only to find, after quite a time, that the signpost had obviously been turned around by the *maquis* in order to confuse the Germans.

'We then set sail for the railway line i.e. in approximately a westerly direction. I believe we laid up for a day on the way to the line,

[1] They were: Captain Tonkin, Lieutenant Weaver, Sergeant Holmes, Corporal Rideout and Troopers Cummings, McNair, Keeble and W. Smith.

but there were two incidents which I recall – firstly seeing a German on a white horse passing the other side of a field near a farm whilst we were on the move, and secondly, passing through a factory. I thought it was a lard factory, but Sam says it was a black pudding factory. We then arrived at the village of Anché early one night. We turned right i.e. heading north and, having proceeded up this road a short distance towards the railway line, guard dogs started barking and several bursts of machine-gun fire came down the road. Sam said we were going to lie up in a copse by the road. This we did for about half an hour until the excitement died down and all was quiet. We retraced our steps through Anché, going over a river and I believe we then laid up for a further night. It is then that I believe the incident of the man lowering his trousers and seeing us, which Sam vividly remembers, took place. The following night we headed for the line at a point south of Anché. We arrived at a haystack and Sam said that he only wanted one of us to go with him. Robert Smith and I tossed and I won. He therefore stayed at the haystack which was a pre-arranged rendezvous point and I went with Sam to the line.

'We skirted a wood to the south and then arrived at the cutting, turned right i.e. north, and came to a point where the line was at its lowest point i.e. the cutting was at its steepest. Sam said that he was going down the cutting himself and wanted me to return to the rendezvous point. This I started to do and hadn't moved five yards before I heard Sam roll down the cutting making quite a considerable noise. I then immediately heard a horse approaching from the south and I went into the wood where there was fairly high bracken. I lay down in the bracken a few yards from the track and was able to watch the German on the horse pass me. I was turning over in my own mind what I was going to do if he stopped at the point where Sam had rolled down the embankment, because I had presumed that he had heard him do this. In the event, I was wrong and fortunately he had not heard the noise. He continued past me and out of sight and I then got up and retraced my steps. After about a quarter of an hour, I found that I was lost and fortunately it was starlight so I was able to orientate my map by means of the north star and my compass and I was soon on my way again. I found Robert Smith at the haystack and we waited for Sam to return. We lay between the haystack and a fence and heard Sam coming down the road, whereupon we got up and apparently caused Sam to be severely frightened! He said we were to make haste and get over the bridge over the river, before the line went up and this we did. The explosion duly happened – a very satisfying time!'

At dawn the three came across a house where some local people were talking in the garden. The troopers were warned to keep away from Verrières because there had been trouble there so they went on and spent the day catching up on sleep in the middle of a cornfield. In the evening they continued and met two young Jewish boys on the edge of the Bois des Cartes who took them to a woodman's house in the centre of the wood. Sam Smith decided to head for the farmhouse at the 'Primo la Coupe' DZ where assistance could be expected. But when they got there the old woman who answered the door slammed it in their faces, clearly in great distress over events at Verrières. More concerned than ever, the two Smiths and Fielding stood in the road outside the farm, at a loss as to where to go next. To their great good fortune, however, a number of *maquisards* passed by in a car and, recognizing the troopers, pulled up. The French took them to Captain Maingard at 'La Roche' where it was originally thought that they were the only three remaining SAS. Maingard discussed with them what their future rôle might be and suggested they could be used for training groups of *maquis*. A good meal was prepared for the weary troopers before, depressed at the thought of the fate of their comrades, they settled down in the barn adjacent to the farmhouse. It was only during the following morning that the survivors started to straggle in. All was not lost.

The next day, 5 July, saw the return of the other party which had the good fortune to be away from Verrières at the time of the attack.

Before the move to Verrières Brigade had requested Tonkin to investigate attacking what were reported to be enemy dive bombers and night fighters on the airfield at Châteauroux, and a second message had subsequently reported flying activity there and thirty Junkers aircraft parked under the trees. When transport and fuel finally allowed, Lieutenant Morris had left camp by jeep on 30 June with Trooper Brown as his driver and Godefroy Koenig (codename 'John') as guide in order to attack the airfield at La Martinerie/Châteauroux. Koenig was the *maquis*' cook and was to be ever-grateful for his selection for the operation. The party left by night and travelled through Gouex, over the bridge at Persac, through Adriers and on until dawn when they joined a *maquis* headquarters in a wood near Azat-le-Ris. From there they were led to the elusive Captain Sadoine's camp in another wood a few kilometres away. In the afternoon of 2 July the group, accompanied by Sadoine, set off for the explosives dump created by the

Phantom team. With Lieutenant Morris at the wheel, the jeep had just taken a sharp bend when it came face to face with a herd of cows. A swerve to the right avoided the herd, but with a telegraph pole immediately ahead, Morris had to wrench the wheel violently to the left and the jeep crashed and turned over, throwing everyone into the road. Of the four, only Sadoine was unscathed; Morris and Brown had leg injuries and Koenig appeared to have cracked some ribs. The jeep was pushed upright, but, with its steering damaged, had to be taken to a nearby farm. The SAS and Koenig spent the night sleeping there with Sadoine's party and at dawn were woken by gunfire in the distance. Later they received the news of the disaster at Verrières. Unable to return to their base camp, their overriding concern was to avoid causing any trouble for the farmer. The jeep was therefore pushed down a small track and covered with foliage. They were driven to the village of Oradour-sur-Vayres where they were hidden in a house while they recuperated for another two days before rejoining Tonkin's survivors near the Forêt de Plessac. Their jeep was now the only one left to the SAS.

Tonkin's party of eleven had regrouped close to the Forêt de Plessachere on the 5th after a move of some 35 kilometres south-east from Verrières. It was an area where the SAS had not yet operated and consequently afforded some sense of security. Having lost the services of Corporal Chick, captured at Verrières, Tonkin was now in urgent need of signals support and therefore immediately sent Lieutenant Weaver and Corporal Rideout, with six *maquisards* and adequate transport, to bring in Sadoine's Phantom group. Tonkin then radioed England the next day to confirm that all his men were now concentrated and ready again for operations. There were just eighteen left out of the original strength of fifty-four.

Tonkin now had to reorganize his survivors into operational groups and looked to make the most of the abilities of those left. Among them, Trooper McNair had shown his resourcefulness in helping Tonkin on the afternoon and evening of the 3rd, immediately after the attack. Tonkin dearly wanted McNair to continue to take more responsibility but was aware of the man's background:

> 'To explain, I had one Trooper whom I had had my eye on right through training as an obvious candidate for promotion. He was a natural. I tried to persuade him on several occasions but he always flatly refused. Just before we were dropped in, I got his Army history. He had been a 2/Lt in the Armoured Corps in the Western Desert in a Matilda with its pop-gun two pounder against the German 88's. Of course, in that bit of war, the tank commander

fought with the hatch open and his head and shoulders out. This 2/Lt had had three tanks brewed up underneath him and had got out each time physically unscathed but with his three crews burned to death. He flatly refused to command any more men, resigned his commission and sought transfer to an infantry fighting unit as a private. When we were in the U.K. he joined the SAS as a trooper and was allocated to my mob.'

On 9 July, and in accordance with Tonkin's decision to stay close to the *maquis*, the SAS moved some 20 kilometres to the west near to Charroux and joined a strong *maquis* camp there. Following Brigade's instructions, Tonkin was to begin to look for a suitable landing ground in the area west of Limoges in order to arrange an air evacuation of his party. In the interim the British concentrated on instructing the *maquis* and planning small-scale sabotage since they could not operate fully without more equipment. Two Stirlings of 190 Squadron had reported successfully dropping containers on the 'Bulbasket' DZ on the night of 3/4 July, but at that time the SAS and *maquis* were still reeling from the Verrières disaster and no reception committee had therefore been arranged at 'Primo La Coupe', the supplies going instead to Sadoine's DZ. It was not until the night of 13/14 July that another resupply drop was arranged. Again, a Stirling of 190 Squadron attempted the task but failed to locate the new DZ south of Usson-du-Poitou and had to turn back. Bad weather on the return journey forced the aircraft to land at RAF Ford on the English south coast.

But at least a little light relief came Tonkin's way when, at the conclusion of a four-day 'active recce' trip with Sergeant Holmes and Trooper Cummings starting on the 10th, the *maquis* invited him to watch their Bastille Day parade in the small town of Luchapt on 14 July. In a ceremony which did wonders for Tonkin's own morale, as well as that of the local population, he took the salute from the smartly turned-out *maquisard* guard and photographed the event for the record. The event was a fitting end to a testing trip for Tonkin and his party. In the remaining jeep they had reached the 'Lot 1' line and successfully cut it two nights running before starting back to camp. The parade at Luchapt gave a welcome opportunity to wind down and for the moment it was easy to forget that the celebrations were taking place in what was still enemy-held territory.

Meanwhile, as the SAS settled to their task again, efforts had already begun back in England to seek retribution against the German units responsible for the Verrières attack and the murder of Lieutenant Stephens and the seven men of the *maquis*.

Tonkin's post-operation report states that he called for an air attack on the Germans on 5 July, just two days after Verrières. This message may have been transmitted to England via Captain Maingard's SOE radio link to Special Forces Headquarters since no record remains of it in the 'Bulbasket' log, but Tonkin believed he already had a map reference for the location of the Germans at Bonneuil-Matours, 22 kilometres north-east of Poitiers. This was a barracks complex, identified as being the sleeping quarters of most of the German troops responsible for the operation at Verrières on 3 July. Even if Tonkin's memory misled him over this point, London certainly knew of the Germans' whereabouts when a Special Forces message on 12 July pinpointed the location. The message came from the Jedburgh team 'Hugh', who, it will be remembered, dropped with Tonkin and Crisp on 6 June. Now operating to the north-east of 'Bulbasket' in the Indre region, Bill Crawshay had obtained the exact location of the headquarters of the so-called 'repression column' which had taken part in the Verrières attack. 'Hugh' had its sights set on the château where the German unit's officers lived, the message reading:

'Request special bombing of HQ Boche Colonel commanding repression columns Indre, Vienne, Creuse et Loire. Situated Bonneuil-Matours. 15 km south of Châtellerault. Château 450 metres south-east of crossroads east of village. 100 metres south of road from Archigny. Defence company in wood 30 metres east of trenches along River Vienne from crossroad TTT 200 yards to south. Also probably tanks.'

The château identified was the Château de Marieville, an imposing residence sited on a hill on the east bank of the River Vienne. The house had been requisitioned by the Colonel commanding the 17th SS *Panzergrenadier* Division's holding battalion and the SS troops themselves were in barracks along the lightly wooded west bank of the river, the latter feature and a nearby bridge providing excellent reference points for an air attack.

From Special Forces Headquarters the message was passed to the head-quarters of the SAS Brigade where no time was wasted in using their established contacts with the RAF to seek revenge. Again the Brigade's Intelligence Officer, Captain Michael Foot, telephoned 2 Group to ask for help.

At this point in time there is no indication that London was aware of the execution of the SAS prisoners, indeed, it remains unclear today as to the extent that the survivors knew of the fate of their comrades. John Fielding thought rumours had circulated that the prisoners had been shot, but, with the passage of time since the war, he cannot be certain. On the other hand, John Tonkin was adamant he knew nothing of the execution until after the liberation of France. Taking into account the measures adopted by the Germans to conceal their deeds at Saint-Sauvant, it seems this is the more likely situation. Captain Foot's call for an air attack has therefore to be seen in the context of an operation chiefly to avenge the death of just one SAS officer, Lieutenant Twm Stephens, and the seven young *maquisards*.

When the call reached the RAF, it came at the busiest time of the war and 2 Group's squadrons were faced with constant demands for round-the-clock air operations, above and immmediately beyond the invasion area. They might therefore have been excused for turning down the SAS's plea for help. Typically, they did not.

The circumstances of the SAS's call touched a raw nerve with 2 Group's Air Officer Commanding, the formidable Air Vice-Marshal Basil Embry. As a Wing Commander, Embry had been shot down flying a Blenheim light bomber over occupied France in May 1940. After only a brief spell of imprisonment he had managed to escape from his captors and had successfully made his way back to England in less than ten weeks. In doing so, however, he had killed three German soldiers and consequently the German High Command had put a price on his head.[1]

This had not deterred the fearless Embry from pursuing a personal crusade against the Germans. He often arrived to fly with his squadrons under an assumed identity and lower rank, contrary to the orders of his own superiors and scornful of the consequences if he were to be shot down and fall into the hands of the Germans. Embry particularly liked to join Mosquito operations, having the highest possible regard for de Havilland's design. He had fought hard to equip much of 2 Group with the type and considered it the finest aeroplane ever built in Britain.

On the 14th Embry was unable to join the air operations, but, as a confirmed German-hater, he considered the task important enough to travel down from 2 Group headquarters (at Mongewell Park near Wallingford in Berkshire) to 140 Wing which had by now moved to RAF Thorney Island near Portsmouth on the south coast. Accompanied by his Senior Air Staff Officer, David Atcherley, Embry personally briefed the fourteen crews detailed to carry out the operation. Although the day had been cloudy, the

---

1 For an excellent account of Embry's escape from France, see *Wingless Victory* by Anthony Richardson, Odhams Press Ltd 1950. Embry retired from the RAF as Air Chief Marshal Sir Basil Embry KCB KBE DSO DFC AFC.

evening promised to be fair and suitable for a precision attack. The operation was therefore timed to reach the target at dusk, Wing Commander 'Black' Smith of the New Zealand squadron making the useful suggestion that the attack should be delivered at evening meal time, in order to catch the maximum number of Germans in the buildings.

Embry made no bones about his feelings towards the task in hand, pointing out that it was Bastille Day and the attack would therefore also serve to raise the spirits of the French people on this symbolic day. This time the attack was only to be undertaken by 140 Wing and so 464 and 487 Squadrons were joined by their sister 21 Squadron, a regular RAF unit commanded by Wing Commander David Dennis.

David Dennis was another example of the able and operationally experienced officers that Embry insisted upon to command his squadrons. Having joined the RAF's Volunteer Reserve in 1937, Dennis joined 21 Squadron on his first operational tour in 1940, flying the Bristol Blenheim light bomber. Surviving a challenging tour of thirty operations, Dennis had then served a supposed 'rest' tour with a training unit before returning to 21 Squadron for a second operational tour, now flying the little more effective Lockheed Ventura bomber. After another thirty-four operational sorties he returned to the training unit, now as Chief Instructor, but was back with 21 Squadron as soon as possible for a third tour as a flight commander with the rank of Squadron Leader. In only two months he had completed the thirty operations of his third tour and promoted to Wing Commander, became the unit's commanding officer. No one could challenge David Dennis' credentials for leading 21 Squadron.

Where time allowed, 2 Group's headquarters staff normally produced a scale model to aid briefing of a pinpoint attack, but Embry explained that this had not been possible in the time available. The Air Vice-Marshal did, however, make it clear that the attack was to be a reprisal operation and revealed that the barracks in question housed a German unit responsible for clubbing to death a British prisoner of war. At the time Embry was under the impression that the Germans involved were from the dreaded Gestapo, and this only added to his resolve that 140 Wing should make a good job of the task. He clearly wanted to fire up his crews with a passion for revenge and Eric Ramsey, a navigator with 464 Squadron, recalls that Embry did not beat about the bush when describing how the Germans had 'bashed somebody's head in'. Six Mosquitos were to be equipped with special new incendiary bombs which were delivered to the airfield by American trucks shortly before take-off. Four aircraft with high explosive bombs would first open up the target; the incendiaries would then be dropped and finally more high explosive would be delivered to spread the effect around. Other aircraft were detailed to patrol the road alongside the River Vienne and shoot up any approaching reinforcements. Describing the plan, Embry cold-bloodedly urged his crews to 'let the bastards burn!', but nevertheless realized that any hint of a reprisal operation could provoke the Germans into 'tit for tat' tactics. His final words were therefore:

> 'If you get shot down and taken prisoner, don't shoot your mouth
> off about retaliation. You can't out-piss a skunk!'

The decision was taken not to attack the solidly built château, but to instead go for the barracks where there would be a greater and more vulnerable concentration of the enemy. There was no mention of any SAS involvement and none of the air crews were aware that British forces were operating so far behind enemy lines.

Of the fourteen Mosquito crews briefed, twelve came equally from 140 Wing's three squadrons and were led by the respective squadron commanding officers. Thus, Wing Commander David Dennis led four aircraft of 21 Squadron, Wing Commander 'Black' Smith four of 487 Squadron RNZAF and Wing Commander Gordon Panitz four of 464 Squadron RAAF. Panitz had only taken over command of the Australian squadron on 22 June after Bob Iredale had been posted on a rest tour to 2 Group headquarters. For Panitz the operation was to round off a hectic day which had earlier seen him fly to RAF Hartford Bridge, with his navigator Flight Lieutenant Williams, where both men were invested with the Distinguished Flying Cross by King George VI.[1]

The squadron aircraft were joined by two crews from the Wing's head-quarters' staff, Group Captain Peter Wykeham-Barnes electing to lead the operation with Flying Officer Chaplin as his navigator and joined by his Wing Commander (Flying), Wing Commander Reggie Reynolds with navigator Flight Lieutenant Ted Sismore, the Wing's navigation leader.

Reynolds and Sismore[2] were a long-established Mosquito team and by now one of the 'star' crews in 2 Group's galaxy. Their most renowned operation to date had been on 30 January, 1943, when Berlin was celebrating the

---

[1] Panitz and Williams were killed only the following month when they were shot down on 22 August while attacking a railway target near Dijon.

[2] Reynolds and Sismore went on to survive the war. Ted Sismore was later to qualify as a pilot and followed a distinguished career in the post-war air force before retiring as an Air Commodore with a DSO, DFC and AFC.

tenth anniversary of Hitler's seizure of power. At 11 am *Reichsmarschall* Hermann Göring was scheduled to address a large assembly at the German capital's Air Ministry and the RAF decided that an accompaniment was called for. Then serving in the Mosquito bombers of 105 Squadron, Reynolds and Sismore led a formation of only three aircraft over the city and released their bombs just in time to disrupt the start of Berlin's radio commentary. Back in England, the other crews of 105 Squadron had listened in delight as the German radio announcer reported a postponement of Göring's speech for an hour. Unfortunately for the morale of the listening German masses, the noise of exploding bombs in the background was all too evident. They recalled that their *Reichsmarschall* had once promised that no British aircraft would ever bomb Germany.

For the operation of 14 July all aircraft took off in the evening shortly before 9 o'clock and formed up into a tidy formation for the trip across the Channel. At 2,000 feet the Mosquitos safely skirted the Cherbourg penin-sula but a few moments later were rocked by explosions as a heavy *flak* battery on the Channel Island of Alderney opened up. The fighter-bombers swiftly scattered in what Flight Lieutenant Gordon Bell-Irving, a Canadian pilot in 21 Squadron, described as 'a relatively disciplined way' before reforming once the guns were out-distanced. Despite the disturbance, the Mosquito crews still took the time to professionally note two small ships in Alderney harbour with a collier or tanker just outside and twelve ships in the Jersey roadsteads. All would be reported at the Intelligence de-briefing on return to Thorney Island.

Over the Bay of St Michel the Mosquito formation was met by an escort of twelve Mustang III fighters from 122 Wing's 65 Squadron RAF, led by Squadron Leader Lamb. Based on the continent at B7 Airfield, Martragny, the Mustangs would be able to afford the Mosquitos extra protection during the daylight stage of their flight over enemy-held territory, the combination of Mosquitos and Mustangs presenting a formidable force should the *Luftwaffe* dare to interfere. Together, and still in strict radio silence, the fighter-bombers and their escorts crossed the French coast near St Malo and then dropped to just 50 feet near Rennes. 60 miles south of Rennes the Mustangs turned back for Martragny which, as day fighters, they planned to reach before night fell.

Shortly before reaching the target, the Mosquito flights climbed to the planned bombing height of 1,000 feet and then swept in to the attack. With no cloud and excellent visibility, the target was easily identified alongside the river and, while small arms fire spat out from a number of doorways on the approach, the only opposition of any real concern was a 20mm gun wildly firing tracer from the roof of a nearby large house. After the first aircraft had released their bombs, smoke enveloped the gun position and the tracer had stopped.

No warning had been given of the fighter-bombers' approach and the townspeople only heard the roar of Merlin engines as the Mosquitos pulled up from the river valley, causing the onlookers to believe that the aircraft had glided in with engines cut in order to surprise the Germans. In actual fact, the sheer speed and low altitude of their attack had ensured that the Mosquitos were upon the target before the Germans had time to hear their approach and organize themselves.

The bombs used were a mixture of eleven seconds' delay and instanta-neously fused high explosive, along with the new American M76 phosphorous incendiary bombs.[1] As the last crews called 'bombs gone' over the target they reported the area and buildings carpeted in flames, the majority of bombs having fallen in the target area with only a few over-shooting towards the neighbouring village and a couple on the east bank of the river.

For the SS troops their ordeal was far from over. As they stumbled from the blasted remains of their barracks a growling crescendo of noise rose above the roaring of the flames as the Mosquitos banked round and dived back into the attack. Through the rising smoke the graceful aircraft streaked in with their nose cannon and machine guns spitting venomously, hosing down any of the black-uniformed figures unlucky enough to be caught in the open. Knowing something of the reason for the raid, the Mosquito men were in no mood for pity.

Night was falling as the Mosquitos left the blazing target and consequently no attempt was made to formate, each aircraft making its individual way back to England where all landed safely at Thorney Island between 0015 and 0045 hours on the 15th. On the return journey Wing Commander Smith jettisoned two unused bombs in a lake nine miles east of Châteaubriant and three trains were spotted and attacked by the Mosquitos, two being seen to stop and emit steam. *Flak* was encountered at a number of points but only one Mosquito was hit, that of Group Captain Wykeham-Barnes which received slight damage from a close burst of heavy anti-aircraft fire.

Behind them the Mosquitos had left a scene of awesome destruction. All

---

[1] Several of the Mosquito crews on this raid, including senior officers, recall that post-war it was claimed this new bomb was effectively the first napalm bomb. If so, then the attack on Bonneuil-Matours constituted the first operational use of the weapon.

seven barrack blocks had been blasted and, as planned, the SS had been caught during their evening meal of lamb stew. They had only just returned after a successful operation in the Indre-Ouest against the 'Gilles' *maquis* in the Bélâbre area and there were estimated to be some 400 enemy troops in camp at the time of the attack. One wayward bomb, on the opposite river bank, had only just missed the Château de Marieville and had consequently given the SS headquarters staff a bad, if unintentional, fright. Throughout the night the town's inhabitants feared reprisals, but happily none were forthcoming as the Germans occupied themselves with transferring their wounded to Poitiers. A number of local men were compelled to help lift bodies into lorries, but otherwise the local people were left unmolested. Quietly, they celebrated the raid which had caused their unwelcome lodgers to choke on their evening meal, the more so as the Germans' stew was made from sheep stolen from local farms. A couple of days later the German camp was completely abandoned when the SS survivors left Bonneuil-Matours for good.[1]

On the 15th Tonkin only learned that the air attack had taken place when he received a radio message from England, asking on behalf of the RAF about results of the bombing. No reply is recorded from Tonkin himself, but a few days later 140 Wing heard that French *Résistance* forces believed 150 German troops had died in the attack and the Jedburgh team 'Hugh' radioed London on the 21st to pass on a report that 200 Germans had been killed. Local *Gendarmerie* records suggest a total of 80-100 killed and wounded, so, allowing for *Résistance* over-enthusiasm, the Police estimate is likely to be the more accurate. Whatever the exact figures, the raid had been a complete success.

In contrast to the drama of the air attack, events in the field were relatively low-key while the SAS regained their momentum. Numbers in camp were increased by the addition of several USAAF evaders brought in by the *maquis*, the first being Lieutenant Harper on 16 July who had been shot down in his Lockheed P-38 fighter when attacking a ground target. Two days later, four more arrived, Lieutenants Bradley and Scott and Sergeants Gross and Norton, who had been shot down some six months before but had then managed to escape from a P.O.W. camp. Another two downed airmen, Sergeants Ward and Hitchcock, were reported as having suffered sprain

---

[1] Today piles of twisted steel-reinforced concrete, alongside a new car park, bear testimony to the accuracy of the RAF's bombing at Bonneuil-Matours. Just one or two stray bomb fragments hit the stone gateway of the large house opposite the barracks site but there was little other damage in the town and no civilian casualties.

injuries and for the time being remained at a farm in the area in order to recover. While most of the Americans were happy to help the SAS with cooking, labouring and general camp chores, there were three exceptions. One of the young Sergeant air gunners was terrified at the thought of what might happen to him if discovered in the company of the SAS and consequently wanted to play no part whatsoever in their activities. By way of contrast, Lieutenant Bill Bradley and Lieutenant Flamm D. Harper could not wait to get to grips with the Germans again, one of them telling Tonkin, 'I see no reason why the lack of an aeroplane should stop me fighting'. They were immediately added to the list of SAS personnel available for operations.

Then, as Tonkin made preparations to receive further supply drops, his plans were again interrupted by reports of German troops moving into nearby Charroux. Concerned at the limited strength of his depleted party, Tonkin moved on to the east and on 15 July joined a strong *maquis* group in their camp at Asnières-sur-Blour, west of the Limoges to Poitiers road.

Asnières was to become the most established of the SAS bases. Under the protection of the large *maquis* group they felt safer from enemy attack and most of the German forces were now some way to the north. A good, easily-identifiable DZ was established immediately next to the camp and on the night of the 16th/17th John Tonkin stood out on the site in the early hours of the morning in order to make a somewhat novel telephone call.

This task was made possible by the S-Phone which had been dropped to the SAS. An ultra-high-frequency radio telephone, first developed by SOE, it enabled a conversation to take place between one party on the ground and another in a circling aircraft above. The day before, Tonkin had been told by Brigade Headquarters that Lieutenant-Colonel Mayne, 1st SAS's commanding officer, would be flying over the DZ and was hoping to speak to him on the S-Phone. But although Tonkin kept his appointment with the circling aircraft, the new radio link would not work and eventually Mayne had to return to England without having made contact. Despite this failure, the viability of the new DZ was proved the following night, the 17th, when a re-supply drop was made by a Stirling of 196 Squadron from Keevil. The pilot reported that the site was easily identified, enabling 24 containers and four packages to be successfully dropped before an uneventful return flight home.

The general area around the new base proved secure enough for the troopers to now enjoy a little of local life. Numerous visits were paid to the café in the village of Asnières, using the kitchen not only for drinking and eating, but also for passing and receiving messages since the SAS' radio set was kept there. In the village square adjacent to the café Sam Smith and John

Fielding took parachute silk to the house of a local woman and, while they played cards, she made up shirts for them from the fabric. Friendly rivalry with their *maquis* comrades also led to the SAS challenging the French to a game of football, recalled by Fielding:

'We played football against the *maquis* on a field north of the farm . . . The result of the match I cannot recall, but I can recall that I played inside right and John played centre forward, his prowess at football not being exactly in the class of Sam! My view of his ability on the football field is that he was probably a far better rugger player than soccer player. During the course of the match, the *maquis* guarded the touch lines and I cannot recall whether or not we had a referee.'

As well as taking time out to relax, the SAS troops also prepared to start operations from their new base. Attention again turned towards railway targets, even though the lines were now known to be heavily guarded. On 20 July a *Résistance* report of thirty locomotives stuck in Poitiers railway station was radioed back to London, this tempting target being too well guarded to permit an attack by the SAS and *maquis*. Instead, Sergeant Johnny Holmes went out that night to the Poitiers-Bordeaux line and laid pressure-operated explosive mines, known as 'fog signals', on the line. These were designed to operate from a pressure fuse and were thus designed to blow up a train passing over them, rather than just blowing the track. Unfortunately, Holmes's mines were twice brushed aside when scoop-equipped trains passed down the line, but, undaunted, he reverted to simpler methods and blew a stretch of line north of Epanvilliers.

The Poitiers-Bordeaux railway was now claiming most attention and on 22/23 July the SAS made another attack on the line. The raiding party, a model of allied co-operation, consisted of Tonkin and Fielding from the SAS, Maurice Dieudonné of the *maquis* and Lieutenant Bradley, one of the shot-down American airmen. John Fielding was designated to guard the jeep while the three others approached the line:

'Our attack on this night was the Paris-Bordeaux railway line between Romagne and Couhé. This is a distance of 44 kilometres in a straight line from Asnières and involved a journey there and back of approximately 100 kilometres. John Tonkin must have therefore had his foot on the floor in both directions.

'He says that he drove to within approximately 150 yards of the line and I was left in charge of the jeep in the middle of a wood. He said that he and the other two ran all the way back from the line to the jeep and came back to me very breathless.'

The hurried return of the demolition party was due to the appearance of a German sentry. Tonkin had consequently not been able to use his pull switches on the line in an attempt to derail a train and it was therefore a disappointed party that returned to Asnières, the 'Bulbasket' signals log showing that this was not managed until a day later. Before planning could start on further operations, a radioed order was received on the 24th – 'Cease Operations'.

As early as 7 July Major Lepine and six SAS troopers had stood by to reinforce 'Bulbasket', but their participation was cancelled at the last moment. Tonkin had also twice called for four more jeeps and had stood by to receive them on 14 July, but again the drop did not materialize and it became clear that Brigade Headquarters had only limited plans for the future use of the 'Bulbasket' survivors. Instead, it was decided to pull out what was left of Tonkin's troop and replace it with a large contingent of French SAS in 'Operation Moses'. Already, two French SAS officers had parachuted in to the west of Parthenay on the night of 15/16 July, accompanying another three-man Jedburgh team, 'Harold'. The new arrivals had visited Tonkin's camp on 22 July when Major Whitty, commanding officer of 'Harold', had used the SAS's radio to report back to England, his own set having been damaged during the parachute drop. Having done so, the newcomers moved on to organize the swelling *maquis* groups in the area, a task with which Tonkin was still struggling due to the lack of any great linguistic ability in his group. Consequently, Tonkin was advised that an officer of 1st SAS would be parachuted in to join him in the near future in order to identify an airstrip suitable for flying out the survivors.

While they waited for this expert to arrive, there were still numerous small tasks for the SAS to carry out. On the 25th details, including an identity disc, arrived from the crash site of an allied bomber, some 15 kilometres to the south of Asnières. The aircraft had come down on the night of 22/23 July with the loss of all eight men on board and, while Tonkin had been away on his railway attack, Lieutenant Weaver and two others attended the funeral of some of the dead in the village of Brillac. Though it was not appreciated at the time, the aircraft was a Stirling of 620 Squadron RAF, one of the squadrons responsible for the regular resupply of 'Bulbasket'. On this occasion Flying Officer Oke was detailed to drop supplies for SOE and it is unknown whether *flak* or a prowling German night fighter brought the four-engined bomber down. When it crashed, fire engulfed the aircraft, making identification of the bodies a grim and difficult task.

At about 0100 hours on 29 July Pilot Officer Hoysted's Stirling bomber of 196 Squadron arrived over the Asnières DZ carrying Squadron Leader Richards, another of the SAS's old friends from the Parachute Training School at RAF Ringway near Manchester. Richards was carrying out the duties of dispatcher for the night and was accompanied at the open hatch of the Stirling by two SAS officers. While Lieutenant David Surrey Dane prepared to jump, Captain Mike Sadler successfully used an S-Phone to talk with John Tonkin on the ground and ascertain that all was well. Satisfied, Sadler nodded to Surrey Dane who disappeared through the hatch into the darkness. A few minutes later, the young Lieutenant himself came up on the S-Phone and reported his safe landing to Sadler. While the equipment had at last worked satisfactorily, there was one drawback which caused unease amongst those on the ground. Reception was so loud and clear that the voice from the orbiting aicraft was heard over something like a quarter mile radius – hardly ideal for clandestine operations.

As the Stirling turned for home, the reception party collected the twenty-four containers and four panniers which had also been dropped, among the supplies being a vital piece of kit which had been personally requested by John Tonkin – a pair of size 10 boots. Surrey Dane was led to the nearby camp where he was warmly received and given a cup of tea. Only then did Tonkin reveal that he had watched Surrey Dane's parachute 'breathe', i.e. close and open, as he came down. Although Tonkin had experienced a few anxious moments, the young Lieutenant had fortunately been wholly unaware of the drama.

Surrey Dane was another of 1st SAS's enthusiastic but operationally inexperienced recruits. As an 18-year-old schoolboy he had volunteered for the army and joined up as an infantry Private. Successful in obtaining a commission, he had then joined the Reconnaissance Corps before volunteering for the Parachute Regiment in 1943. After earning his wings he was posted to the 4th Parachute Brigade and it was while there, still kicking his heels in the spring of 1944, that he heard the SAS was expanding and looking for volunteers. He joined 1st SAS in April and in May moved with the Regiment to the secure camp at Fairford. As very much the 'new boy', Surrey Dane only had a brief opportunity to become acquainted with his fellow officers, including John Tonkin and Twm Stephens, before he and Lieutenant MacReady were sent on an RAF-run course to train in the selection, preparation and operation of clandestine airstrips. When the SAS then dispatched its first operations in support of the invasion, Surrey Dane was still undergoing this training and so again missed the opportunity to get out of England in his pursuit of active service. In joining 'Bulbasket', he at last had his search for adventure fulfilled.

Before his departure the young Lieutenant had been briefed by the RAF at SOE's Baker Street headquarters in London. He had been advised of three possible sites to be reconnoitred and was provided with the instructions for an evacuation airlift of all 'Bulbasket' personnel back to England. On arrival, he found his fellow SAS in good spirits and looking forward to going home. Despite the setback of Verrières, Tonkin showed no signs of flagging and Surrey Dane would later comment:

> 'At the time I thought that the good morale I found was largely due to his courage and leadership.'

Without delay Surrey Dane set about his task and on 30 July was sent off by John Tonkin in search of a suitable airstrip. After the loss of three of their four jeeps at Verrières, the survivors had been compelled to requisition local transport and Surrey Dane was therefore taken on this trip by Lieutenant Morris in a battered Citroën car which looked not unlike the one used by Inspector Maigret. It had no clutch or starter motor so the passengers had to push start it and then jump in when it was going. Fortunately, Lieutenant Morris proved adept at changing gear without a clutch once the car was on the move. Despite these shortcomings, the car served its purpose adequately and the two officers headed north to look at the sites suggested to Surrey Dane back in England.

The trip about the French countryside proved eventful and served as a good introduction to Surrey Dane as to how things were in the field. On their first sortie of over 100 kilometres, he could not believe that he, Morris and their driver could trust not to run across the enemy at some point. He was proved correct:

> 'As it turned out we did just that, but fortune was on our side. We found ourselves driving past an Army barracks guarded by two smartly dressed French North African soldiers wearing red tarbooshes. They were obviously being employed by the other side. When they saw us they sprang to attention and presented arms. Our surprise and pleasure at being greeted in this way was short-lived.
> 'Further down the road were two German soldiers, tunics undone, strolling casually back to the barracks carrying their mess tins. Lieutenant Morris told us to keep our guns down and look

27. (L to R) Lt Harper (USAAF), with Troopers Cummings, R. Smith and Fielding in front of Capt. Maingard's SOE car. (*Dr D. Dane*)

28. A Mosquito, its shadow in the foreground, records damage to the Caserne des Dunes barracks the day after the air raid of 1.8.44 (*Air Cdre E. Sismore*)

29. (L to R) Capt. Maingard of SOE, Lt Peter Weaver (with beige SAS beret) and Lt Cameron of 3rd SAS. (*Dr. D. Dane*)

30. At 'Bon Bon' – (L to R) Tpr Keeble, USAAF Sgt (unidentified) Capt. Tonkin, Sgt Holmes, Tpr Cummings, Tpr Smith, Lt Harper (USAAF), Tpr Fielding (standing), Sgnm Plumb (Phantom), Phantom signaller (unidentified). (*Dr D. Dane*)

31. Lt David Surrey Dane (left) greets the French 3rd SAS of 'Operation Moses' on their arrival in the USAAF Douglas C-47. (*Dr D. Dane*)

32. The C-47 (Dakota) at 'Bon Bon' — taken by time-lapse exposure. (*Dr D. Dane*)

33. An autopsy under way in the Saint-Sauvant forest, December, 1944. (*Miss I. Crisp*)

34. Executed maquisards in the forest at Verrières. (*R. Picard*)

35. The three wounded troopers who disappeared from the Poitiers *Feldkommandantur*: (L to R) Joe Ogg, Henry 'Sam' Pascoe, John Williams. (*D. Braddick and A. & C. Peterkin*)

6. Col Clifford Heflin, pilot of he C-47. (*J. Abrahams*)

37. F/L Mussett (left) and P/O Burrows, shot down 1.8.44 attacking the Caserne des Dunes barracks in Poitiers. (*S. Chambon*)

38. The memorial at La Couarde on the edge of the forest at Verrières. (*Author*)

39. The grave of Lt Lincoln D. Bundy, the USAAF fighter pilot who was captured and executed with the SAS. (*Author*)

40. The Saint-Sauvant memorial erected in 1973 and, on the right, the track where the SAS prisoners faced their firing squad. (*Author*)

41. Hundreds of local people paid their last respects at the re-burial ceremony. (*Miss I. Crisp*)

42. Major John Tonkin MC, back in the Vienne, July, 1987. (*D. Chansigaud*)

43. 50 years on, John Fielding pays tribute at Saint-Sauvant to his executed colleagues, July 1994. (*Author*)

44. At the Saint-Sauvant 50th anniversary ceremony, former Résistance members Albert Dupont (left) and Denis Chansigaud recalled their days with the SAS in 1944. (*Author*)

straight ahead. As we drove past them the Germans showed no interest, which was probably just as well for all concerned.

'From its bonnet the Citroën was flying a Free French flag, which was an ordinary French flag adorned with the Cross of Lorraine. It was difficult to see the Cross of Lorraine from a distance and the sentries probably took us for *Milice*. The two Germans may also have thought it improbable that a hostile vehicle would drive past their barracks and we certainly had not done so intentionally! Later, when we were looking for the second of the map references the RAF had given me, we saw what appeared to be an armoured car a mile away across some open fields. Eventually, to our relief, it moved away without showing any sign of wanting to take a closer look at us.'

Of the three possible sites identified by the RAF, Surrey Dane and Morris visited two unsuitable ones on their first sortie but the next day found a much better location, north of Montmorillon and close to the hamlets of Haims and Villemort. The two SAS officers approached and introduced themselves to the farmer owning the site who, to their relief, was everything they could have hoped for: intelligent and very much on their side. Surrey Dane appreciated that it was a risky business allowing a field to be used as a clandestine airstrip. The people using the airstrip spent a relatively short time there and those who had not left by plane could melt into the surrounding countryside, but the farmer had to remain behind, hoping the Germans had not pinpointed the landing site. This farmer also revealed to the two officers that, in November, 1943, another pick-up had been carried out from one of his fields when a RAF Lysander delivered two agents and returned to England with two members of the SOE 'Zetland-Dahlia' network and a downed RAF flyer. The particular field used then was not, however, large enough for the Lockheed Hudson aircraft which the RAF now planned to send to pick up John Tonkin's party, the twin-engined type ideally needing a strip 1600 yards long by 800 wide. Luckily, there was another adjacent field which appeared suitable if a tree in the flight path were cut down. Surrey Dane code-named the potential airstrip 'Bon Bon' and subsequently radioed its description and location to England on the 31st:

'Surface stubble looks clover. Security OK. One excellent strip can be cleared, hedges trimmed to 2 metres and one tree felled, given one day's notice.'

While at Asnières, Surrey Dane also soon discovered that life in the camp had its sombre side:

'The morning after I had parachuted in to join John Tonkin, he took me to visit a group of *maquisards* hidden a few hundred yards away from the SAS camp. They were using an old pigsty as a shelter and I can remember having to bend down to look inside and greet their leader. Sitting next to him on the floor was a young woman whose head had been shaved. This made a lasting impression on me as she was the first shaven-headed woman collaborator I had seen. It was explained to me that they were holding her until some enquiries about her collaboration had been completed. I never saw her again.

'When I returned to camp one evening after being away during the day, one of the SAS soldiers told me what had happened to her. Word must have come through that she had committed a serious crime. Perhaps she had been the mistress of a German officer. The trooper saw her being taken past the SAS camp to a nearby wood by two members of the local *maquis*. One carried a spade and the other a Sten gun. After a while there was a burst of automatic fire and later the two men reappeared, one carrying the fur coat she had been wearing. They said that before they shot her she removed the coat and gave it to them saying that it would be of more use to them than to her.

'I thought at the time and have thought many times since how lucky we were in Britain not to have been occupied by the Germans. It meant we were spared this sort of killing.'

Troopers John Fielding and Sam Smith also never forgot the incidents involving the alleged spies and collaborators, Fielding remembering:

'I believe there were two executions by the *maquis*, one being the French/Canadian spy and the other one a woman. These two were executed in the wood adjacent to the DZ.

'Both the man and the woman were brought through our base and I also recall seeing the woman being informed of her pending execution the following morning – she was taken into the field between our base and the farmhouse and the group could be seen standing on the horizon.'

The young woman was alleged to have fraternized with the Germans and had been held prisoner in the camp for some time. She was in her thirties, a graduate of Poitiers University and spoke perfect English when she chatted amiably with the British soldiers. She had no great fear for her own fate, for she did not think her crime serious. Sam Smith found it particularly difficult to accept the 'crime' of the woman and before his death in 1989 he wrote of his bad memories:

> 'At this base, 'Topper' Brown and I had rather good relations with the senior *maquis*. At one drinking session, an invitation to witness the execution of the Belgian spy was accepted. At 8 a.m. the following morning, we gathered at the execution site and the grave was dug. The Belgian (half-carried and half-dragged) was brought into the opening. After his cry for mercy was rejected, he pulled himself together, stood to attention and when asked if he wanted to say anything, pleaded with the firing squad (I was asked to join this but declined) not to shoot him in the throat.
>
> 'The other prisoner was a woman from Poitiers. I got to know her very well – not intimately. She was a university graduate and a very intelligent person. Her 'offence' was socialising with the Germans. She asked Brown and I to visit her in Poitiers after the war. One afternoon, drinking with the French, she was singled out and taken to the far side of the field. I asked if she was being told to leave as she had told us that this is what she was expecting. The reply that she was to be executed next morning horrified me – could I have done anything?
>
> 'This is something I have lived with all these years.'

The memoirs of the communist *maquis* leader Camille Olivet (alias 'La Chouette') pour scorn on such accounts. Responding to similar discriptions[1] that collaborators and spies were executed by the *maquis* while they were with the 'Bulbasket' team, Olivet claimed: 'All these assertions are false and would be worthy of a serialized novel'. Olivet may be sensitive about such things but it is nevertheless fact that survivors of 'Bulbasket' definitely recall at least three such executions after Verrières, and Tonkin believes there to have been five. The Belgian 'spy' referred to by Sam Smith was in fact a former *maquisard* named Van Hellepute who had deserted and had been involved with arms smuggling and looting. He had faced a military trial at

---

[1] See *Das Reich* by Max Hastings.

Colonel Chêne's headquarters where his defence had been provided by Albert Dupont. Found guilty of such serious crimes, the Belgian was bound to face a death penalty. The French-Canadian spy mentioned by Fielding was a more mysterious case into which Tonkin himself was unwittingly drawn.

Tonkin was called to Maingard's headquarters where a supposed Canadian soldier had arrived, having been passed down an escape line from the fighting in Normandy. Maingard, for whatever reasons, had suspicions and when the SAS officer, in full uniform, entered the room, Maingard barked at the suspect, 'Don't you stand to attention when an officer enters the room?' The man sprang belatedly to attention, whereupon Maingard stared coldly at him. After a few moments' silence the SOE agent observed, 'He has his hands flat against the sides of his legs. No Canadian soldier stands to attention like that'. The stranger was led outside and immediately shot.

Tonkin also went as far as to record the methods adopted by the *maquis* to undertake their executions:

'As I've said before, war is a ruthless business, but one doesn't have to be brutal. The technique for these executions (we had five) was to have a firing squad ready at the far side of a big field, tell the person what was going to happen, march him/her between two guards, with one guard behind, towards the field, then the instant they entered the field and the prisoner could see the firing squad at the far side, the guard behind would shoot the prisoner through the back of the head. One could be cynical about the motives behind the concept, but it was as humane as killing ever can be.'

The beginning of the new month saw time running out for 'Bulbasket'. Yet, conversely, the first two days of August brought two more devasting air attacks prompted by the SAS.

Back in July, Tonkin had first heard on the 24th of enemy forces massing in Poitiers for a major sweep against the *maquis*. Their assembly point was the Caserne des Dunes, a pre-war permanent barracks of the French Army which stood on a prominent hill on the city's eastern edge. The Caserne des Dunes was now not only a German barracks, but also the training school for the local *'Francs-gardes'* of the *Milice*, the militia of the pro-Nazi French Vichy government which was commanded locally by Louis Aussenac, a former officer of the French Navy. Despite an extensive recruitment drive and the offer of high wages, only some 300 young men, largely under 30 and from the lower strata of French life in terms of ability and intellect, had volunteered in the Poitiers region. Nevertheless, these numbers added considerably to the resources of the Germans in combating the *Résistance* and they were despised by loyal Frenchmen above all others.

A radio message to England therefore suggested the barracks as a bombing target, along with an enemy headquarters building and a telephone exchange which were both in the vicinity, the Quartier Abboville district of the city. Colonel Chêne of the *Résistance* had then become increasingly concerned as reports, albeit open to exaggeration, indicated the enemy's strength in the barracks to be approaching 2-3000, indicating the imminence of a major action. At the same time another enemy force, 1800 strong, had been identified at St Germain, some way to the south. The Vienne *maquis* feared a concerted pincer movement against many of their units who, along with the SAS, risked being caught between the two enemy forces. Tonkin's first message had failed to elicit any action, so, on 1 August, Colonel Chêne again implored Tonkin to bring as much pressure as possible to bear on London and further details on the southerly force, now south-east of Confolens, were radioed back to England.

From here on a combination of the 'Bulbasket' radio log and Tonkin's post-operation report have, over the years, served to confuse the true sequence of events.

In his official report Tonkin states that an RAF attack was mounted on 1 August only four hours after he radioed to England with the location of the enemy force to the south. In fact the RAF raid which was mounted was on the Poitiers barracks target, first identified by Tonkin on 24 July. No air support was forthcoming for the *maquis* groups seeking to confront the southerly German force which was the target pin-pointed at 1645 hours on the 1st. To add to the confusion, a radio message on 2 August from Tonkin advised that the Germans subjected to air attack on the 1st had regrouped close to the town of Champagne-Mouton. Champagne-Mouton is only a few kilometres to the west of the Confolens area where the southerly enemy forces were located and this led several post-war *Résistance* historians to conclude that an RAF fighter-bomber attack had taken place in this area on 1 August. However, the Germans regrouping at Champagne-Mouton were those survivors of the RAF's 1 August attack on Poitiers, seeking to join up with the southerly force. It is worth repeating – *no* allied air attack is recorded in the Vienne area on 1 August, 1944, other than the one on the Caserne des Dunes barracks in Poitiers. Records of the RAF's 2nd Tactical Air Force, RAF Bomber Command and the USAAF's 8th and 9th Air Forces have been carefully checked to confirm this. Indeed, nothing should be allowed to detract from the Poitiers attack which was another classic example of the professionalism displayed by the Mosquito squadrons of the RAF's 2 Group.

2 Group were finally informed of details of the target on the morning of 1 August by Special Forces HQ and an operation was quickly planned for the same evening in the belief that, like the operation against Bonneuil-Matours, this could catch most troops in the barracks. Again there was no time for a target model to be made, but the barracks were a prominent and easily identifiable feature on the outskirts of Poitiers. Aircrew were told that the barracks were filling with troops for an anti-*maquis* sweep and the operation was to be a purely 140 Wing show of twenty-five Mosquito crews who were briefed at 1800 hours. Group Captain Wykeham-Barnes again chose to join and lead the attack, this time with Ted Sismore as his navigator, along with ten aircraft from 21 Squadron and fourteen, including two reserves, from 487 Squadron RNZAF. Twelve crews of 464 Squadron RAAF were briefed for a second attack after dark.

First into the air at 1940 hours were Group Captain Wykeham-Barnes and the 21 Squadron formation led by Wing Commander David Dennis. Within this flight, Mosquito 'K' of 21 Squadron carried the unusual name 'Folly' on its nose since its pilot was Flight Lieutenant Keith Freeman, son of Air Chief Marshal Sir Wilfrid Freeman who had proved so instrumental in securing the Mosquito design's future in the RAF. Still a schoolboy when his father had pushed through the RAF's first order for fifty aircraft, Keith now had the perfect opportunity to demonstrate the value of Sir Wilfrid's conviction in 'Freeman's Folly'.

Immediately behind 21 Squadron, Wing Commander 'Black' Smith led the 12 main force and two reserve aircraft of 487 Squadron. By now Smith's able flight commanders, Ellacombe and Runciman, had received their promotions to Squadron Leader and as usual were behind Smith in the formation which lifted off from Thorney Island.

At the French coast, five miles west of Avranches, the Mosquitos were to be met by a fighter escort, again provided by 122 Wing, in the form of twenty Mustangs, twelve from 19 Squadron RAF led by Squadron Leader Loud and eight from 65 Squadron RAF led once more by Squadron Leader Lamb. Now based at B12 Airfield at Ellon in newly liberated Normandy, the Mustangs were briefed to accompany the Mosquitos all the way to the target in Poitiers. Although the fighters missed the rendezvous on the coast due to poor visibility, they picked up their charges a little later. By this time it had been decided that the two reserve Mosquitos were not needed and they had turned back over the Channel for Thorney Island. It was therefore a combined force of twenty-three Mosquitos and twenty Mustangs that thundered on over the French countryside.

The plan called for an approach from the south, all aircraft armed with instantaneously fused bombs attacking in a shallow dive from 1-2,000 feet and those using eleven seconds' delay fuses coming in as low as 100 feet. The weather was clear with visibility at 10-12 miles and Peter Wykeham-Barnes recalled that the only impediments to good aiming were the thousands of dead insects plastered over his cockpit windscreen after the low-level flight across France. The Wing Leader was also full of praise for Ted Sismore's navigational skills which brought them spot-on to their target. Sismore clearly deserved his reputation as the 'ace' navigator of 2 Group.

Despite the Caserne des Dunes being a permanent and well-established barracks and therefore undoubtedly defended by *flak* guns, the speed of the Mosquitos' approach ensured the crucial element of surprise. The enemy had no time to react before the roar of aero engines and the crump of exploding bombs told them of the RAF's arrival, the fighter-bombers wheeling around the hill-top like hornets disturbed from their nest. The majority of bombs were seen to fall in the target area where several buildings, including three large ones and two smaller ones, were severely damaged. The last aircraft to clear the area also reported it covered in smoke from the incendiary bombs which had taken a good hold. In just minutes the deadly attack was over and the Mosquitos streaked for home.

An amusing postscript to the attack comes from Albert Dupont, who had the following scene described to him by a resident of Poitiers who had watched the Mosquitos with great satisfaction.

In order to shelter from the bombing, two German officers scrambled into the cellar of a building. They were just in time, as a near miss blocked the entrance with fallen masonry just after they entered. But the officers then discovered that their temporary prison possessed an unsavoury amenity. Instead of a proper toilet, the cellar could only boast a latrine channel, already brimming with deposits. A moment later, another bomb falling nearby cleared the exit and sucked the air out of the cellar. The out-rushing air, however, had an unpleasant side-effect for the two Germans. As the Mosquitos and Mustangs left the area, the two officers stumbled from the ruins and one, surveying his comrade's uniform, was heard to remark 'Ach! In die scheisse für Hitler!'

Accompanying their charges right to the target, the Mustang fighter escort had circled protectively overhead while the Mosquitos went about their business. 65 Squadron's pilots were later to record their praise for the accuracy and weight of the Mosquitos' attack, saying they had 'never seen a target so thoroughly pranged'. No enemy aircraft were encountered and neither was any *flak* reported, so the Mustangs were released to make their own way home at low level.

19 Squadron's Mustangs took advantage of their release by sweeping low along the Alençon-Domfront road on the way back where Flight Sergeant Fellows spotted and attacked a number of German vehicles, leaving one smoking. 65 Squadron were deterred from similar activities when allied anti-aircraft guns opened up on them near Caen. The squadron's daily log wryly noted:

> 'No doubt the gunners like to practice, but we certainly feel it an imposition on our normally sunny dispositions when they expect us to join their little romps without even asking us.'

The Mustangs were not the only ones to suffer from anti-aircraft fire. On the return journey the Mosquitos encountered accurate *flak* two miles north of Ancenis and one aircraft suffered slight damage. On returning to base between 2255 and 2345 hours, a total of four aircraft were found to have minor damage from bomb splinters and Flying Officer White in 'E' of 487 Squadron returned with all bombs hung up. Of greater concern was the failure of 'T' of 21 Squadron to return. At de-briefing, other crews reported a lone Mosquito trailing behind on one engine shortly after leaving the target, but no other details were forthcoming. The missing aircraft from 21 Squadron was 'T-Tommy' NS183, crewed by Canadian Flight Lieutenant Drummond Mussett and his English navigator, Pilot Officer George Burrows.

Soon after they had turned away from the target, *flak* hit Mussett's Mosquito and immediately stopped one engine. Unable to maintain enough power on the remaining engine, the pilot realized he could not keep 'Tommy' airborne for much longer and he frantically searched ahead for a suitable spot to put the Mosquito down. Close to Mazières-en-Gâtine, some 50 kilometres west of Poitiers, Mussett found a large field and successfully brought the aircraft in for a safe forced landing.

The two flyers' first concern was to set fire to their aircraft and, this accomplished, they distanced themselves from the spot as quickly as possible. They then hid in a field for three nights until they were reasonably certain that any search for them would have been called off. Emerging from hiding on their fourth day in enemy territory, Mussett and Burrows set off to walk southwards, considering this was a safer direction as most German units were concentrating north of Poitiers. 120 kilometres later they reached the village of Jarnac, on the River Charente near Cognac, where they were taken in by the Chambon family. Madame Chambon's first marriage had been to an Englishman and her daughter had been born in Bishops Stortford. This gave 17-year-old Simone something in common with the 30-year-old navigator as George Burrows had been born in the same town and she was to treasure for many years the two small photographs taken of their visitors. Simone recalls that it was difficult to keep the two fliers a secret, the danger of betrayal to the Germans being ever-present. But Monsieur Chambon was *'un grand résistant'* and, despite four villagers having already been taken away for anti-German activities, he insisted on sheltering the two men until the allied invasion overran the area.[1]

Back at Thorney Island the Australians of 464 Squadron had been disappointed not to join the early operation, but were nevertheless looking forward to delivering the follow-up night operation. To their disappointment, however, orders were received at take-off time cancelling the strike due to worsening weather conditions.

In the following days good aerial reconnaissance photographs were obtained showing considerable damage inflicted on the target and in his '2 Group Operations and News Bulletin' of 5 August, Air Vice-Marshal Embry congratulated his crews warmly:

> 'Reconnaissance photographs have since shown that this was a very clean attack; only three bombs have fallen outside the barrack area and these have not damaged civilian property. Nearly all the bombs have found their mark in barrack buildings. Of three large barrack blocks, one is 3/4 destroyed and the other [sic] is completely destroyed by high explosive at its western end and the western part has suffered severe fire damage, causing partial collapse of the roof.
>
> 'Seven other buildings and buildings lining the walls of the barracks have been destroyed or gutted by fire, containing possibly 40 or 50 motor transport vehicles. The activity of the barracks is confirmed by the presence of horse exercise rings and ambulances are seen at the main entrance, some twelve hours after the attack.

---

[1] Mussett and Burrows remained safely in Jarnac until the Allies liberated the area in September, 1944, and they were flown back to England from Angoulême by RAF Hudson. Leaving behind a Union Jack flag inscribed with the details of their adventure and thanks for the Chambons' shelter, the airmen flew back to England on the 16th and returned to 21 Squadron at Thorney Island five days later, none the worse for their experiences. Happily, both men went on to survive the war.

'It has been reported that 150 enemy troops were killed and more than that number again injured.'

The casualty report came from a *Résistance* claim radioed back by Tonkin on 3 August, '150' appearing to be a popular local assessment of enemy casualties in response to a Mosquito air attack. Local post-war historians, Racault and Picard, cite only ten *Milice* killed and thirty wounded during the attack, but a *Milice* document discovered after the war lists a total of forty-three French personnel killed. Numbers of *Milice* wounded, and German losses, were not recorded.

One final aspect of the attack clearly shows the extent of the political rivalries ever-present in occupied France. In yet another, quite remarkable, abuse of the facts, communist FTP *Résistance* leader Camille Olivet described a totally different version of events in his post-war memoirs. Claiming it was he who identified the enemy force in the Dunes barracks, he described how he then pressed SOE agent Captain Maingard to radio for a bombing attack. While this aspect may be true, Olivet went on to relate how he supposedly listened as Maingard's radio operator succeeded in diverting four Mosquitos already taking part in an attack on the railway station at Tours. He describes the Mosquitos' leader speaking over the radio in an American accent until it was discovered that he was, in fact, another Frenchman. In reality there was no such air operation over Tours; there were no means by which anyone on the ground in France could have spoken by radio to the Mosquitos; twenty-three Mosquitos participated, not four; the RAF leader was Englishman Peter Wykeham-Barnes, not a Frenchman.

The factual and courageous achievements of the *Résistance* are legion and indisputable, they require no fictional embellishment for the sake of personal or political posturing.

The day after the Poitiers attack the RAF's Mosquitos again sought out the SAS's enemies on 2 August. On this occasion it was 107 Squadron, from RAF Lasham's 138 Wing, which was to deliver the final blow.

Tonkin's surviving party had been informed by local sources that the German SS troops battered in the air attack of 14/15 July at Bonneuil-Matours had since relocated to the Château du Fou, 11 kilometres south of Châtellerault. Tonkin had therefore again radioed England for a retaliatory strike by the RAF and from SAS headquarters Captain Michael Foot made another telephone call to 2 Group for help.

Taking off at 1920 hours, Wing Commander W. J. Scott (who had recently replaced Wing Commander Mike Pollard) led seventeen aircraft of his own squadron, plus a Mosquito Mk IV aircraft of the RAF's Film Production Unit

(FPU), attached to 138 Wing at Lasham. The FPU aircraft was a glass-nosed variant of the Mosquito which was able to carry a 35mm cine camera. Professional and experienced cameramen from Pinewood Studios were commissioned in whichever service they were attached to and the aim of the FPU was to produce good quality films for propaganda purposes, to be used in newsreels etc. The daylight attack on the Château du Fou was thought to hold good potential for dramatic footage of a precision low-level attack and so Flight Lieutenant Vic Hester, with cameraman Flying Officer Oakley, found himself attached to the third attack wave.

By this stage of the war 107 Squadron's aircrew ranks were being filled more and more by overseas personnel as the RAF types rotated on to rest tours. While nominally an English squadron, 107's crews for the raid of 2 August give a good indication of the unit's international flavour. Among the pilots, McLurg, Ballachey and Taylor hailed from Canada, Slayden was an American serving in the Royal Canadian Air Force, Captains Brown and Hunt were from the South African Air Force and Lieutenant Commander 'Skav' Skavhaugh came from the Royal Norwegian Navy. Among the navigators, the Dutchman van der Helstraete and Jamaican Karl Aiken added more variety, the latter officer being particularly popular on the squadron as his parents insisted on keeping the unit well supplied with strong Jamaican rum. Less popular was Skavhaugh's burning ambition to take the squadron on an anti-shipping strike among the Norwegian fjords he knew so well. Perhaps fortunately, 'Skav' never managed to persuade his C.O. to follow up the idea!

For the trip to the target area, Scott had briefed his three waves of six aircraft each to fly at 3,000 feet until past the French coast, Squadron Leader Wallington leading the first wave, himself the second and Flight Lieutenant McLurg the third.[1]

---

[1] Canadian McLurg had a reputation for a keen shooting eye during his time with 107 Squadron. In April, 1944, he had spotted an aircraft heading away from the Thames estuary which he identified in the grey dawn light as a German Dornier bomber. McLurg was hampered by his reflector gun sight being stuck on maximum illumination, but he nevertheless was able to confirm that his quarry had the twin fins and two engines of a Dornier Do 217. Opening fire, McLurg was gratified to see both engines immediately hit and stop but as he watched the aircraft commence a gliding descent, he saw his mistake – the aircraft was a B25 Mitchell medium bomber, sporting RAF markings. Only one member of the Dutch crew baled out, but the aircraft's pilot managed an excellent forced landing and none of the crew were badly injured. At the subsequent Court of Inquiry, McLurg was perhaps fortunate to be exonerated due to the problem with the illumination of his gun sight.

Leaving the English coast at Selsey Bill, the Mosquitos crossed into France over the Cap de la Hague and dropped to low level for a zig-zag course in order to confuse the enemy's radar. This time there had been enough time for 2 Group's planners to build an accurate scale model of the château, working from aerial reconnaissance photographs. All crews were told that the target housed SS troops but there was no mention of a link with earlier operations, nor of the reprisal nature of the attack.

Each wave was given a portion of the target upon which to concentrate, the first two groups attacking in quick succession at ground level with delayed action bombs and the third in a shallow dive with instantaneously fused bombs. Weather conditions were excellent, with no cloud and visibility of 15 miles and the moderate but inaccurate *flak* experienced en route did nothing to distract the aircrews from their task.

The crew of Flight Lieutenant Jack Whittle and Flying Officer Denis Shanahan found themselves in Wing Commander Scott's second wave, with orders to attack the front elevation of the château. Navigator Shanahan recalled an approach over beautiful formal gardens and a fine courtyard before he released their bombs right in through the front entrance area. Both Whittle and Shanahan felt regrets at destroying such a magnificent building but had no sympathies with its present occupiers, many of whom could be seen fleeing the château for the supposed safety of nearby woods. Like a pack of wolves, the Mosquitos broke formation and dived back into the attack at ground level. Streams of canon and machine-gun fire snaked after the fleeing troops, mowing many of them down before they could reach the cover of the trees. Even those who did were not left in peace. The aircrews had been warned that some of the Germans were camped in the woods, so the Mosquitos comprehensively strafed the trees before the flyers, satisfied, called it a day and turned for home. At least twenty-eight bombs hit the target, the centre and south wings were left burning and the north wing was also hit several times.

The return to England was to prove a trial for 107 Squadron's crews. Most returned singly and, apart from the necessity of avoiding a little *flak* en route which caused minor damage to Flying Officer Staple's 'J', the crews enjoyed a beautiful clear evening over France. Over the Channel, however, solid low cloud cover was met and on reaching Lasham from 2300 hours onwards the Mosquitos were also warned of fog. Only a few crews elected to make the nerve-stretching approach, one being Canadian Flying Officer John Ballachey in aircraft 'Q'. Ballachey had already had a major electrical failure to contend with but his 'GEE' navigational aid was still working and his English navigator, Flying Officer Jim Arnold, concentrated on using it to steer a course for Lasham. Loath to divert elsewhere due to his very low fuel state, Ballachey was determined to find Lasham. Fortunately, Arnold's confidence in his 'box of tricks' was vindicated when the Mosquito eventually let down out of the cloud at just 200 feet and found itself directly overhead Lasham's control tower. With his fuel gauges now on empty, Ballachey fired a red Verey pistol flare and landed immediately. Other crews with less critical fuel states diverted to clearer conditions at Odiham and Thorney Island and were all safely down by 2325 hours with the exception of Captain Hunt.

Hunt had suffered an engine failure near to the target and had initially only hoped to make the safety of the American lines for a crash landing. Encouraged by his Mosquito's performance, however, he continued on towards England at much reduced speed on his one remaining Merlin engine. This he had successfully managed until his fuel gauges showed empty approaching the English coast and he therefore chose to put down at the first available aerodrome, RAF Thorney Island. When Lasham's station personnel were telephoned of Hunt's whereabouts, the Flying Control staff at Thorney Island were of the opinion that Hunt and his navigator, Flight Sergeant Collins, were very fortunate to be alive. A dramatic crash-landing had been followed by the stricken Mosquito disintegrating into ever smaller pieces as it careered across the airfield. Staff in the control tower could then only stare in amazement when, from the tangled wreckage, Hunt and Collins struggled out smiling and virtually unscathed.

Interpretation of most of the photographs taken proved impossible due to under-exposure and Oakley's filming in Flight Lieutenant Hester's FPU Mosquito was hindered by dense smoke from the target. There was no subsequent report from the SAS in the field, so it must be left to 107 Squadron's log to record a conclusion on the operation:
'All those taking part thoroughly enjoyed themselves.'

6

HOME

With the conclusion of 'Bulbasket' now imminent, SAS Brigade headquarters continued with plans to replace Tonkin's survivors with 'Operation Moses' of the French 3rd SAS Regiment. On the night of 2/3 August, eight men were therefore parachuted onto the Asnières DZ, including Lieutenant Cameron, their British liaison officer. All landed safely save for a sprained ankle and several burned hands from kit-bag ropes and, with their arrival, Tonkin was then free to leave the area and move closer to the site chosen for the return to England.

'Bon Bon', Surrey Dane's choice for an evacuation airstrip, was some 40 kilometres north-east of the Asnières camp. The fields to be used were part of the 'Foussac' farm, but were still in need of a considerable amount of hard labour in order to get them to the standard which would be required by the RAF. A north-south strip, 1000 metres long, was needed and would entail the removal of several hedgerows. Work therefore began, using the remaining jeep to pull an agricultural harrow, and the combination of wholesome toil and glorious weather further helped memories of the Verrières disaster to lift from the young men. Peter Weaver[1] later admitted that he had initially written himself off and did not expect to live to see England again, but now a sense of optimism and well-being pervaded the party as they looked forward to going home. They were organized by David Surrey Dane and, somewhat unexpectedly, Trooper McNair. It transpired that McNair

---

1 Post-war Weaver chose to stay in the regular British Army and served in Crete and then with the Sudan Defence Force. He later joined the Royal Berkshire Regiment in Eritrea and Egypt and served with the British Military Mission in Greece. On his retirement from the Army in the rank of Major, he took up chicken-farming in Essex before retiring again to Swanage where he died in 1991.

was a farmer's son well versed in use of a harrow and so, despite his reluctance, the Trooper again naturally came to the fore. While McNair supervised the physical work, Surrey Dane dealt with another somewhat more sensitive aspect:

'"Bon Bon" required some modification before it complied with RAF specifications. A strip of ground needed harrowing to smooth it down and this was done by one of the SAS troopers who had worked on a farm, but the most urgent need was to get rid of a tree obstructing take-off. It turned out to be a walnut owned by the next-door farmer and I had to pay him the equivalent of £40 before he would agree to cut it down. Fortunately, I had been sent to France with an emergency supply of francs so this did not present a problem.'

For four days the SAS and their American evaders sweated in the fields and during the day of the 5th, a move was made to a site north of Lathus-St-Rémy to be close to 'Bon Bon'. The remaining USAAF evaders, Ward and Hitchcock, were called in from the outlying farm where they had been recuperating and on the 6th, with all preparation finished, Tonkin tuned in to the BBC for confirmation of the air-lift. First came the BBC News in French and then the announcer said as usual: *'Voici les messages personnels'*. A long string of coded messages followed until eventually the SAS's own message was broadcast – two aircraft would be landing that same night. The men whooped with delight.

Only the RAF's Special Duties squadrons were experienced in pick-up operations and therefore it was again 161 Squadron from RAF Tempsford which was called upon, the same unit which had originally dropped Tonkin and Crisp from a Halifax in the early hours of D-Day. This time the logistics of the operation called for a smaller aircraft to fit into 'Bon Bon' and the squadron's 'C' Flight provided two twin-engined Lockheed Hudsons for the job.

On the outbound journey the Hudsons carried not only a cargo of arms to re-supply the *maquis* but also a total of eleven more French SAS to replace the 'Bulbasket' team. First into the air from Tempsford was Flying Officer Ibbott in Hudson 'M', followed a quarter of an hour later by his C.O., Wing Commander Alan Boxer[1], in 'P'. While Boxer was well

[1] Today Air Vice-Marshal Sir Alan Boxer KCVO CB DSO DFC.

experienced in this type of clandestine operation, Harold Ibbott was making his first solo pick-up and his other three crew members were relative newcomers to the squadron. Nevertheless, it was Ibbott who forged the way with five French SAS aboard and a quantity of ammunition. Despite no Eureka/Rebecca aids, he navigated blind on to 'Bon Bon' with no difficulty and, receiving the required response from the ground reception party, dropped successfully into the field at 0130 hours. Other than finding the ground 'not too good', Ibbott was satisfied with the landing strip chosen by David Surrey Dane.

As the first Hudson landed, Alan Boxer arrived overhead, having made good time behind Ibbott from England. He was able to watch his junior colleague's approach to the strip quite easily but he realized that it would be some minutes before the field could be cleared for his own arrival. There was also the danger that the circling aircraft might serve to draw attention to activities on the ground. Boxer therefore flew on away from 'Bon Bon' before returning 10 minutes later and safely delivering his load of six French SAS, personal kit and small arms ammunition. For Surrey Dane, it was the culmination of his airstrip training:

'It was exciting waiting for the planes to arrive as this was the first real life pick-up that any of us had seen. In training I had worked with the much smaller Lysander and the only previous time I had seen a Hudson was in Northern Ireland. It was a Coastal Command plane which crashed and blew up in spectacular fashion when coming in to land at Aldergrove aerodrome with a full load of depth charges on board. I kept this memory to myself. Dead on time we heard an aircraft in the distance and set fire to the small bonfire which was to act as a beacon. The first of the Hudsons appeared against the moonlit sky and as it circled our airstrip, we exchanged a pre-arranged morse code signal and then turned on the five torches that formed an inverted 'L' marking the 'runway'. Without further delay the Hudson came in to land, switching on its landing lights at the last moment. The plane bounced high into the air after touching down and then disappeared in a cloud of dust. A couple of anxious minutes later it reappeared taxiing to the take-off point. I cannot recall whether it had brought any incoming passengers, but very soon half our SAS party were aboard and the Hudson was starting down the 'runway' for take-off. Again it disappeared in a cloud of dust and there were more anxious moments before we saw it climbing away safely. The second Hudson had been circling the airstrip and now came in to land. It made a smoother landing and took on board as many of the remaining members of Bulbasket as it could, leaving a few of us to be picked up on another occasion. I cannot remember how long it took from the time we heard the first Hudson until the second one was airborne and away. It was probably less than twenty minutes. All lights had been on for the shortest possible time and I was fairly confident that the operation had passed unnoticed by our enemies.'

The combined capacity of the two Hudsons had enabled Tonkin and twelve other SAS, Sadoine and two of his signallers, three USAAF evaders (Sergeant Norton and Lieutenants Bradley and Harper) and Maingard to be picked up, the latter being temporarily returned to London. For those aboard, the flight was relatively uneventful although the trees at the end of 'Bon Bon' had appeared uncomfortably close. Light *flak*, with tracer, had searched for them at one point, but did little to trouble the pilots. In the second aircraft, John Fielding gave his head a nasty bang when the Hudson suddenly dropped like a stone in an air pocket. As the aircraft went down, Fielding went up and met the fuselage roof. Before long the English coast was in sight and, low on fuel and warned of foggy conditions back at Tempsford, the Hudsons let down to the south-coast fighter airfield at Tangmere, frequently used as a forward base by the Special Duties squadrons. All passengers were off-loaded and, while Maingard headed for SOE headquarters in London, the SAS underwent a day's medical tests before being taken to a reception centre at Nettlebed near Reading.

Back at 'Bon Bon', David Surrey Dane had stayed behind with two of the Phantom signallers (Corporal Stephenson and Signalman Bell) as a radio link for the five American flyers still to be evacuated. Their wait was to last three nights until another aircraft successfully found 'Bon Bon', this time a Douglas C-47 Skytrain twin-engined transport of the USAAF, better known by its civilian title as a Dakota.

Surrey Dane was later to learn that Wing Commander Boxer had reported 'Bon Bon' to be unsuitable for Hudson aircraft and consequently SAS Brigade Headquarters were left to cast around for a more suitable last-minute replacement. Though bigger, the sturdy Dakota was considered to be up to the job and in view of the American flyers awaiting evacuation, an approach was made to the USAAF.

The USAAF's own special duties squadrons, 'The Carpetbaggers' of the 492nd Bombardment (H) Group, had recently started to carry out the same type of pick-up operations as the RAF's 'Moon' squadrons. Using the

Dakota[1], their most experienced pilot and pioneer of the technique was Colonel Clifford Heflin, the group's commander at the American base of RAF Harrington in Northamptonshire. Heflin had commanded the very first 'Carpetbaggers' of the 406th Bomb Squadron which formed in November, 1943, and in January, 1944, began operations using B-24 Liberators to drop agents and supplies. On the night of 6/7 June, 1944, Heflin had performed the Americans' first behind-the-lines Dakota landing in France for the Ain *maquis* and thus was a natural choice for the operation. Without hesitation, Heflin agreed to fly into 'Bon Bon' on the night of 9/10 August and his only moment of drama arose when, on his final approach, he lined up the torch-lit runway lights between his wheels, rather than to the port side as was normal practice. Since each torch was held by a member of the reception party, the Colonel's landing run caused considerable alarm and some panic, as Surrey Dane himself was only too aware:

'The Dakota, which was piloted by a big, bluff American named Colonel Heflin, appeared over 'Bon Bon' on time looking a good deal larger than a Hudson against the night sky. All went according to plan until the last moment before touchdown. When the Dakota's landing lights were switched on it became obvious that, instead of landing with the row of torches on his left, Colonel Heflin was going to land with them between his wheels. There were three or four of us manning the torches ensuring that they were switched on for only the minimum length of time. I just managed to get out of the way myself, but with the noise of the engines there was no chance of shouting to the others to jump clear. Fortunately, like me, they all managed to avoid getting run down, but with the dust cloud thrown up by the propellers it was a minute or two before I realized this. When I explained to Colonel Heflin what had happened he apologized, but I do not think he realized just how near he had come to writing off half the people he had come to collect!'

The Dakota had, as planned, brought a supply of heavy weapons for the 'Bretheral' *maquis* group, in order to defend Colonel Chêne's headquarters, and another eight French SAS of 'Operation Moses', towards an eventual total of forty-six. But Surrey Dane was not expecting the American airman who jumped out of the Dakota behind them. Carrying a large camera with flash attachment, he introduced himself as an official USAAF photographer and insisted on recording the handover between the French and British SAS. While the latter obediently posed for the shots, their *maquis* helpers muttered curses as the powerful flash bulbs exploded, threatening to attract any Germans in the neighbourhood.

Formalities over, the remaining party of Surrey Dane, the two Phantom signallers (Stephenson and Bell) and five USAAF evaders (Lieutenants Scott and Banks and Sergeants Ward, Gross and Hitchcock) quickly climbed aboard the Dakota, eager to leave the hullabaloo behind. At the last moment two shadowy secret service agents also climbed aboard and, sitting apart from the others near the tail, uttered scarcely a word for the entire flight. This was in marked contrast to the USAAF evaders, overjoyed to be back amongst their own kind. One of these Americans in particular had caused Tonkin some concern when he was first brought into camp by the *maquis* who had found him cycling enthusiastically towards the Spanish frontier 250 miles away.

Lieutenant Bill Banks of the USAAF's 474th Fighter Group had baled out of his P-38 Lightning near Tours after a dog-fight, acquired a bicycle and then set out for Spain following the advice given to pilots shot down over occupied France. When he was brought in on 4 August he seemed over-wrought and with appropriate gestures described over and over again exactly how he had been shot down. Wondering if he were the genuine article, the SAS asked the American airmen already with them for their opinion. Surprisingly, they too were unsure of him, so the newcomer was politely asked for his hand-gun and a guard placed over him while he slept. As a precaution, a radio message was sent to Brigade headquarters in England asking for information about the pilot and for an identifying question that could be asked of him. The reply came back that a pilot of his name had been lost at the right time and in the right place and that he was to be quizzed as to what his nickname was at school. It was a name the American found embarrassing, but his reply reassured the SAS that he was the genuine article. When last seen by Surrey Dane he was having a joyful reunion with pilots of his own squadron who had come over to Harrington to welcome the Dakota when it landed at 0400 hours on 10 August. Not many airmen were able to enjoy such a quick return from enemy territory and the American had been happy to forgive the SAS for double-checking his credentials.

As a parting present, the *maquis* had given Surrey Dane a *petit cochon* which they had killed only that evening. Before sewing it into a sack they showed the SAS Lieutenant a Cross of Lorraine which they had cut on its side and offered it as a gift to meat-starved England. Surrey Dane expressed himself suitably grateful but in the event could not do justice to the gift. By the time he had been de-briefed and sent on leave, hot weather and blow flies had been too much for the pig, but Surrey Dane's mother came up with a solution. Some years before, she had been told by a local gardener that figs needed feeding on flesh and, having a fig tree in the garden, the uneaten pig was buried beneath it with due ceremony.

Back in England, Surrey Dane knew little of the trouble which the reported shortcomings of 'Bon Bon' had caused the SAS HQ staff, but he later heard that, after the USAAF Dakota had made its successful trip, Brigade had sent a telegram to the RAF announcing this and ending: 'Bulbaskets to you Boxer!' It may have seemed a suitable message at the time from headquarters but the survivors of 'Bulbasket' were more than grateful for the efforts of 161 Squadron's two Hudson pilots. Despite having had to wait for the Americans to pick him up, Surrey Dane had no reservations over Boxer's decision:

> 'I met the pilot of the second Hudson about a year later and he told me that he had found our 'runway' not too bad. In retrospect, I am glad that W/C Boxer felt as he did. He was experienced and was probably right. His decision led to Col. Heflin of the USAAF offering to fly his Dakota into 'Bon Bon'. Dakotas were more suited to this type of airstrip, though being unarmed they had not been used over this part of France until the German air defences were more fully occupied elsewhere'.

In any final analysis, the combination of RAF Hudsons and USAAF Dakota performed an excellent job without loss.

7

A GRIM DISCOVERY

As Christmas of 1944 approached, the Poitiers area bore relatively few lasting reminders of the enemy's occupation. While war still raged on the borders of Germany, the French countryside gradually settled back into its traditional way of life. Although incidents such as the massacre at Oradour-sur-Glane had left terrible, permanent scars, rural life in the region was largely untouched. Here and there poignant roadside crosses or memorials already bore testament to the actions and sacrifices of the *maquis*, but no large-scale battles had devastated the countryside. Even in Poitiers itself the Germans had withdrawn or surrendered meekly, leaving the city more physically damaged by the RAF than by four years of German occupation.

It was to this background of returning peace that in mid-December of 1944 *la chasse* resumed, with the first wild boar hunt hosted by Monsieur Fossembas on his land in the Forêt de Saint-Sauvant. An area of dense thickets, the forest's Bois de Guron was just over the administrative boundary in the Deux-Sèvres *département*, not far from the village of Rom.

The huntsmen were alongside a forestry track, the Borne Vezêtre, when they noticed an area of broken branches just inside the tree line. Investigating, they found three patches of displaced earth and a cautious exploratory dig soon revealed the reason. Not far below the surface were the decaying, yet still clothed, remains of a number of bodies.

The traumatic find blighted the hunt, yet the discovery of bodies in shallow graves was not an uncommon event in the France of 1944. Not only had the Germans often disposed of *maquisards*, killed in action or executed, in this way, but the *maquis* itself had quietly buried many bodies – Germans, *Milice* or condemned civilian collaborators. Furthermore, it was known that a pitched battle had taken place in the area that summer between the Germans and a *maquis* group. It was therefore not an immediate priority to alert the police, and Monsieur Fossembas waited until he returned home to write a letter to the *Gendarmerie* in the town of Melle.

On the morning of 18 December Maréchal des Logis Chef Albert Charron, and Gendarmes Rene Bizard and Jean Brunner left Melle for Saint-Sauvant. On the way they collected Auxiliary Gendarme André Rivière from Lezay, the nearest police post to the forest, and Monsieur Eugene Lagorre, Mayor of Rom. In the forest the police took careful note of everything they found, two ditches being discovered on the left and a third on the right of a foot-path leading to the Borne Vezêtre. The nearest dwelling was the 'Touche-Moreau' farm, some 1800 metres to the south-west. As described in Monsieur Fossembas' letter, the ground had clearly been disturbed. Carefully, they excavated one grave and found five bodies, dressed in uniform. A label on the left inside pocket of a battle dress tunic bore the inscription: 'BATTLE DRESS BLOUSE 1940 PATTERN, SIZE 7. T.H. CROMBIE and Co.' There was little doubt that the bodies were of allied soldiers.

While gendarmes Bizard and Rivière remained on guard in the wood, police chief Charron immediately returned to the *Gendarmerie* to alert his Commander on the telephone. The next day saw a host of officials descend on the site in the morning and shortly afterwards an FFI detachment under the command of Commandant Jomeau also arrived and started to excavate the three graves fully. The police continued their descriptive record of what was unearthed:

'The first grave measured 3 metres long, 1.8 metres across and 1.2 metres deep. It contained eleven bodies (Nos. 1-11). Of these eleven, ten were dressed in blouses with flap pockets and trousers with two front pockets which fastened with a band and three press-studs. The 11th wore the same type of trousers but had no blouse, though this was found in the grave.

'All these bodies were placed close to each other along the right side.

'The second grave measured 3 metres long by 2 metres across, and was 1.2 metres deep. It contained nine bodies (Nos. 12-20), all wearing the same type of clothing with one exception, which wore a pullover with zip-fastener. Eight were placed as in the first grave, and the ninth was placed along the feet of his comrades.

'The third grave, which measured 5 metres by 1.80 and was 1.30 deep, contained eleven bodies (Nos. 21-31). Seven were placed on their right side and the other four were placed head to feet on their comrades. Ten were dressed in a manner similar to their comrades in the first grave, the 11th wore drill trousers, a leather waistcoat and laced shoes.'

On the morning of the 20th Doctor Maupetit visited the wood to carry out autopsies on the bodies. Fittingly, fifteen German prisoners of war, accompanied by their guards, arrived to carry out the actual exhumation of the bodies. As darkness fell in the gloomy forest, Dr Maupetit returned home after completing his work on ten of the bodies. He returned the next day to record his findings on the remaining twenty-one bodies.

The *Gendarmerie's* report contained the doctor's autopsy details for every one of the thirty-one bodies. The document makes grim reading. With two riflemen to each prisoner, the Germans had conducted the exercise with ruthless efficiency.

A formal inquest was quickly arranged in Niort and heard evidence from a number of local people. First to speak was Alexandre Esteve, a keeper for Madame Baritault at 'Le Parc', Celle-Levescault. On the afternoon of 6 July, 1944, he had seen six or seven German lorries, escorted by three or four motor-cycles, arrive and park at 100 metre intervals at the edge of the wood. He noticed only enemy soldiers in the vehicles and thought that they might have remained there for the night as the next morning, Friday the 7th, he had heard firing from the woods. Two days later on the 9th he had walked through the area:

'The following Sunday, that is to say two days after the presumed date of the crime, I was walking through the wood and took the path which passes the three graves, but I did not notice anything abnormal. However, I did notice that a number of people had walked along the path and along the edge of the wood, but I thought that troops had camped there during the night.

'Troops and vehicles had left signs of their presence at the point of the forest called La Borne Vezêtre, and I noticed that bundles of twigs had been dragged along the path for a distance of some 60 to 80 metres; I now presume that this was done in an effort to hide their tracks. At the time I thought that they were searching for the *maquis* in this area, for they had placed guards at the various junctions of the paths and roads leading to the graves.'

Auguste Cousson, a gardener at 'L'Embraille', had likewise seen the activity of the lorries on the 6th and was able to describe in more detail the gunfire heard the next morning:

'On the 7th, towards 0530-0600 hours, I heard several bursts of machine-gun fire and two rounds of cannon fire, followed by several single shots, in the direction of La Borne Vezêtre, that is to say a short distance from the graves.

'As it was only a few days after an attack made against the *maquis* of the Saint-Sauvant forest, I thought that these troops were commencing a new attack, as the previous one was carried out in the same manner.'

Another gardener, Henri Leon from 'La Pierre Brune', had also seen Germans in the area on the 6th and confirmed Cousson's recollections:

'At approximately 1500 hours [on the 6th] I saw a side-car, driven by an officer with two men, who were looking for the La Ferrière road, which leads to the crossroad La Borne Vezêtre. I noticed that it was marked on their map in blue pencil, as well as the wood containing the graves. I thought they were going to a new attack against the *maquis* and that the wood in question was to be guarded.

'The following day, 7th July, between 0530 and 0600 hours, I heard two rounds of cannon fire and some machine-gun fire, near La Borne Vezêtre. I thought that the attack had commenced.'

Leon's son had also walked through the woods on the Sunday and noticed that something had been dragged along the ground at the start of the path leading to the area of the graves. Almost certainly, the 'something' had been the bodies of the murdered soldiers.

Finally, Capitaine Paul Alleau from the Air Ministry in Paris gave evidence. In July, 1944, Alleau had comanded an FFI group in the Saint-Sauvant area and, knowing a little more of the wider picture, confirmed:

'At the end of June or beginning of July, 1944, precise date unknown, a group of approximately 30 British parachutists and several French patriots was captured at Verrières (Vienne) by a German detachment. Their ultimate fate is unknown.

'I can certify that the bodies discovered in the graves in the Guron wood are definitely those of parachutists, by reason of their clothing.

'No personnel were dropped by parachute in the district of Saint-Sauvant forest, where the *maquis* under my command were stationed.

'It is quite possible that the group of British parachutists and French patriots captured at Verrières (Vienne), may be the victims, for amongst those bodies discovered No. 22, the only one wearing shoes (laced shoes) and French underclothes, could very probably be a Frenchman.'

Positive identification was made difficult as it became clear that most of the dead soldiers' 'dog tags' had been removed. Nevertheless, the identity discs of Trooper Livingstone and Corporal Allan had been overlooked and Lieutenant Crisp's name was marked inside his battle dress. From initials on rings, Trooper Brophy and Trooper Simmons could also be tentatively identified. The body dressed in French civilian clothes gave rise to a number of theories but was eventually realized to be that of Lieutenant Bundy, USAAF. Since the pilot had been hidden for a while by the French, he had undoubtedly been fitted out with appropriate civilian clothing. As Capitaine Alleau had correctly guessed, the thirty-one bodies were therefore deemed to be Bundy, twenty-eight of the thirty-one SAS taken prisoner at Verrières, plus Sergeant Eccles and Corporal Bateman captured previously at St Benoît. Of Trooper Biffin, missing at Airvault, and Troopers Ogg, Pascoe and Williams, captured wounded at Verrières, there was still no sign.

The French police then made little effort to identify the German unit responsible for the crime, observing merely that it was thought to have been a formation which was passing through the area. As a military matter, this stance by the civilian police was understandable and the report was passed to the allied military authorities for any further action.

Meanwhile, following the completion of Dr Maupetit's autopsies, the bodies had been placed in coffins on 21 December, in the presence of the Mayor of Rom. Each body was wrapped in a shroud and a plate was nailed at the head and outside each coffin, bearing a number, 1-31, in Roman numerals. On each body a corked glass tube, sealed with wax, was placed. This showed the same number as on the coffin and contained a description of the victim and the result of the autopsy. Finally, a number of strands were taken from the hair of each victim and were placed in numbered packets, together with all personal belongings found on the bodies. The packets were then placed in a locked box in the care of the *Gendarmerie* for later forwarding to the British authorities.

On the evening of 21 December the coffins of the soldiers were taken to

Rom and were tended by the FFI until the morning of the 23rd. They were then taken to the Town Hall where they lay in state until the afternoon. At 3 o'clock, watched by a huge crowd of local people come to pay their respects, the thirty-one bodies were re-buried with full military honours in a corner of the village graveyard in Rom.

8

JUSTICE?

At the end of the war the SAS's operational units gradually filtered back to their headquarters base in England, now at Wivenhoe in Essex. Most of the men were demobbed to return to civilian life while the regulars were posted back to the regiments from which they had originally volunteered. Against the Service itself old jealousies now gathered strength and it was eventually deemed there was no need for such a specialist and élitist unit in the post-war army. By October, 1945, the Special Air Service Brigade, with all its constituent units, was ordered to be disbanded.

But not quite. One small group managed to linger on for four years while attached to the British Military Reparations Committee in Greece. And in north-west Europe, Lieutenant-Colonel Brian Franks, C.O. of 2nd SAS, was determined that there was at least one more task to be completed. As the Allies' war crimes investigations increasingly concentrated on mass atrocities, such as those committed by the staff of Belsen concentration camp, Franks became concerned that crimes against SAS personnel were being ignored. In May, 1945, soon after the war's end, he had therefore authorized a small unit of six men to travel to the continent to determine, in particular, the fate of 2nd SAS personnel captured during 'Operation Loyton' in the Vosges region of France from August to September of 1944. The unit, impressively named the 'SAS War Crimes Investigation Team' (WCIT), was commanded by Major E. W. 'Bill' Barkworth, ably assisted by Company Sergeant Major Fred 'Dusty' Rhodes and four troopers. When the small party left England in just a jeep and a lorry, no one could foresee that it would be 1949 before their work was completed.

Bill Barkworth, from Sidmouth in Devon, had originally served in the Somerset Light Infantry before transferring to the SAS. He had been 2nd SAS's wartime Intelligence Officer and was well-suited to the job in hand, being fluent in German and almost as capable in French. Above all, he was a skilled interrogator and a cunning hunter of his quarry. His unorthodox methods, however, which on one occasion even included a startlingly successful séance, won him few friends among the British Army authorities with whom he was supposed to liaise. One important ally proved to be a young British Army Captain of Russian royal lineage with an English mother. Prince Yuri Galitzine had worked his way through France investigating evidence of German atrocities on behalf of the Political Warfare Department of SHAEF.[1] Determined to play a part in finding those responsible, he had been less than impressed by the disinterested manner with which the British Army authorities were pursuing war crimes. For many of the Army's officers, war crime duties were simply another delay to their long-awaited demobilization. Thus, when offered a posting to the War Office's War Crimes Investigation Branch back in London, Galitzine leapt at the opportunity to make a more strategic contribution and consequently found himself ideally placed when Barkworth and his team were orphaned by the SAS's disbandment in October, 1945. From his office in Eaton Square, Galitzine maintained radio contact with the WCIT and managed, with the help of Lieutenant-Colonel Franks' influential connections, to maintain administrative and logistical support to Barkworth and his men, even to the extent of arranging for their pay to come directly from the War Office. While the British Army considered the days of the SAS as over, the six members of the WCIT therefore managed to keep the Service's proud origins alive and once their investigations into 'Loyton' were completed their brief was extended to investigate the deaths of men from both SAS regiments.

For the 1st SAS Regiment the priority was clearly 'Bulbasket'. In January, 1945, John Tonkin had been alerted by a newspaper report covering the burials at Rom and, fearing the worst, had quickly crossed to France with Sergeant Bob Holmes to investigate. At Rom their fears were confirmed and there was little they could do other than attempt to help with some of the indentification difficulties by studying the autopsy reports and the locks of hair taken from each body before burial. In Poitiers the hospital authorities confirmed that the three wounded troopers, Ogg, Pascoe and Williams, had disappeared from the Hôtel-Dieu around 8 July, but there the trail went cold. Tonkin subsequently prepared a report in February, 1945, on the discovery of the graves at Saint-Sauvant but had then had no time to follow up the matter further, as, promoted to Major, he returned to active service

[1] SHAEF – Supreme Headquarters, Allied Expeditionary Force – was by now based in Paris.

leading D Squadron through the remainder of the North-West Europe campaign.

Up until the discovery of the bodies at Saint-Sauvant, all the men had only been listed as missing in action and a number of families, particularly the father of Trooper Eades, had been pressing for confirmation of identities. Sadly, confirmation of the finding of his son's body reached Mr Eades after an American Army pathologist was able to use dental records to fill in the gaps left by the autopsies of Doctor Maupetit at Saint-Sauvant. But for the families of Biffin, Ogg, Pascoe and Williams there was just a chance that the missing men were prisoners of war. The parents of Ogg, Pascoe and Williams were at least informed of their sons' stay in hospital in Poitiers and in June, 1945, the London *Evening News* ran an article on their disappearance. Seemingly, the German military authorities had informed the Hôtel-Dieu's medical staff that the three men had been transferred to a hospital in Tours. This hospital had been evacuated during the retreat of the Germans on 13 or 14 August, 1944, and it was thought that the troopers may then have been sent on to a P.O.W. camp in Germany.

In July, 1945, the families had heard from Professor Daniel Villey, the former Director of Regional Information in Poitiers and recently returned to his position as a member of the Law Faculty at Poitiers University. Villey had been making efforts to determine the fate of the three wounded from a personal point of view. In 1944 he had been actively involved in the *Résistance* and Trooper Joe Ogg had been the first allied soldier seen by Villey since the German occupation. The meeeting was at a farm near Chasseneuil, north of Poitiers, which Ogg had reached, alone, on his way to join up with the main party. This almost certainly places Ogg as the third member of Corporal Kinnevane's 'Lot' party which was dropped into the town square at Airvault on the night of 10/11 June, 1944. While Trooper Biffin was believed to have been captured and subsequently disappeared, Corporal Kinnevane and the other trooper had escaped singly and were later reunited before continuing on to the main party. It would therefore appear that Ogg's encounter with Villey had been shortly before he joined up again with Kinnevane.

Villey had then thought no more of the young soldier until, on 4 July, 1944, he happened to be in the Hôtel-Dieu hospital in Poitiers and saw three wounded British soldiers under German guard. To the Frenchman's surprise, one of the three quietly called to him during a moment's inattention by the Germans – 'I have met you already'. Looking more closely, Villey was startled to recognize Ogg, the Trooper whom he had briefly met at Chasseneuil. Due to the presence of the Germans, there was no opportunity to speak further, but the next day Villey returned to the hospital and was able to visit the young Scot and his companions in their beds. They chatted for a while and, before he had to leave, Villey took their addresses so that they could correspond after the war.

It was thus by taking the addresses that Villey was able to contact the families in July, 1945, soon after the end of the war in Europe. He had been in touch with the hospital authorities in Tours who were only able to confirm that Ogg, Pascoe and Williams had not been among the twenty-eight wounded allied P.O.W.s left with the French by the retreating Germans. Indeed, there was no evidence whatsoever to support the claim that the three troopers had ever been transferred to Tours and from this point onwards the fog of war had obliterated any certainties. For the time being Professor Villey could progress no further.

When Barkworth and his team therefore turned to 'Bulbasket', the only material they had to start their search came from an original SHAEF Court of Inquiry which had included investigations made in Poitiers. Frustratingly, SHAEF War Crime files are today still not open to the public under a 75-year closure ruling, but some details survive in the form of evidence used in later court proceedings. The questioning of key French witnesses in Poitiers was undertaken by Lieutenant-Colonels Boraston and Cutting who conducted interviews among the staff of the Hôtel-Dieu hospital. Monsieur Georges Polet, the Director, and interne André Clert who clearly recalled the arrival and care of Ogg, Pascoe and Williams, were of particular help.

The only other documentation released from the SHAEF Inquiry was a summary of the Court's findings which concluded that:

'31 allied military personnel met their deaths at the hands of the German armed forces in the Bois de Guron, near Rom, Deux-Sèvres, France, on or about Friday 7th July 1944. Of the 31, the bodies of only 17 had been positively identified beyond all doubt and these were:

R Crisp	H Mullen
J R Jessiman	S Ryland
R Chick	E Simmons
J Govan	A Spooner
W Allan	V White
M Brophy	Lincoln D Bundy
G Budden	G Cogger
L Eades	D Livingstone
A McLeod	

'Despite inconclusive evidence, the bodies of the remainder were found in all probability to be:

D Eccles	J Aspin
K Bateman	A Ashley
R Heavens	D Gray
J Kinnevane	R Guard
L Long	H Hill
J Baker	D Phillips
E Adamson	W Richardson

'Sergeant Eccles and Corporal Bateman were captured by the Germans on or about 29th June 1944, while on an independent operation south of Poitiers.

'The remaining 29 personnel were captured by the Germans in the action which took place on 3rd July 1944 in the Forest of Verrières.

'The Germans also captured in the Verrières action three other allied personnel who were wounded, namely:

H J Pascoe

J Ogg

J R Williams

'The said remaining 29 allied personnel, together with the said three wounded personnel were conveyed by the Germans to Poitiers as prisoners of war on 3rd July 1944.

'On or about 7th July 1944, the 17 allied personnel positively named above, together with the 14 allied personnel probably identified above were conveyed by the Germans to the Bois de Guron, near Rom, Deux-Sèvres, France, and were there shot, so that they died.

'The three wounded personnel captured on 3rd July, 1944, were admitted to the Hôtel-Dieu, Poitiers, suffering from wounds, and on 8th July 1994, while still requiring hospital treatment, were removed by the Germans to an unknown destination.'

The Court also clearly confirmed that the thirty-one men were prisoners of war at the time of their deaths, having been in the custody of the Germans for three or more days, and should have been entitled to the privileges and immunities accorded to prisoners of war by the 'well recognised laws and usages of war and the terms of the Geneva Convention of 1929'. There was no evidence to suggest that the prisoners had done anything to deprive themselves of the protection of the Geneva Convention.

Without doubt then, the Allies were convinced that a war crime had been committed. In a formal signal from SHAEF, SAS Brigade headquarters were notified that:

> 'The Germans actually responsible for the murders are not known but there is a *prima facie* case against Major HEROLD, the senior [*sic*] German authority at POITIERS at the time.'

The signal, passed on to the SAS's WCIT, at last gave Major Barkworth a name and a starting point and by May, 1946, he was able to inform Lieutenant-Colonel Franks back in England that:

> 'Major Karl Hermann Herold (*Kommandeur* of Poitiers district *Sicherheitspolizei*) and *SS-Hauptsturmführer* Doctor Walter Linn (*Kommandeur* of *Sicherheitspolizei* for the Departement of the Vienne) named as wanted in connection with the murder of the 'Bulbasket' personnel.'

In beginning to try to find his suspects, Barkworth immediately struck gold. The American military authorities confirmed that Herold was already in their custody and in June Barkworth arranged for the German to be extradited from the US zone of Germany into his custody where interrogation began at once. But the SAS Major soon realized that his pursuit of Herold had not been entirely justified. It became apparent that the SD had not played the major part in the execution of the prisoners, Herold indeed claiming that he had assumed 80th Corps had decided not to shoot them and that it was only a week later that he had learned of the prisoners' execution. By October, 1946, Barkworth had to report:

> 'Major Herold and general SD involvement in the atrocity discounted after detailed investigation and interrogations. Unit responsible for executions of 7th July 1944 identified as the Recce. Squadron of the 158th Division, 80th Corps, German Army. Accused and suspect accused now named as:
> 1) *General der Infanterie* von der Chevallerie, General Commanding, 1st Army.
> 2) General Feyerabend, Chief of Staff, 1st Army.
> 3) Major Hay, Senior Intelligence Officer, 1st Army.
> 4) General Gallenkamp, General Commanding, 80th Corps.
> 5) *Oberst* Koestlin, Chief of Staff, 80th Corps.
> 6) *Hauptmann* Dr Schönig, Intelligence Officer, 80th Corps.
> 7) *Oberst* Haugk, *Feldkommandant*, Poitiers.
> 8) *Oberleutnant* Vogt, O/C Recce Squadron, 158th Division.'

It was further noted that Generals Feyerabend and Gallenkamp were already in British Army custody in Wuppertal prison, Germany. *Hauptmann* Dr Schönig was known to have a dental practice at Ebingen and *Oberleutnant* Vogt was understood to have been a protestant priest at Tuebingen.

As the scent grew stronger, Barkworth and his men worked tirelessly for the next four months to track down and interrogate the suspects and on 17 October, 1946, at Barkworth's request, Schönig was arrested at Ebingen in the French zone of occupation by British military authorities from Baden-Baden.

Despite the chaotic conditions of post-war Germany, Barkworth's 'wanted' list was continually refined, either in the light of questioning or due to the deaths of some of the suspects. *Sonderführer* Hönigschmidt, who had acted as interpreter to the prisoners, was missing and *Oberleutnant* Vogt, leader of the firing squad, was then confirmed as having been killed in action *Oberfeldwebel* Allendorf, who had been the NCO in charge at the *Kommandantur*'s prison, had been killed in April, 1945, in the Friedrichsbrunn/Harz area of Germany. Yet by February of 1947, the key players in the affair were identified as General Gallenkamp, *Oberst* Koestlin and *Hauptmann* Schönig of 80th Corps headquarters and all had been gathered under the watchful care of the 2nd Battalion of the Grenadier Guards at Wuppertal in the British occupied zone of Germany.

It was at Wuppertal that the British Army had established a series of military courts to judge alleged war crimes against their own personnel and it was here that Barkworth finally concluded, in late March, 1947, his interrogations. In addition to the three main suspects, Hesterberg, Weber and Deter, also of the former 80th Corps headquarters, and Doctor Tönshoff, late of the Poitiers *Kommandantur*, were in custody. The case against Generals von der Chevallerie and Feyeraband had been dropped, but instead, General Blumentritt, former Chief of Staff at OB-West, had been added to the charge sheet. Herold and Linn of the SD were also held, but now purely for use as prosecution witnesses, and no longer among the accused.

While still reticent as to the extent of their own personal responsibility, the former German officers made little or no attempt to hide the true story. For Barkworth, as he pieced together the final pieces of the tragedy, the Germans' statements therefore provided sad confirmation of the fate of the SAS prisoners following the attack at Verrières on 3 July, 1944. Yet before a court could convene, one of Barkworth's accused almost slipped from his grasp.

General Curt Gallenkamp was already a broken man, the consequences of the SAS executions seemingly having lain heavily on his conscience. Even as the last 'Bulbasket' survivors had left France in August, 1944, the General had asked to be relieved of his command, claiming ill-health, and on 10 August, 1944 his wish was accepted. He was 54 years old. From then until the final German surrender in May, 1945, Gallenkamp had refused all offers of any other command duties and took no further part in the war. Now, faced with the shame of being branded a war criminal, the General could take no more and sometime in the early hours of the morning of 6 February, 1947, he unsuccessfully tried to take his own life in his prison cell in Wuppertal. The prison's Chief Inspector, Heinrich Heubrock, found a statement and a letter penned the previous evening by Gallenkamp to his interrogator:

'To Major E. A. Barkworth,

'My voluntary departure from this life takes place under the impression of the terrible things which happened in the Corps HQ which I commanded.

'I am unable to endure the exposure of my name and my honour as a General to be drawn through the mud in a public trial.

'Enclosed is a statement made before my Heavenly Judge, from which you see that I gave my consent to a merciful injection for the wounded Englishmen after it had been expressly explained to me that they were bound to die (*Todeskandidaten*). Then I believed that I was helping the men.

'Today I have to realize that I was perhaps not correctly informed. That I was silent about this until now was because I wanted, under no circumstances, to burden one under my command by my statement. You accorded me the right to do so on the first day. Since numerous witnesses are now available who will state all details, I no longer consider my reticence to be necessary.

'I hope that you, as an officer, will understand my attitude towards those under my command who are involved.

'My last request is that the greatest possible leniency may be shown to my former subordinates and that my accidental absence from Poitiers may not be considered as increasing the punishment against my Chief of Staff. He acted, no doubt, under unavoidable compulsion.

'Respectfully yours
    Curt Gallenkamp.'

The General's attached statement read:

'STATEMENT OF GENERAL CURT GALLENKAMP
(5.2.47 2000 HRS)

Standing before my heavenly judge, I declare:

1. I did not order the shooting of the 31 Englishmen.

2. I knew nothing about any torture of the prisoners.

3. I did not prohibit the medical treatment of the wounded in Hôtel-Dieu hospital.

4. I did not order the transfer of the wounded to the military prison.

5. I did not know that the wounded received no medical treatment there.

6. I had no knowledge of the assessment of the sanitary conditions made by Dr Hesterberg on his first visit to the military prison.

7. Later, when I was told that the wounded were condemned men, I simply gave Dr Hesterberg my consent to liberate them from their already dead bodies by means of an injection.

    I am not able to say what the reason for this consultation with Dr Hesterberg was.

    I stress that the wounded Englishmen were described to me throughout as beyond saving.'

But Gallenkamp's attempted suicide failed and Barkworth interrogated him on several occasions between 5 and 27 February, 1947. Concerned at the General's obviously poor state of health, the SAS officer took the precaution of having him observed by a psychiatrist, Dr Wilhelm Philipps. Only after Dr Philipps had confirmed that Gallenkamp was well enough did Barkworth then take a formal statement, on 28 February, 1947. Sufficiently recovered, Gallenkamp stood as the major suspect when, on 11 March, 1947, a Military Court was convened at Wuppertal to investigate formal United Nations charges in respect of two cases involving 'Operation Bulbasket'. The Court President was Colonel B. C. Fletcher DSO MC, late of the Highland Light Infantry and then serving at the headquarters of the 1st British Corps. The five other members of the Court were Majors Landrock, McPherson, Bayham and Stewart-Smith and Captain Hewitt.

The first case charged that General Blumentritt, General Curt Gallenkamp, *Oberst* Herbert Koestlin, *Hauptmann* Erich Schönig and *Oberleutnant* Egon Deter were concerned in the killing of 30 members of the 1st SAS Regiment[1] and Lieutenant Lincoln Bundy of the United States Army Air Force, all while prisoners of war. The second case again named Gallenkamp, Koestlin and Schönig, and added Doctor Paul Tönshoff, Doctor Georg Hesterberg and Doctor Walter Weber as being implicated in the killing of Troopers Ogg, Pascoe and Williams while wounded prisoners of war. Herold and Linn acted as the third and second prosecution witnesses.

The prosecution case against Gallenkamp was that the General should have made attempts to save the prisoners and his defending lawyers therefore stressed the efforts made on 4 July, 1944, to transfer the captured men to a P.O.W. camp of the *Luftwaffe*. Efforts had still been continuing on the 5th when Gallenkamp had left Poitiers. Herold and Linn of the SD had suspected 80th Corps HQ of misleading OB-West over the report that questioning was still continuing and Gallenkamp had even thought he might face a court martial over the matter. Here Gallenkamp's defence gave strong emphasis to Hitler's infamous *Kommandobefehl* issued on 18 October, 1942, and intended to stamp out raids by allied special forces parties. This order was ultimately to be held responsible for the execution of up to 300 captured uniformed troops. As Gallenkamp's defending lawyer stressed:

> 'May I repeat . . . .an order of the *Führer* was binding on those to whom it was given, and indeed legally binding, even when the order was contrary to international law or other traditional values.'

It was also pointed out that when Gallenkamp had returned from his tour of inspection on the late afternoon of 7 July Schönig was able to confirm that the General appeared very surprised to learn that the executions had already taken place. Despite 1st Army's denial of transmitting any orders on the fate of the prisoners, it was still claimed by Gallenkamp and his officers that such an order had been received, but from the even higher authority of OB-West. The order had to be immediately destroyed after reading so there could be

---

[1] The formal charge sheet for the trial still listed one of the 30 SAS as being unidentified. This was in fact Trooper Mullen who had been positively identified at the time of the earlier SHAEF Court of Inquiry. Mullen was executed with the others at Saint-Sauvant and is buried at Rom.

no definite proof of its existence. It would surely have been OB-West's involvement, argued the General's lawyer, which enabled, as quickly as 5 July, the BBC's Monitoring Service to pick up the communiqué from Hitler's headquarters which reported the liquidation of a British sabotage party in central France.

In the event, although Gallenkamp had thought it must have been General Blumentritt, or his OB-West staff, who had pressured Koestlin to carry out the executions in Gallenkamp's absence, the prosecution had little to offer in the way of evidence against Blumentritt. A distinguished soldier, and generally regarded as being one of the *Wehrmacht's* best staff officers of the war, Blumentritt cut a dignified figure in court and resolutely maintained that he had not been aware of any direct contact between OB-West and 80th Corps over the order to execute the prisoners. He said that he had seen the statements of Gallenkamp and Koestlin but he had known nothing about the shooting until a few days before the trial. Blumentritt was certain that no order concerning the *Kommandobefehl* could have gone out to 80th Corps from OB-West without his knowledge.

Blumentritt was also able to cite the fact that it had been OB-West who had gone as far as to request the Führer's HQ to rescind the *Kommandobefehl* in their area of operations in June, 1944. This request had been turned down, and though a supplementary order from Führer HQ on 23 June, 1944, had reminded all commands of the Führer order of 18 October, 1942, Blumentritt stressed that OB-West had done much, in person and by telephone, to water down the order. There had never been disciplinary action against any officer refusing to carry out this order.

Koestlin's evidence also stood Blumentritt in good stead:

'So far as I remember, no pressure was exercised in a call to me in order to hurry on the execution, or to carry it out.'

Barkworth was thus left with no evidence to link Blumentritt in person to the events and, in the face of the General's denial, could do little more than use him as a witness.

When Koestlin himself took to the stand, his defence, like that of Gallenkamp, made much of Hitler's ultimate personal culpability for the *Kommandobefehl,* and Koestlin took care to stress his own opposition to the edict:

'I always gave expression to my mental repugnance for this order in the form of applications, which were made each time in agreement

147

with my superiors. The first time this happened was when the order was made known, and when I still was in the East. I made an application for this order to be rescinded since, as a result of three-dimensional warfare, a distinction between enemy soldiers at the front, immediately behind the front, and far behind the front could no longer be made.

'The second attempt to change or rescind the order was at 80th Corps HQ. On the occasion of a visit of the commander of the 1st Army or of OB-West, General Gallenkamp, after a previous conference with me, submitted that the execution of the *Kommandobefehl*, even if the fundamental considerations against it could not be taken into account, could no longer be justified in view of the impending invasion with frontal contact with the enemy and with the possibility of the infiltration of reconnaissance and fighting patrols. This application must also have been passed on by 1st Army or OB-West, for I recollect a reply by teleprint in which the demand for the execution of the *Kommandobefehl* was renewed, or words to that effect, and which bore the signature of Keitel or that of Warlimont. Application and reply occurred before the capture of the English.'

On behalf of Koestlin, considerable support had been martialled, particularly to emphasize the compassionate and Christian nature of his conduct during the war. General Walter Hahm wrote glowingly of Koestlin's good service in Russia with the 260th Infantry Division. There Koestlin had looked after Russian P.O.W.s 'in a warm-hearted manner' and Hahm went on to say that Koestlin's alleged crime was 'incompatible with his Christian belief'. General Dr Franz Beyer too wrote of Koestlin's religious tenets, saying he could not credit the latter's guilt 'by reason of his Christian and military views on life' and General Gustav Wilke considered it impossible that such an 'avowed follower of the Christian church' would not have used every effort to avoid carrying out the execution order, even if it were the *Kommandobefehl*. General Erich Dethleffse had shared a P.O.W cell in Germany from May to November of 1946 with Koestlin and wrote with praise of the latter's 'Christian conviction'. Dr Karl Frank, Mayor of the German town of Ludwigsburg, described how he and Koestlin had contrived to surrender the town to the Allies without fighting, thereby saving much unnecessary bloodshed. This had not been done without Koestlin facing possible reaction from SS elements in the area. His lawyers claimed that Koestlin had in fact been labelled too much of a 'pessimist', he had already been by-passed for promotion and his posting to the quiet backwater of 80th

Corps was the reaction of higher command who felt he had too much 'human sympathy towards his subordinates'. Many examples were given where, late in the war, Koestlin had ordered withdrawals from situations which he considered to be 'military nonsense' and unnecessarily risking lives.

Summing up, Koestlin's defence therefore maintained that the Chief of Staff had received 'a very clear and unmistakeable order' from Gallenkamp, that he had not acted over Gallenkamp's head and was in touch with him during the whole period of the General's absence between 5 and 7 July. Moreover, Koestlin's lawyer pointed out that neither in his previously given statement nor in court had Gallenkamp made any claim that he had reprimanded Koestlin for the action which the latter had taken.

Hauptmann Dr Erich Schönig had fully admitted his part in the affair to Barkworth as early as October, 1946. He made no attempt to hide or deny the fact that he had been ordered to attend the execution as 80th Corps' observer and to see that the formalities were observed. He acknowledged it had been his task to make the decision known to the British officer (Lieutenant Crisp) and he then remained during the shooting, collected the prisoners' identity discs and reported to the Red Cross authorities that they had been killed in action. Schönig summed up his evidence by stating, 'I was frankly revolted'.

Last to be questioned, *Oberleutnant* Egon Deter, Schönig's deputy, was soon accepted to have held little responsibility for events, although he too had been present at the execution. It was acknowledged that, to his credit, he had been involved in attempts to transfer the SAS prisoners to the *Luftwaffe* P.O.W. camp at Oberursel by claiming that the SAS were really British air force personnel. On this somewhat more positive note, proceedings were completed in respect of the first charge.

For the second case, Gallenkamp, Koestlin and Schönig continued as the accused and were joined by two of 80th Corps' medical officers – *Hauptmann* Dr Georg Hesterberg and his commanding officer, *Oberst* (former Major) Dr Walter Weber, along with Major (formerly *Hauptmann*) Dr Paul Tönshof, the Poitiers *Feldkommandantur's* doctor.

Apparently worn down by the earlier proceedings, General Gallenkamp made little effort to disguise his actions in connection with the wounded men, though he resolutely denied having been aware that they had been denied proper medical attention. Loyally, however, the General initially attempted to protect former Chief of Staff Koestlin by saying during his original interrogation that he had spoken only to Dr Hesterberg about arrangements to speed the men's deaths. He was later to admit that he could not be sure that this was so and as Hesterberg refuted any such contact, then the doctor must be correct. What would appear to be the facts are that Gallenkamp discussed the matter not with Hesterberg but with Koestlin. Gallenkamp was later to concede that he had tried to cover up Koestlin's and Schönig's involvement in the affair; the supposed conversation with Hesterberg would therefore appear to be an example of the General's efforts on behalf of his immediate subordinates. His statement can thus be accepted as having been directed to Koestlin:

> 'I spoke to [Koestlin] around the 10th or 11th July when I had heard that all the men were bound to die so I told him 'then do not let the men suffer unnecessarily, but help them'. By this I understood an injection of morphia or similar.'

For his part, Koestlin had seemed vague in his first attempts to answer questions on the second charge concerning the three wounded SAS troopers, albeit he too did not seek to hide his complicity:

> 'Until the day of 26th February 1947, when I was confronted with *Hauptmann* Schönig in the office of Major Barkworth, I did not know anything about the fate of the wounded men. But if Schönig says that I gave the order to kill them then that will be correct, even if I do not remember it. I cannot explain why I remembered the execution, which I shall never forget, whereas I forgot the order to kill the wounded SAS men. And I have no explanation for myself either . . . I cannot free myself from guilt.'

Soon, however, Koestlin's memory, or perhaps his conscience, gathered strength. He admitted that he had given the order, via Schönig, for the wounded men to receive a quick and painless death from Dr Hesterberg, possibly via injections. He confirmed that he and Schönig were determined that the wounded troopers would not have to be shot in their beds.

Schönig himself continued to make a clean breast of his involvement. Yes, he had received an order from Koestlin for the three wounded men to be killed and yes, he had passed this order on to Dr Hesterberg. Damningly, Schönig repeated:

> 'Three or four days after the transfer of the wounded to the prison, Hesterberg came to see me again in order to inform me that he had given lethal injections to the three troopers.'

Doctor Hesterberg's defence clearly faced an up-hill struggle to clear their client in the light of the statements of Gallenkamp, Koestlin and, particularly, Schönig. Nevertheless, his lawyer methodically set about a defence which first of all concentrated on depicting a humane and caring man. Hesterberg had ended the war in a P.O.W. camp in Shalstone, Berkshire, and had remained imprisoned there until January, 1946. From Shalstone, the camp's C.O., Lieutenant-Colonel Charles Moore MC, had written:

> 'In my opinion he was a first class doctor and looked after the health of the camp very well . . . his behaviour was extremely correct.'

The Court was reminded too of Hesterberg's small clinic for the local people in Poitiers, a facility by which, it was claimed, he attempted to 'mitigate the burden of occupation for the civil population'. Here then was another seemingly compassionate professional, caught in the turmoil of war and the rigid discipline of an army.

But even though Hesterberg's general good character might be accepted, his stand against the charges looked decidedly weak. The doctor's opening claim was that the medical attention of the wounded SAS in prison was never his responsibilty as a medical officer of 80th Corps HQ and he had never received any particular instructions to take over the medical attention of the three. Hesterberg nevertheless admitted to three visits to the prison, but maintained he had only ever done his best to help ease the troopers' suffering in the context of their not receiving full treatment for their wounds. Twice he had given attention to the wounded without orders to do so. He admitted to receiving the order to administer lethal injections, but denied, despite Schönig's damning evidence, that he had done so. Instead, Hesterberg claimed that the three men had eventually died from their wounds. He made the point that he had not been approached for the filling in of death certificates, nor in connection with any burial. He stressed that those others of the accused who were making statements to his disadvantage had personal interests and reasons to do so, hence he found himself standing alone. Finally, seeking to divert blame for the lack of medical attention given to the wounded, Hesterberg said that he had relied upon the support of Dr Tönshof to save the wounded, but this support had not proved forthcoming.

Dr Paul Tönshof was the *Feldkommandantur*'s 49-year-old doctor normally responsible for the treatment of prisoners in Poitiers' military prison. Despite Hesterberg's condemnation, his defence was relatively straightforward. Tönshof was quick to point out that Hauptmann Maurer, who was also the *Feldkommandantur*'s Intelligence Officer, was the officer with overall responsibility for the military prison and it was from the *Kommandantur* that he, Tönshof, had been informed that the SAS prisoners were the responsibility of the 80th Corps medical officer, Hesterberg. He confirmed that he had seen two of the wounded on his first visit to the prison and he had wanted to transfer them to a military hospital. The *Feldkommandantur*, however, had told Tönshof of 80th Corps' involvement and he had therefore been happy to leave the care of the wounded to Dr Hesterberg who was better surgically trained.

Some two weeks later Tönshof heard that at least one of the wounded had subsequently died, but, he claimed, he had no suspicions of any irregularities, reflecting only that the death might not have occurred had the wounded been transferred to hospital. Other than this statement, Tönshof was able to maintain that he had no other involvement in the matter and was generally unaware of the circumstances surrounding it.

Last to take the stand was *Oberst* Dr Walter Weber, Hesterberg's immediate superior and senior medical officer at 80th Corps HQ. Weber's defence was even shorter. He claimed he had not known about the SAS operation and did not even recall the brief mention of the SAS wounded which Hesterberg claimed to have made to him. The prosecution was unable to offer any evidence of his direct involvement with the wounded.

Overall, the Court took three weeks to hear the two cases. At the trial's conclusion all the accused pleaded 'not guilty' to both charges and, apart from their individual defences, the general defence of all was that they would have been court-martialled had they not carried out the *Kommandobefehl*.

On 1 April, 1947, sentences were announced by the Military Court, subject to confirmation. General Blumentritt, Doctor Walter Weber, Doctor Egon Deter and Doctor Paul Tönshoff were acquitted, the remaining accused were all found guilty. Erich Schönig received five years imprisonment. Herbert Koestlin, having played a pivotal rôle, was sentenced to life imprisonment. But it was General Curt Gallenkamp and Doctor Georg Hesterberg who were judged to have borne the most guilt. By unanimous decision of the Court, both were to suffer death by hanging.

Yet the verdicts at Wuppertal were far from the final word. All the convicted men submitted appeals, Gallenkamp and Koestlin against sentence only, Hesterberg and Schönig against both finding and sentence. On 2 May, 1947, the sentences were reviewed by the Deputy Judge Advocate's Office at the headquarters of the British Army of the Rhine (BAOR). There, it was the responsibility of Colonel Williams to provide advice for the Commander in Chief of the British zone in Germany, Lord Sholto Douglas, before confirmation of the sentences.

Williams noted the argument used concerning the *Kommandobefehl* and conceded it was an issue which could be taken into consideration in mitigation of sentence. Nevertheless, he felt that the findings in respect of the first charge were sound and that they might properly be confirmed.

With regard to the second charge, however, Colonel Williams had considerable concerns and concluded that the evidence in support of this charge was unsatisfactory. He accepted that there was indeed evidence that Koestlin had given an order for the three wounded men to be killed by lethal injections. Likewise, there was no doubt that Schönig had passed the order on, that Gallenkamp acquiesced in it and that Hesterberg had acknowledged it. But, Williams argued, there was still no satisfactory or conclusive evidence as to precisely how the three men had died. While he was happy with the findings and sentences in respect of Gallenkamp, Koestlin and Schönig, the Colonel's report to his Commander in Chief concluded in respect of Dr Hesterberg:

'I therefore advise that you refuse confirmation of the finding in respect of this charge.'

The onus was then left with Sholto Douglas, one of the RAF's most celebrated wartime leaders. Now, in peacetime, he held the unenviable responsibility for confirming the findings of military war crime courts including, under Regulation 12 (War Crimes), deciding upon application of the death penalty. Perhaps not surprisingly, the airman followed the advice of his army legal advisor. The finding guilty of Galllenkamp, Koestlin and Schönig was confirmed. Hesterberg, however, could not be conclusively proven guilty as to the second charge and was to be set free. Finally, Sholto Douglas considered Gallenkamp's death sentence. The *Kommandobefehl* of Hitler was, he agreed, a mitigating factor. Sentence of death was to be commuted to life imprisonment.[1]

And there the story of justice might end, but for a final bout of soul-searching by the British.

In 1949 a committee was appointed to review all sentences pronounced in war crime trials. In June of that year it is known that Koestlin's lawyer, Dr

---

[1] Gallenkamp was unable to completely hide behind the Führer's order since it was known that at least one German commander, Rommel, had chosen to ignore the Kommandobefehl in the desert campaigns of the Middle East and North Africa. Perhaps because of his standing, Rommel had received no punishment for his stance.

Zierenberg, petitioned for a pardon for his client and in August the War Crimes Review Board was forwarded a letter, addressed to the Secretary of State for War, from no less than the Bishop of Chichester. The Bishop backed the view of Doctor Martin Niemoller and argued that Koestlin's sentence of life imprisonment merited review. But the yellowing files of the Judge Advocate General's Office then fall frustratingly mute on the subject and no record remains as to whether a further appeal was ever permitted. In the case of Gallenkamp, however, much more remains on record of a final twist to the tale.

Petitioning against his sentence had begun in April, 1947, when Gallenkamp's brother-in-law, General Tippelskirch, had pleaded to the authorities for clemency to be shown. He explained how his wife, Gallenkamp's sister, had been forced to leave her mortally ill mother behind when fleeing the Russians. To lose her brother as well as her mother would undoubtedly break her, Tippelskirch claimed. In the same month, a petition signed by thirty-one former *Wehrmacht* Generals, general staff officers and Admirals, headed by Major Generals Blaskowitz and Guderian, had also pleaded for mercy. These pleas were backed up by a letter from Cardinal von Preysing, Bishop of Berlin, and in May, 1947, a moving and impassioned plea was made by Gallenkamp's son, Hans-Georg, directly to the Lord Chancellor in London. All this the committee took into account, along with the fact that Gallenkamp still seemed very much a broken spirit, rarely in good health. In a decision of remarkable compassion, the sentence was reduced to ten years, dating from 1 April, 1947. On 22 February, 1952, Gallenkamp then came up before his Remission Board at Werl penitentiary. His lawyer, Dr Lüdecke, again stressed that the General was a tired and broken man in poor health. Making allowances for pre-trial custody served and good conduct and industry in prison, the Board concluded that Gallenkamp was worthy of remission and four days later, on 26 February, 1952, he walked from the prison a free man.

9

BETRAYAL?

One final element remains to be uncovered in the account of 'Operation Bulbasket'; yet it is an element that has been deliberately omitted from the remaining SAS files which languish in the depths of the Public Record Office.

On 6 July, 1944, Special Forces Headquarters had received a radio message from SOE agent Captain Maingard. The message, which was subsequently copied to SAS Brigade HQ, included confirmation from Tonkin of the Verrières attack, with his belief that the group had been 'betrayed and surrounded'. While Tonkin and his party then sent over seventy more recorded radio messages before their evacuation from France, no further mention of betrayal seems to have been made. Neither do the official after-operation reports, prepared by both Tonkin and Sadoine within a couple of days of their return to England, touch on the subject. Nevertheless, as early as 10 August, 1944, the Director of Tactical Investigation at the War Office had written:

> 'There is no evidence to show why this group was subjected to attack so early. It is reported, however, that it was caused by betrayal.'

Even Captain Maingard, the experienced SOE agent and surely one of those best-placed to know all the details, was to comment:

> 'To my mind, the location of the camp of Captain Tonkin and his men was certainly betrayed to the German SS.'

Yet for what reasons was betrayal so strongly suspected?

Since the war several French sources have been critical of the SAS's operating methods: some of the 'Bulbasket' troopers had been incautious in visiting local cafés and bars and they, or their *maquis* comrades, had received visits from local girls in the camp. The latter incident had made Jean

155

Dieudonné furious and was later to lie heavily on his mind: 'I feel that all our misfortune stems from that'. Consequently one theory, chiefly from the French point of view, is that the Verrières camp was given away by a combination of the SAS's high-profile and incautious movements, reported to the enemy by local informers.

But it is the opinion of Denis Chansigaud that, despite Dieudonné's preoccupation with them, the local girls were not the cause of the group's betrayal to the enemy. He recalls that there were only two or three of them; they lived close by and were simply in search of adventure.

Chansigaud himself raises three possibilities, the first concerning the American flyer, Lieutenant Lincoln Bundy. Chansigaud was not alone in knowing that the SAS were suspicious of the arrival of Bundy and had immediately radioed to London to check his identity. No answer was received before the Verrières disaster, nor indeed after it. This in itself led to speculation post-war that Bundy had been a German imposter and had been able to report on the camp's location. In reality, however, Bundy's identity was confirmed. He was executed with the SAS at Saint-Sauvant and is buried with them at Rom.[1]

Chansigaud also recalled that a man from a nearby hamlet had warned Dieudonné's *maquis* of a suspected radio direction-finding vehicle which had been seen touring the area. While this sighting was not confirmed, such a method would have been usual practice for the German armed forces and intelligence services. With the likelihood that the SAS were remaining in regular radio contact with England, it would also have meant that the Germans would have stood a fair chance of at least monitoring some of the transmissions.

But Chansigaud's strongest suspicion centres on another incident:

'As to whether we were betrayed, I believe that yes, we were . . .

'There was certainly the possibility of radio location by the Germans but I also recall clearly the incident the day before the attack when three [sic] men, dressed as gendarmes, were brought into the camp. They were armed with machine guns, claimed to be part of a *maquis* group, had a convincing alibi and were able to adequately answer the testing questions put to them. On reflection,

[1] Intriguingly, though there is little or no doubt that Bundy is buried at Rom, official American records still leave room for conjecture. The headstone on Bundy's grave at Rom only states 'believed to be buried here' while in England, his name appears on a USAAF memorial to those missing in action with no known grave.

however, I believe they were really *Milice* and that it was they who guided the Germans on to us.'

In raising this incident, Chansigaud probably comes closest to the truth as it is only now, more than fifty years after the happenings of 1944, that the full story can be revealed, along with events deliberately omitted from the official reports after the operation by both Tonkin and Sadoine.

It will be recalled that on 1 July, 1944, shortly before the attack on Verrières, Tonkin had received an urgent message to attend a meeting with the SOE agent, Maingard. A car was provided and Tonkin was rapidly driven some 70 kilometres to the south-east where Colonel Chêne then had his FFI headquarters. There, Tonkin found Maingard in a grave mood, along with Chêne, Capitaine Blondel ('Michel'), leader of the Haute-Vienne *maquis* and Capitaine Robichon of the 'Vauquois' *maquis*.

The Frenchmen had startling news for the SAS Captain. Reports had reached them from absolutely reliable and trusted *maquis* group leaders that Captain Sadoine of the Phantom party was not only reluctant to join Tonkin, but had been actively encouraging the *maquis* forces to keep away from the SAS group. Sadoine seemingly considered that the SAS's mode of operations represented not only a danger to themselves, but also to any Frenchman helping them and also to his own team of Phantom signallers. Apparently Sadoine had become obsessed by the idea that the SAS operations would lead to his own capture and execution. In view of the allied invasion having begun, he no longer saw any purpose to 'Bulbasket' and it was even reported that he had gone as far as to suggest that the only solution was the elimination of Tonkin and his officers.

Tonkin was stunned by the information, yet both Maingard and Colonel Chêne were clear in what they thought he should now do: court-martial Sadoine in the field and execute him. But Tonkin could not bring himself to do so. Sadoine was from another unit and, as such, was not Tonkin's direct responsibility. To execute a brother officer was a grave decision to have to make and, instead, Tonkin pledged to have Sadoine placed under close arrest as soon as possible. This having been agreed, Tonkin was driven back to Verrières.[1]

---

[1] Before Tonkin's departure, and in contrast to the gravity of the meeting, Colonel Chêne used the SAS officer's camera to take a group photograph of Maingard, Jacques Hirsch, Captain Blondel and John Tonkin, standing against a backdrop of the high country around the FFI headquarters. See Illustrations.

For the next few days Tonkin was fully occupied with the aftermath of the disaster at Verrières, but when Sadoine and his party eventually joined him Tonkin wasted no time in acting. As he was to reflect many years later:

'I had been told by London on 14 June where Sadoine was and on 16 June that he had been instructed to join me. On 16 June I told U.K. to send all important messages to my and Cpl Chick's codes. By then I was beginning to wonder why he hadn't joined or sent word.

'I set out to find him and my men on 18 June but was misdirected. I will never know if it was *Résistance* jealousy (they had a private source of abundant arms, explosives, petrol and food which they wouldn't want to lose), or deliberate action at Sadoine's direction. You may speculate from what follows.

'Four days may sound like a long time now, but I was trying to get the jeeps parachuted in, and further supplies so that we could operate more effectively. (Jeeping beats walking at any time, but particularly at night.) We were also being hunted by strong German forces and had to move fast on the 13th and 18th – my own men, the attached *Résistance* groups and all our supplies.

'Anyway, I went back on 19 June in a newly dropped jeep and found him. I picked up Sgt Eccles and four of my men and the Eureka and left Cpl Bateman (another veteran) with two SAS to help Sadoine build up a reserve of supplies until I could provide transport to get them. Lt Morris went and got the SAS on 23 June, but, as I recall it, Sadoine wouldn't come at that time as he wasn't prepared . . .

'Hindsight is easy, particularly when you have time to set things down in unhurried, peaceful sequence, but at the time I put Sadoine's attitude down to status problems arising from our equal rank and his being 'under command'. I do recall not minding much as I had my own radio link and Sadoine would be useful in building up a reserve of supplies in a relatively safe place, so I let it be. In retrospect, it was a stupid decision.'

On 22, 24 and 29 June England had radioed additional commands to Sadoine to join the SAS and on the 27th he had been reminded 'You are alternate W/T source for Bulbasket'. But still the Phantom leader would not move, even though he had transport. Clearly, in the light of Sadoine's strange actions to date, there therefore had to be some truth in the accusations of the French on 1 July.

After Verrières a car had been sent by Maingard to collect Tonkin and the SOE agent had stressed his continuing concern about the activities of Sadoine. Consequently, Tonkin sent a party led by Lieutenant Weaver, with transport, to collect Sadoine's Phantom group. They returned on the afternoon of the 5th and Sadoine was quietly taken to one side where Tonkin, Maingard, Weaver, Morris and three other SAS assembled. Coming straight to the point, Tonkin confronted the Phantom officer with the *maquis'* reports of his treachery. By way of response the Belgian simply paled and began to tremble, offering no words in his own defence. Continuing, Tonkin told Sadoine he should now consider himself under close arrest. He would be guarded around the clock by the three 'old hand' troopers let in on the affair, Troopers Brown, R. Smith and W. Smith. They would operate on an eight-hour guard rota and they had orders to shoot to kill. Still Sadoine offered no explanation. Apart from the three guards, Tonkin only told Lieutenants Morris and Weaver, Sergeant Holmes and Corporal Stephenson, the Phantom NCO, the full details of his suspicions. The latter was now Tonkin's only radio link, since Corporal Chick had been captured at Verrières. Despite the circumstances, Stephenson never batted an eye and quickly proved to be a first-rate man. While the other SAS troopers were not privy to the full facts, they were nevertheless aware of Sadoine's arrest and their C.O.'s general dissatisfaction with him.

Sadoine returned to England by Hudson with Tonkin and Maingard on 7 August, 1944. Upon debriefing, Tonkin reported the issue to Paddy Mayne and, while he could not be certain, expected that Maingard had confirmed it. Former senior Phantom officers recall that Sadoine was certainly removed from his duties soon after his arrival back in England, yet not before the GHQ Liaison Regiment's war diary had recorded in June 'he [Sadoine] passed back many bomber targets, which were bombed, including 11 petrol trains'. This, of course, was totally wrong. Sadoine and his team had not even arrived in France when the SAS pinpointed the petrol trains at Châtellerault. Thereafter, while Phantom's headquarters seem to have assumed that Sadoine was fulfilling his duties in reporting the other targets, it was only on the return of the survivors that the truth emerged. Sadoine was swiftly returned to his original unit, the Irish Guards,[1] and no further part was directly played by Tonkin, the SAS or Phantom in his eventual punishment.

And so, despite their strong suspicions of Sadoine's treachery, the SAS

[1] Personal recollections of Sir John Astor, former Major commanding F Squadron, Phantom, and Colonel John Morgan, second in command of Phantom.

survivors heard no more of the mysterious Belgian until, twenty-seven years later, circumstances combined to resurrect the matter.

In 1971 a reunion was held in Paris of former *résistants* from France, Holland and Belgium and among those present was Albert Dupont, who had briefly been attached to 'Bulbasket' by Colonel Chêne as interpreter. At the reception Dupont found himself seated next to a veteran of the Belgian *Résistance*, discussing their respective wartime experiences. On hearing that Dupont had operated in the Vienne region, the Belgian sat up in his seat and interrupted his French comrade. There was, he told Dupont, a man in a mental home in Belgium who also claimed to have fought in the Vienne. At some point this individual had been badly wounded during the war and had ended up in the psychiatric institute at Leuze, suffering from total amnesia for over twenty years or so. Over the last four years, however, he had slowly started to recover some memory and about two years ago he had started calling himself Captain Tonkin and claimed that he had operated with the *Résistance* in the Vienne.

Albert Dupont was both astounded and excited at the news. Since the war he had heard little of the fate of the 'Bulbasket' team yet he clearly recalled the name of Tonkin. Pressing the Belgian for more details, Dupont was then stunned by the news that 'Tonkin' had stressed that the SAS had been betrayed, repeating again and again that 'it was the radio operator who betrayed the group to the Germans'.

This was shocking news for Dupont and the other former *résistants* of the Vienne as it was thought that the finger could therefore only be pointing at Pierre Hirsch, hitherto accepted to have served Maingard and SOE loyally as a radio operator since April, 1943. Hirsch, a war hero and by then a respected senior civil servant, suddenly found himself under the gravest suspicion of having been a double agent of the Germans. The matter required urgent resolution.

As a first step Albert Dupont had written to the patient in Leuze and discovered that he was registered under the name of Octave Dupont. In an exchange of correspondence, however, there could be no doubt that 'Tonkin', or Octave Dupont, had definitely been involved with 'Bulbasket', possessing as he did detailed knowledge of many aspects of the operation. Determined to pursue the matter, Albert Dupont then travelled north to visit his namesake in the mental institute. He found a wreck of a man whom he could not identify for certain after the passage of so many years, but they talked of incidents that only a participant could have known. 'Tonkin' revealed that his true nationality was Belgian and that he had never uttered a word in French during the war for security reasons because of his relatives in Belgium. Having only met the SAS officer for a few days in 1944, Albert Dupont was prepared to believe that the patient was indeed John Tonkin. Returning to France, Dupont reported the matter to the *Résistance* veterans' headquarters in Paris who in turn contacted Colonel Maurice Buckmaster, former head of SOE's French Section, in England. Buckmaster maintained contact with many of his former agents and therefore had no difficulty in writing to Maingard in Mauritius, where he had returned post-war to a successful career in commerce. Maingard was immediately suspicious and concerned. The physical description and photograph of 'Tonkin' supplied via Albert Dupont did not match Maingard's recollections at all; the height and hair colour were both wrong. Above all, he could not begin to believe that Pierre Hirsch had been other than a loyal and extremely brave SOE radio operator.

While controversy continued to rage in France, Colonel Buckmaster was hard at work using his extensive network of contacts to try to get to the bottom of the affair. Using Foreign Office and M.I.6 sources, he soon confirmed that the real John Tonkin did not match the description of the mental patient discovered by Albert Dupont. Indeed, Tonkin was known to have been a mining engineer in northern Australia from 1953 to 1961 and his last known address was in Melbourne.

This information was relayed back to Albert Dupont via Paris and, by a remarkable coincidence, Dupont had a brother in Melbourne whom he therefore telephoned without delay. Yves Dupont rang the first J. E. Tonkin he could find in the telephone directory and reached John Tonkin's wife who, initially somewhat suspicious and cautious, rang her husband at work.

Tonkin lost no time in calling Albert Dupont in France, his initial thoughts and concern being that the hospital patient might be one of 'Bulbasket's' missing troopers – Biffin, Ogg, Pascoe or Williams, or even Trooper Guard whom Tonkin mistakenly thought had not been among those exhumed at Saint-Sauvant and buried at Rom.

Accompanied by his wife Heather, Tonkin set off as soon as he could, first for England where he had asked the SAS to do some checking for him. Before continuing on to Belgium, Tonkin knew the identity of the man in Leuze. David Dane[1], the former SAS Lieutenant who had chosen the 'Bon Bon' landing ground, had been sent the photograph of the patient taken by Albert Dupont. Despite a drastic change in facial features, Dane believed the patient to be Captain Sadoine, commander of the Phantom signals team attached to 'Bulbasket'.

[1] Postwar, David Surrey Dane had shortened his family name to simply Dane.

161

Buckmaster had passed this identification to the Belgian authorities for further research, but it became apparent that the Belgians had known nothing of Sadoine's British Army service. All they were certain of was that, on the liberation of Belgium, he had been called up for service in his own country's army as an infantry private under the name of Octave Dupont. After just two months he was quite badly wounded in the lower back, in action on the Rhine, in early 1945. He was taken to the Canadian hospital at Nimegue and after his physical injuries had healed as best they could, he was found to have amnesia. When able to speak, he had no memory of his past, no relatives could be traced and there was not even proof that Octave Dupont was his real name. In such condition he was transferred to the psychiatric institute in Leuze and had remained there ever since, working in the gardens and calling himself either Octave Dupont, Don Varrenes or, latterly, John Tonkin.

Before leaving for the Continent, Tonkin took time to consult a medical friend, a senior brain surgeon, on Sadoine's reported condition. There was no known case of injury-inflicted amnesia recovering after so long a time and therefore Tonkin was advised that the cause of Sadoine's amnesia had to be hysterical, the condition of a man who had a strong reason not to want to identify with his old self.

On arrival at the Saint-Jean-de-Dieu Institut Psychiatrique in Leuze, Tonkin and his wife first met the Institute's staff to discuss the nature of their visit. After a while, Sadoine was brought into the room. He immediately greeted Tonkin by name but appeared terrified by his presence. Gently, Heather Tonkin did her best to reassure Sadoine that he would come to no harm and even John Tonkin, despite his bitter memories of the man, could not help but feel sympathy for the wretched individual before him. Clearly the Belgian had paid a terrible price for what amounted to a combination of severe stress and battle fatigue. He had obviously been completely unsuited to duties behind enemy lines, and even his later service in the Belgian Army had been erratic and plagued by absences. When Sadoine again insisted that it had been a radio operator who had betrayed the SAS, Tonkin began to perceive what he believed to be the reality behind the Belgian's rambling. If Sadoine truly believed himself to be Tonkin, then surely his accusation against a radio operator could, in effect, be directed against himself, Sadoine, as the chief radio operator attached to the SAS. Thus, the real John Tonkin believed that he was witnessing an inverted confession to the betrayal by Sadoine, confirming the wartime reports of the *maquis* and so absolving Pierre Hirsch from any blame. His quest completed, Tonkin continued on to France where he had already agreed to be present at the raising of a memorial in the forest at Saint-Sauvant. He confirmed that Pierre Hirsch could be restored to his rightful standing as one of the most steadfast *Résistance* workers France had known. Looking back today on the period when his reputation was in doubt, Hirsch describes how he was happy to be cleared of suspicion, but sad for Sadoine and his state of mind. In the circumstances, Hirsch's concern for Sadoine can only be another indication of the Frenchman's true worth.[1]

Returning to Australia, Tonkin was satisfied that he had at last confirmed the truth surrounding the betrayal of his operation to the Germans, and was content to leave Sadoine in what measure of peace remained to him. Indeed, so concerned was he that Tonkin drew up a legal document purporting to clear Sadoine of any culpability for Verrières. Instead, the document suggested, blame should more likely attach to the SAS's own lack of caution in the area. Privately, however, Tonkin remained convinced that Sadoine had betrayed the SAS to the enemy in order to relieve the pressure on his own Phantom team.

And yet, Tonkin had still not discovered the whole story, for the truth lay hidden in the minutiae of the war crime trial transcripts held by the Public Record Office and was only uncovered during research for this book.

It will be recalled that when Sergeant Eccles and Corporal Bateman were surprised on the railway at Saint Benoît on the night of 28/29 June, 1944, the two SAS NCOs had no option but to surrender and were quickly taken into Poitiers for questioning at the *Feldkommandantur*. Here the *Wehrmacht* learned no more than the name, rank and number of their captives, along with the information that they belonged to the Special Air Service. Shortly afterwards, in accordance with the requirements of Hitler's *Kommandobefehl*, they were handed over to the SS Security Police for interrogation.

The SD would have known it was critical to break the men in order to locate the other SAS, and would therefore have undoubtedly used all the brutal means at their disposal. While one German report suggested that Eccles and Bateman were transferred for questioning to Tours, this was almost certainly a smoke-screen to cloud local responsibility since only a few days later it was known that they were still in Poitiers. *Hauptmann* Schönig, 80th Corps' Senior Intelligence Officer, had carried out the initial and

---

[1] To make absolutely certain that Pierre Hirsch was cleared of all suspicion, Maingard also returned to France in May, 1973, and visited the Vienne region to publicly pledge his support of Hirsch to the local Résistance veterans and historians. This was in spite of his memories of many tragic events and his previous reluctance to return to the Poitiers area.

fruitless questioning of the two SAS NCOs immediately after their capture. A couple of days later however:

> 'I was all the more astonished when the SD informed me that the interrogation of the two prisoners by the SD had resulted in the disclosure of the hiding places in the woods near Verrières . . .
>
> '*SS-Obersturmführer* Hoffmann and *SS-Hauptsturmführer* Linn came to see the Chief of Staff and told him in my presence that one of the prisoners had made definite statements. The man claimed that he belonged to a detachment of about thirty-five men which was in a wood in the neighbourhood of Poitiers and that they were in contact with the *maquis* there. They said that the detachment was well equipped with weapons such as machine guns, machine pistols and that three [*sic*] jeeps and a complete wireless set for reception and transmission were in its possession. By means of this wireless set the detachment was in contact with the motherland several times daily . . .
>
> '. . . on the day before the operation the SD, as a result of the interrogation, sent an agent into the Verrières wood to track down the hiding place. I assume that the interrogation of the two prisoners by the SD was made under pressure.'

One can only guess at how the SAS prisoner was forced to talk 'under pressure' but even the 80th Corps officers who learned of the information had no illusions as to the torture that would have been used. What is clear, and what is extremely important, is that the SD did not manage to extract the information until after Tonkin had moved camp and no more could have been expected of the two captured SAS men in the circumstances. Certainly, in the SOE, even experienced agents were expected, and trained, to resist determined interrogation for no more than forty-eight hours, enough for their comrades to disperse. This, it would seem, Eccles and Bateman managed – but to no avail. The SAS main party had been given the chance to move, and did so, but then returned to Verrières at the very moment that the Germans began to look for them there.

Denis Chansigaud and John Fielding may well therefore be right in suspecting the two men found apparently trying to repair a motor cycle puncture near to the camp. If these were the local French agents of the SD, then they were given the perfect opportunity to pinpoint the SAS when they were taken into the camp for questioning. They produced *maquis* credentials which could not be fully checked but, given the benefit of the doubt, they were allowed to continue on their way. In retrospect, Fielding wished that he had shot them outright.

Although both Herold and Linn of the SD were interrogated and made statements during the SHAEF Inquiry, their submissions were only referred to at the war crime trial in 1947 and no doubt concentrated on the two charges concerning the shooting of the prisoners and the murder of the three wounded men. The SD's part in the torture of Eccles and Bateman was therefore a peripheral issue to Major Barkworth's investigations, and one which was never followed up. Public Record Office files which may include Herold's and Linn's statements from the original SHAEF investigation are closed until the year 2020.

To return then to the initial subject of this chapter, it has to be acknowledged that Sadoine was certainly guilty of at least dereliction of duty in the field, and indeed attempted treachery against the SAS if the *maquis* report of Capitaine Blondel was accurate. Fortunately, the *maquis* proved loyal to Tonkin and any further consequences of Sadoine's failings were therefore limited. This, however, was undoubtedly the guilt with which Sadoine had then persecuted himself for the rest of his life. It fell short of the betrayal that he had been suspected of, that of actually revealing the location of Tonkin's camp to the enemy, but was nevertheless enough for him to have been dismissed from the British Army on his return to England. Quite simply, he had not been up to the stress of operating behind enemy lines and his nerve had failed him almost immediately after dropping into France.

While Sadoine's memory had appeared to be recovering at the time of Tonkin's visit, his general condition then began to deteriorate. He lost the ability to write and could eventually barely speak. On 21 April, 1986, Sadoine, alias Octave Dupont, alias Don Varrenes, alias Captain Tonkin, died in the psychiatric institute in Leuze-en-Hainaut, Belgium.

10

CONCLUSIONS

Some fifty years on from the summer of 1944, a combination of hindsight and access to most of the relevant official records makes it all too easy for the armchair historian to reach facile conclusions. That fact acknowledged, it is still useful to summarize the parts played by the various participants in the affair, and to analyse the background to some of the more contentious issues.

Firstly, while 'Bulbasket' was essentially an SAS operation, it must not be forgotten that several other agencies contributed significantly, not least of which, both in terms of supply drops and fighter-bomber support, were the squadrons of the Royal Air Force and its Commonwealth allies.

From the very beginning the RAF's 161 (Special Duties) Squadron deserves specific mention. Despite poor weather conditions, Tonkin, Crisp and the 'Hugh' Jedburgh team were dropped on target, on time and right on top of their reception committee. For the evacuation, Boxer and Ibbott coolly landed their two Hudsons behind enemy lines and brought back twenty men without incident. While Alan Boxer subsequently declined to make a third trip, David Dane was satisfied that the experienced Wing Commander had made the right decision: the rugged Dakota was much more suited to the terrain at 'Bon Bon'.

When 38 Group came on to the scene, however, they faced a number of problems. More than half of the expected sorties did not reach Tonkin and Sadoine, leading to shortages of such vital commodities as petrol for the jeeps. At one point Tonkin was unable to mount an immediate attack on the airfield at Châteauroux until sufficient fuel became available. Yet considering the poor weather conditions of the period and the lack of a Eureka aid in Tonkin's party, the demands of the task were often akin to finding a needle in a haystack at night. Brigadier McLeod himself, believing the

Eureka to have been damaged rather than lost, had acknowledged on 11 June:

'It is essential to get another Eureka into Bulbasket if resupply missions are to be carried out properly and the Eureka at present there does not appear to be working.'

Despite this observation, Tonkin had to manage without a Eureka for some time. Remaining records contradict themselves, and the memories of survivors differ again, but the SAS headquarters' radio log mentions still trying to drop the aid to Tonkin at the time of the attack on Verrières. Tonkin believed that in the period 18 June to 3 July, nine out of ten planned supply drops did not succeed owing to aircraft not locating the DZ. But closer examination of the reasons for missed drops reveals problems in communications and bad weather conditions rather than a failing on the part of the Stirling crews. During this period five operations were scrubbed due to the weather and one due to late notification of a new DZ by Tonkin. On two consecutive nights the RAF were sent when the SAS were apparently not manning the DZ and on one occasion the reception party could not light the signal fires as Germans were close by. Only on two sorties did the RAF actually fail to locate the DZ.[1]

Unfortunately such difficulties also led to problems other than just a shortage of supplies. It was not unusual for a reception party to sit out on a DZ for four to five hours per night, waiting for a resupply drop. With the need for operations during daylight hours, everyone consequently began to get very tired and it was all too easy to let one's guard slip as a result.

The SAS also suspected that the pilots did not always appreciate the effects of a slightly inaccurate drop, a one-second delay meaning a difference of about 100 yards, even before allowing for any wind. It was no easy matter for a small group to carry twenty-four containers weighing 500 lbs each for 400 yards through woods and across ploughed fields in the dark, in a hurry and in silence. On the other hand, Tonkin accepted that the SAS had not appreciated the need to have DZs near an easily seen topographical feature. Nor had it been anticipated that a great many patriotic Frenchmen quickly learned that, if one heard a low-flying bomber and lit a fire, one might quite well receive gifts from the gods. The result, naturally, was that the countryside was dotted with hopeful little fires and flashing lights. Nevertheless, 38 Group's crucial contribution of fifty-five sorties, which included nineteen

[1] See Appendix V for a detailed break-down of operations by 38 Group.

tons of arms and four jeeps, enabled the operation to continue for two months.

When considering the RAF's offensive operations in support of 'Bulbasket', there can be little argument over the value of the part played by the Mosquito fighter-bombers. At this stage of the war their skilled pilots and navigators were flying with great professionalism and were equipped with a superb tool for the job. Before his death in 1995 Air Marshal Sir Peter Wykeham, former leader of 140 Wing, recalled his conversion to the Mosquito with the opinion that:

'At last I felt I had an aeroplane that was as good, or better, than anything the Germans could put up.'

And Squadron Leader Vic Hester, the Film Production Unit pilot, had continued to volunteer for operational flying due to his belief in the Mosquito:

'It was an aeroplane which usually brought you back and gave you confidence that you could get through a tour safely.'

Certainly Mosquito operations on behalf of 'Bulbasket' supported Hester's belief. From a total of sixty-seven sorties flown in the four attacks only one aircraft failed to make it back to England. Considering the daylight and low-level nature of the attacks, a loss rate of just 1.49% is therefore highly creditable. Even more praiseworthy is the fact that no aircrew were lost since 21 Squadron's 'T-Tommy' made a successful forced landing and its crew were back at Thorney Island by the autumn after their successful evacuation from France. The loss rate of Mosquito aircrew was thus nil. All targets attacked were comprehensively damaged or destroyed in what were almost surgically precise strikes, involving relatively few civilian casualties.

By way of comparison, it is worth recalling that Bomber Command's single raid on the night of 12/13 June, 1944, against the railway yards and station at Poitiers had indeed pulverized the target but had also caused heavy damage to residential areas. Over 1200 houses were damaged or destroyed and 562 civilians were killed or wounded. The operation involved 116 aircraft.

In contrast, 140 Wing's attack on Châtellerault was carried out by just twelve Mosquitos. All the petrol trains were destroyed and the target left an inferno. The town itself suffered only slightly with eleven dead and twenty wounded among the civilian population.

One final aspect of the RAF's involvement should be mentioned. Amidst a constant flow of operational demands, the RAF aircrews involved in 'Bulbasket' operations normally had only the vaguest notion of the wider picture. This was especially so for the crews of 38 Group, their log books only showing the bland entry of 'SAS Operations'. For these airmen, their involvement and knowledge ended when their passengers or supply loads dropped into the darkness of an isolated French field. For the Mosquito crews, their appreciation of the situation was a little better, due to the very nature of their 'close-up' attacks, yet even so, they were never made aware of a link with the SAS and there was rarely more than scant feedback on results. This was a constant irritant, especially to squadron commanders such as 'Black' Smith of 487 Squadron RNZAF:

'At the time I was devoid of any historical sense or interest, lived from day to day and looked no further. Only rarely did I hear how well or how badly we had performed and often, what information we did receive was so garbled and had been through so many hands that it was rarely accurate. This was a continuous grouse of mine at the time but I never achieved an improvement.'

It is only now, with the weaving together of the varied aspects of 'Bulbasket' for this book, that the former airmen have been able to appreciate their involvement, after so many years of 'I often wondered what was behind that operation'. For participants like Ray Gough, the Halifax bomb aimer responsible for dropping one of the jeeps at 'Primo la Coupe', for Peter Banks, the Mustang fighter escort pilot shepherding a purposeful formation of Mosquitos heading for a distant target, this account at last gives the full picture and purpose to their efforts. As one former Mosquito crew member put it:

'I have always had a great deal of time for the SAS and was grati-fied that the RAF was in a position to mete out some 'punishment' on their behalf. To say 'revenge is sweet' would not go down very well in some quarters in these 'enlightened' times.'

But much as 'Bulbasket' was reliant on its air support, it was the local French *maquisards* of the newly co-ordinated FFI who fought shoulder to shoulder with the British and who are thus best remembered by the SAS veterans. Headquarters had stressed that one of the major aims of 'Bulbasket' was to arm and train the *Résistance*, but Tonkin found that SOE, in the person of

Captain Maingard, had already laid much of the groundwork. As a conse-
quence, many *maquis* groups were quite capable of offensive operations
without much additional encouragement. The communist *maquis* of the FTP
in particular had always been ready to attack the enemy, no matter what
reprisals were subsequently forthcoming. And while the *maquis* proved to
be inadequately trained or equipped to protect the SAS against opposition
in force, John Tonkin held no reservations about their worth:

> 'The encouragement of the *Résistance* to active insurrection and
> sabotage was a major part of the plan, together with arming them,
> instructing them in the use of sabotage devices and teaching them
> certain military skills. I saw this as important and we spent much
> time over the sixty-three days we lasted doing just that. In return we
> got a great deal of help and protection and I do not underrate the
> active sabotage which the *Résistance* in my area did. They accounted
> for the great majority of successful attacks on the railways in our
> area of operations on a total basis . . . From information in the field
> at the time, both local and by wireless intelligence from the U.K.,
> the *Résistance* groups north of Châteauroux kept 'Lot 1' almost
> continually cut . . . .
>
> 'The assistance was material. The intelligence was limited as to
> local matters (few of them were local people) but was good when
> passed through the *Résistance* chain on major matters such as the
> use of aerodromes . . . and concentrations of German troops. As far
> as I recall, we always got at least some advance information of
> German sweeps or convoys in our area, except of course at
> Verrières.'

While the same could not be said of all *Résistance* groups in France, those
of the Vienne were without doubt well co-ordinated by Colonel Chêne's FFI
headquarters, ably assisted by Maingard and the material support of SOE in
England. The latter contribution should also not be overlooked. Maingard
performed a courageous and effective rôle throughout the Indre and the
Vienne, deserving in itself of full description some day. From the day of
Tonkin's arrival, Maingard ensured that 'Bulbasket' received the best
possible assistance, both from his own SOE network and from the local
Résistance groups with whom he enjoyed the best possible affinity. This
contrasted somewhat with SOE/SAS relations at the highest levels, where the
SAS's Brigadier McLeod complained to Airborne Corps HQ soon after D-
Day about the type of operation the SAS were being asked to undertake:

'Some of these requests are undoubtedly the result of SOE sugges- tions and I have the impression that SAS troops are regarded as a military adjunct of SOE to undertake those tasks that SOE cannot undertake. It seems that the policy for the employment of SAS troops is becoming a short-term one and is largely governed by the advice of SOE. There is therefore a grave danger of SAS troops being employed on the advice of Special Forces HQ rather than on the advice of the Commanding Officer, Airborne Troops, and I am not satisfied that there is any clear policy in existence for the employ- ment of SAS troops.'

The comments of the Jedburgh team 'Hugh' were also indicative of the rivalry which often prevailed between SOE and the SAS. 'Hugh' was critical that the SHAEF planners required the SAS to operate so openly and felt that such tactics only served to draw danger upon themselves and the *maquis*. Another symptom of rivalry between the two organizations was shown in the radio messages of the Jedburgh where 'Sad Athletic Sacks' was used as a tongue-in-cheek code for the SAS.

Fortunately, neither Tonkin nor Maingard were aware of this enmity during 'Bulbasket', much to the benefit of the operation. When Maingard returned with Tonkin by Hudson on 10 August he reported back to Baker Street on progress to date – progress that included 5000 men in the Vienne, 3000 in Haute-Vienne, 2000 in Deux-Sèvres and 2000 in the Vendée ready for action. During this visit Maingard was promoted Major, decorated by General Koenig with the *Croix de Guerre avec Palmes* and then parachuted back in to France on 13 August with David Surrey Dane acting as Dakota and weapons expert for his circuit. He returned to England on 14 September, 1944, and was awarded the Distinguished Service Order by the British. Maingard's final tally of achievements included the organization of some 125 landings or parachute drops, involving over 4,000 containers and pack- ages, with enough arms for 6,000 men.

And finally, what of the SAS itself?

Any analysis of the results of 'Bulbasket' must start not only with the plan- ning of the operation, but also with the use that was determined for the SAS Brigade in its entirety. Throughout the early years of the Second World War a number of so-called 'private armies' had been able to take root and claim some success, but, as preparations were made for the huge conventional battles of 1944 onwards, so the planners at SHAEF grew impatient with the demands of these irregular forces to be involved. The SAS insisted they should be employed because they had trained hard and were ready to go, but much of the Brigade was ultimately used in a similar rôle to SOE's three man Jedburghs – encouraging *maquis* groups, carrying out sabotage and locating targets for the allied air forces. The value of small parties in such a rôle cannot be denied, but the use of large groups of SAS was asking for trouble. 'Bulbasket', never reinforced beyond a strength of fifty-four men, fell between two stools. Its size made it impossible for all the men to be gainfully employed at any one time, yet it was too small, and too lightly equipped, to deal with the substantial enemy reaction which it inevitably attracted.[1] In comparison, the full three-troop strength of 1st SAS's A Squadron fared considerably better when undertaking 'Operation Houndsworth' in the Morvan region of France. In addition to more men and more jeeps, 'Houndsworth' were dropped mortars and even two six-pounder field guns, adding a valuable extra dimension to their capabilities. In contrast, John Tonkin's requests for, and expectations of, reinforcements of material and men after Verrières were denied. 'Bulbasket' was cut short and brought home at a time when the other two troops of B Squadron, led by Major Lepine, should have been inserted according to the original plan. Instead, the French SAS replaced 'Bulbasket' with 'Operation Moses', a continuation of Tonkin's efforts in all but name. Why this should have occurred remains unclear, but political considerations, including General de Gaulle's personal suspicions over allied special forces operating in France, may have had much to do with the decision. The French leader had already made it clear that the operations of SOE's French section should henceforth fall under the direction of the Free French command.

Lacking the ability to fight pitched battles with the Germans, John Tonkin had thus appreciated from the very beginning that his only realistic hope was to delay and harass the enemy, to hit and run, and to report. In retrospect, therefore, it must be said that 'Bulbasket' could surely have accomplished as much, if not more, by using only a quarter of the men. Operations were rarely undertaken by more than three or four men at a time, and four groups of such size, using the four jeeps, would probably have been adequate for what

[1] At least one other account of 'Bulbasket' has suggested that the entire SAS party had been sent from England with only .45 pistols as personal weapons and the Vickers guns on their jeeps. While this was true of some of the operation's elements, such as Tonkin and Crisp, and the 'Lot' parties, it is clearly wrong in general. Local French historians noted that the SAS were equipped not only with Colt revolvers but also with American Remington carbine rifles and this is backed up by contemporary photographs. It is also confirmed in an official equipment list attached to Captain Sadoine's report in the Public Record Office. The SAS, moreover, would have been able to take their pick of the Sten and Bren machine guns dropped to them.

was achieved. A smaller party would also have been much less conspicuous and would not have needed a large camp, such as that at Verrières, which was easier for the enemy to find. Again, the planners were to blame in trying to deploy a relatively large-scale highly visible party behind the lines for what should have been an essentially low profile, small-scale task. After David Stirling's capture and imprisonment by the Germans in 1943, the SAS had expanded so much that its very size ultimately contributed to the manner of its use on operations like 'Bulbasket'. The more resources one has, the more one attempts to use.

The plan then for 'Bulbasket' was simply the end result of a series of conflicts of interest and compromises. In 1973 John Tonkin discovered a task description for the 'Bulbasket' reconnaissance party[1] which he had never seen before and which, in his opinion, made no sense for a half or even full squadron operating in the Poitiers area, let alone just he and Richard Crisp. He commented:

'It would have to have been someone's pipe dream for all four squadrons of the 1st SAS for it covers an enormous area, and how two men would be expected to assess it is beyond me.'

The task was further complicated by inadequate transport, both in view of the size of the area the party was supposed to cover and in respect of the need to move camp regularly, due to the impossibility of keeping such a large body of men hidden. With only four jeeps, the SAS therefore had to rely on the French for additional, low-grade, local vehicles.

Once in the field, the mistakes of the planners were recognized in the very first discussions between Tonkin and Maingard. The latter pointed out that news of the arrival of armed British paratroops in uniform was bound to spread like wildfire and it would have been impossible to keep the SAS's presence hidden. It was therefore decided to capitalize on the situation and word was circulated that the SAS would appreciate news of German petrol reserves, troop movements, etc. This approach soon proved the right one when information arrived of the petrol trains at Châtellerault.

These tactics also served to help Tonkin with the distractions faced by his men:

'One point to be watched carefully is the general state of alertness. It often happened that we went several days without a flap. When

[1] See Appendix III.

driving around in daylight all the villages were very friendly and the girls looked very nice. No Jerry was seen in the area, consequently the men tended to forget they were behind the lines and liable to be attacked at any moment. They wanted to stop in the villages and there was a general tendency to relax . . . The highest discipline must be maintained to prevent them wandering away from camp. The British soldier's aptitude for scrounging will make him see no harm in going to the nearest farm for eggs, whereas such a thing is highly dangerous.'

Thus, when critics of 'Bulbasket' point to the high-profile nature of the SAS, it should be remembered that, in the circumstances, this was both deliberate and arguably successful.

But in addition to the successes of 'Bulbasket', there was also tragedy, both in the form of the surprise enemy attack on the Verrières camp and the subsequent murders of the men who surrendered. Let us consider both in more detail.

At Verrières we now know that the Germans had tortured their basic information from either Eccles or Bateman and had refined this by the use of local agents in order to pinpoint the camp site. The SAS had been in the forest for eight days, and while normal procedure was to move after not more than four days, we have heard how such a precaution twice failed due to enemy troop movements in the area and the lack of an adequate water supply. It was also necessary for Tonkin to remain close to his DZ where he was awaiting a crucial re-supply drop of petrol, explosives and food. Again it must be stressed that the information extracted from one of the two captured NCOs was only of importance due to the combination of circumstances which prevented the main party from having moved on before the Germans came looking for them. No blame can attach to the tortured man and it is also understandable why Tonkin was still at Verrières after such a relatively long time.

Camille Olivet, the FTP *maquis* leader, was highly critical of the surprise achieved by the Germans' attack, saying of John Tonkin:

'He let himself be lured by false considerations which no commander had the right to ignore. And then, when the Germans attacked, there were no sentries whatsoever in place.'

From the accounts of the survivors of Verrières, Olivet's assertion regarding sentries could be true, but the situation was no simple oversight of the young

SAS commander. Tonkin already knew that the Germans normally mounted an attack only after encirclement of their target from as far away as five kilometres. He had therefore reasoned that short-range sentries provided little or no additional security. Instead, he relied upon the advance warning of enemy troop movements which was normally forthcoming from the local *maquis*. At Verrières, the Germans were sure of the exact location of their quarry and thus needed no extensive search operation during daylight. They would have been able to deploy their forces at dead of night, when no *maquis* informers could report their presence. Again, circumstances contrived to defeat Tonkin's assumptions.

And what then of the fate of the men of 'Bulbasket' who were taken prisoner? There have been claims that the contents of the infamous *Kommandobefehl* were deliberately withheld from allied special forces personnel and, in particular, there is controversy over what information was given in advance to the men of 'Operation Bulbasket'.

Officially, it was not until late 1944, when the first bodies of murdered SAS prisoners were uncovered in liberated France and a copy of the *Kommandobefehl* was discovered in Italy, that the Allies became aware of the order's existence. Even then, it was not until March, 1945, that the resultant outrage reached the highest echelons of the allied forces and General Eisenhower made a wireless proclamation warning the Germans of his intention to treat them as war criminals for such atrocities. By then the murdered men of 'Bulbasket' had been dead for eight long months.

But how much did the allied high command already know of Hitler's order before 'Bulbasket'? Even within the SAS itself, there had been a number of earlier occasions when evidence of such an order was strongly suggested. During the Brigade's operations in Italy in 1943 Lieutenant Hughes of the 2nd SAS Regiment had been captured while attacking a *Luftwaffe* airfield. His captors, who were of the regular *Wehrmacht*, warned Hughes that, as a member of the allied special forces, he could not be treated as an ordinary prisoner of war and should be handed over to the local *Gestapo* or SD. Hughes had then managed to escape, however, and was able to prepare a report on his experiences which was forwarded to Airborne Forces headquarters some time before D-Day. Astonishingly, headquarters concluded that the Germans had merely been trying to frighten Hughes into talking, and they likewise shrugged off reports of other SAS and Commando prisoners who had disappeared in captivity. Such reports, said headquarters, were simply an indication that the Germans would not admit to the success of allied special forces operations. But John Tonkin had encountered a similar ordeal to that of Lieutenant Hughes when he himself had been captured at Termoli. His experience was put down as another example of the type of bluff played against Hughes, but Tonkin was unconvinced and David Dane is certain that the matter was discussed in the officers' mess with Paddy Mayne, some weeks before 'Bulbasket'.

The issue does not seem to have generally had the same airing among the men. John Fielding is quite positive in recalling that he received no briefing regarding the *Kommandobefehl*. Indeed, his view is that had there been such a briefing, then there might well have been a few men wanting to pull out of the operation. Other commentators have also suggested that fewer of the SAS would have surrendered at Verrières had they known they were more likely to be executed than treated as P.O.W.s.

And yet, in his defence at the Wuppertal trial in 1947, General Curt Gallenkamp claimed that interrogation of the prisoners had revealed:

> 'Since it had been pointed out to them before they left England by aeroplane that in the case of failure of their mission they must expect to be shot, they had been prepared for it.'

So what is the truth of the matter? After so long it appears impossible to say with any great degree of certainty, but it may be that the officers, and perhaps also the 'old hands' among the other ranks, speculated and guessed at the dangers involved, without revealing their concerns to the other men. Certainly it would have been important to maintain morale at the time and there could well have been an informal understanding to shelter the relative newcomers like John Fielding from the full picture. At least some of the officers accepted the possibility of capture and execution as no more than an occupational hazard, given the nature of their operations. The SAS themselves were rarely in a position to take or hold prisoners, yet were not told what to do if the enemy tried to surrender. The SOE's principles were no more liberal, documentation from the 'Hugh' team admitting:

> '. . . it was extremely inconvenient to take prisoners . . . we avoided it as far as possible without inhumanity.'

John Tonkin therefore had few illusions at the treatment that captured SAS could expect from the Germans:

> 'I have always felt that the Geneva Convention is a dangerous piece of stupidity, because it leads people to believe that war can be civilized. It can't.'

Of some 100 SAS personnel captured by the Germans after D-Day, only six survived.

By way of final analysis of the results of 'Bulbasket', it is also important to consider the official view reported soon after the operation. Despite John Tonkin being awarded the Military Cross for 'Bulbasket' on his return to England, in his report of 10 August, 1944, the War Office's Director of Tactical Investigation wrote:

> 'In comparison with the achievements of the other SAS groups, 'Bulbasket' has not, on the evidence available, been so successful as a source of information. This group has from time to time reported a few bombing targets, and also the results when the targets were taken on by the RAF. There is nothing to show that SAS troops have taken part in arming or organizing the *maquis* in this area . . . 'Bulbasket' has, however, played an important part in making the movements of German troops in the area difficult, in conjunction with RAF bombing . . . They have also employed many German troops in action.'

A crucial phrase here is 'on the evidence available'. This report was drawn up just three days after Tonkin's return from France and in all likelihood had nothing more than that officer's own first-hand account to draw upon. Without access to the radio log of 'Bulbasket', Tonkin omitted several achievements from his report which was all the more rushed as he was anxious to depart on leave at the time.

The War Office rather disparagingly mentions 'a few bombing targets' which were radioed back. In fact, Tonkin was responsible for four, and possibly five, air attacks, the bombing raid on the petrol trains at Châtellerault being a particularly successful example of liaison between special forces behind the lines and conventional air forces. With their petrol stocks destroyed, the 2nd SS *Das Reich* division was further delayed on its movement northwards and a journey which could have been made in three days ultimately took seventeen. The gravity of the attack's results can be judged from the following *Wehrmacht* radio message which was picked up and decoded by the 'Ultra' code experts in England:

> 'Urgent request for allocation of fuel for 2 Sugar Sugar [SS] Panzer Division from Army Fuel Depot, Châtellerault. Addressed to AOK 1 at 1100 hours, 13th June.'

The three air attacks against enemy troop concentrations – at Bonneuil-Matours, the Château du Fou and the Caserne des Dunes, killed and wounded scores of the enemy and extensively damaged the targets. And lastly, the possibility of a link between 'Bulbasket' and the allied air raid of 12/13 June on Poitiers appears to have hitherto been overlooked. The attack represented the first occasion that Poitiers suffered the attention of RAF Bomber Command, the target being the railway station and adjacent marshalling yards. Can it then be purely coincidental that the onslaught was unleashed just a day after Tonkin had radioed back to England on the evening of the 11th with a report on *maquis* sabotage against the railway in Poitiers – and with the further intelligence that the Germans were planning to run thirty-five trains a day through the city? Hardly. In all likelihood therefore, the heavy bomber raid was a fifth example of the success of 'Bulbasket' in reporting targets.

There were also other targets reported which were never acted upon. The passage of *Das Reich* up the N147 road was in itself a lucrative target and one which was reported to England on 12 June. It is interesting to speculate what havoc the medium bombers and fighter-bombers of the RAF or USAAF might have wrought against the slow-moving armoured vehicles on the long straight road through largely open countryside. But the opportunity was missed. Other potential targets which were radioed back included: railway traffic through Parthenay, and the fact that the bridge there had been repaired following ineffective bombing; the discovery of two enemy-controlled crude alcohol factories; enemy units moving north on the Bellac – Lussac road; trapped locomotives, a vital telephone exchange and an enemy headquarters in Poitiers; details of flying operations by Condor aicraft of the *Luftwaffe* from an airfield near Cognac; and enemy troop concentrations at Champagne-Mouton. In all, some fourteen possible bombing targets were therefore reported by 'Bulbasket', of which only four or five were actually attacked. With the demands of the invasion, such a ratio is not surprising, but the War Office's report of 'a few bombing targets' does the SAS considerable injustice.

The same report concluded that there was no evidence that the SAS had taken part in arming or organizing the *maquis* in the area. The answer to this observation is simple – there was little need. Colonel Chêne's FFI headquarters, with Maingard's SOE support, already had this task comfortably in hand and the *maquis* were happily engaged in active operations by the time 'Bulbasket' arrived. Nevertheless, Tonkin and his men forged a good working relationship alongside the local *maquis*, especially the 'Amilcar' group. The SAS gave training on weapons, sabotage and explosives, unarmed combat and ambush techniques when time permitted, and the French joined some of the sabotage missions, nominally as guides. There is also no doubt that just the known presence of the SAS served to encourage recruitment to the *Résistance* and enabled them to step up their actions in the region, tying down large numbers of the enemy in wild goose chases around the countryside. In the Vienne alone an estimated strength of 3300 *résistants* in June, 1944, increased to 11500 by September.[1]

And yet there still persists in many accounts that touch upon 'Bulbasket' the notion that because of Verrières, and the scent of betrayal, the operation was a disaster. The deaths of thirty-five men out of a total of fifty-five[2] equate to the loss of some 64% of the party, a sobering statistic by any measure and certainly a temptation to think in terms of a disaster. But to balance this, we must return again to the operation's achievements in order to judge whether this sacrifice of young lives was justified. 'Bulbasket' initiated four confirmed air attacks and a possible fifth, with the resultant killing of upwards of 150 German troops and *Milice*; it was responsible for the destruction of crucial petrol stocks and the consequent delay of the 2nd SS Panzer Division; and it contributed to slowing the movement northwards of both the 276th Infantry Division from Bayonne and the 277th Infantry Division from Carcassonne. No less than twenty-three successful road and rail sabotage operations were completed and continual disruption and mayhem in the enemy's rear was achieved at a time when the Germans had more than enough to concern them on the invasion front. By any military judgement, the loss of thirty-five men for such a tally of achievement can only be considered as acceptable. The sacrifice was not in vain.

[1] Roger Picard, *La Vienne dans La Guerre 1939/1945*.
[2] This total reflects the original forty-five men of Tonkin's troop, Corporal Allan of the RAMC, three SAS drivers, five Phantom radio operators and the later arrival of Lieutenant Surrey Dane.

11

IN MEMORIAM

Former Trooper John Fielding first returned to the Vienne in 1960, by which time a memorial had already been erected at La Couarde on the edge of the forest at Verrières, close by the spot where Twm Stephens and the seven young *maquisards* had met their deaths. On the front of the memorial a relief of a dying man is depicted before a cross of Lorraine, while on a side face the names of the eight dead are engraved. Some 20 metres down the grassy track to the right of the memorial a plain granite plinth marks the exact spot where the Germans shot their prisoners. Up until the 1960s a concentration of bullet holes and scars among the trees bore evidence of this deed, but today young saplings have taken over, innocent of such acts.

In the village cemetery at Verrières Twm Stephens's final resting place would not be spotted by the casual observer as he was buried in one of the small, chapel-like vaults of two local families. It is a gesture of the feelings of the local people that Stephens was literally taken into the community in death, his own wartime burial cross standing in one corner of the vault and still displaying the SAS cap badge and 1st SAS shoulder flashes which John Tonkin had given to the Mayor of Verrières when identifying Stephens's body on 3 July, 1944. A simple stone plaque, amongst those of the family members, records his death.[1] Each year the villagers hold a memorial church service and walk first to Stephens's grave, then to the forest memorial, in order to honour the fallen. Even today both sites are rarely without a wreath or fading flowers and in recent years a card left at the cemetery shows that Twm Stephens's sister has visited her brother's grave. Guest of honour at La

---

[1] The stone erroneously quotes 4 July, 1944, as the date of Stephens' death. The 4th was probably the date of burial.

Couarde is normally Denis Chansigaud, a survivor of the attack and now retired from a career in the *Gendarmerie* in Paris to return to the Vienne village of Persac.

Likewise, the people of the commune of Rom have never forgotten the legacy of the German occupation left in the form of the thirty-one graves in their cemetery. Not content with merely honouring the graves, support gathered for a memorial at the site of the execution in the Saint-Sauvant forest, where the shallow impressions of the three mass graves could still be seen. A committee was formed by Messieurs Quintard, Demarbre and Marnais and subsequently, on 23 June, 1973, a tall granite stone was raised adjacent to the forest track where the German firing squad performed their dark deed at dawn on 7 July, 1944. At the memorial's base a plaque lists the names of the thirty SAS men and the American fighter pilot, Lieutenant Bundy, while behind the grassy plot the three mass graves are marked by small plain granite stones. A huge crowd attended the memorial's inauguration ceremony to hear John Tonkin, returned for the first time from Australia,[1] make a moving speech in memory of his murdered troopers. As well as a host of French generals, civic leaders and former *Résistance* fighters, many SAS representatives travelled from England, including the Regiment's then commanding officer, Brigadier Simpson.

In 1979 three of the SAS survivors of 'Bulbasket' – John Tonkin, John Fielding and Sam Smith – teamed up to make a return journey together for the annual ceremonies in the Vienne and were joined in Verrières by another survivor, Les Keeble, the former SAS party's cook. As well as paying their respects in Verrières and Rom, the group toured many of their wartime haunts. Fielding and Smith managed to retrace the route which they had taken to the railway line south of Anché and identified the cutting where Smith had carried out his demolition job. In Asnières Madame Lavarret still lived close to the café which had been popular with the SAS troopers camped just outside the village, and at the site of the 'Bon Bon' landing ground Fielding happened upon a local man who had helped the SAS prepare the field for the arrival of the Hudsons.

---

1 Tonkin had finished the war in the rank of Major and commanding 'D' Squadron of the 1st SAS Regiment. He received the Military Cross for 'Bulbasket' and was Mentioned in Dispatches. After the war he had followed a restless trail for several years: exploring the Antarctic with former 1st SAS colleagues Paddy Mayne and Mike Sadler, drilling for oil in Holland and Brunei, and uranium mining and treatment in Rum Jungle, North Australia. In 1961 he settled in the Melbourne area where he remained until his death in 1995.

For John Tonkin a highlight of the trip was returning to the very spot where he had landed on D-Day, 1944. At the hamlet of Moncousinat he had no difficulty in identifying the field into which he, Richard Crisp and the Jedburgh team 'Hugh' were dropped on that historic night. Although the Girault family had moved from the exact farm, the farmer's son, Narcisse, was still in the area and was able to come to meet Tonkin in the farm's field, much as he had done in the early hours of 6 June, 1944. That Tonkin was alive came as a great surprise to Narcisse Girault as he had heard that the English officer had been killed by the Germans. Instead, they laughed when remembering their first meeting, Tonkin holding a gun in one hand but chocolate and cigarettes in the other. Narcisse admitted that he too had been one of those who refused to believe Tonkin's news that the invasion was under way.

Together the two men walked the field and looked over the farm's barn where the group had spent their first night in enemy territory. Narcisse Girault had been involved at the very beginning of 'Bulbasket' but had then been almost totally unaware of what had later happened. John Tonkin's visit at last fitted the missing pieces into the Frenchman's puzzle.

As an example of the emotions and memories still strong among the relatives of the murdered men, the following account from the nephew of Lieutenant Richard Crisp was published in the journal of the SAS Regimental Association and describes a family pilgrimage of three generations, made in July, 1988:

'VERRIÈRES – SAINT-SAUVANT – ROM, JULY 1988
BY RICHARD G. T. CRISP

'Lieutenant Richard Crisp, of 1st SAS Regiment and 'Operation Bulbasket', would have been my uncle, had he not perished along with so many during the last world war.

'As I was born two years after the end of the war, I grew up without having experienced the loss of an uncle, and as my family were deeply affected by the circumstances of his death, questions that I asked as a child can only have reawakened painful memories. My aunt (Richard's sister), however, in spite of the intense feeling of loss and loathing of war from the viewpoint of a nurse, visited the area in 1948 with two friends, travelling by bicycle and public transport.

'This year, with my son aged thirteen to act as navigator, and my aunt in good health, we undertook a five-day motorised camping trip, with the specific aims of joining the Remembrance gatherings at Verrières on Sunday, 3rd July, visiting the memorial in the Saint-Sauvant forest, and placing flowers on Richard's grave at Rom.

'The trip was planned with the invaluable help of John Fielding, a survivor of 'Bulbasket', with whom my aunt had corresponded previously, and who of course has written of his visits in previous editions. Having read the article of his 1982 trip, and discussed with him details of possible events over that weekend and the location of the various sites, as well as obtaining a couple of names of people to contact, I had an idea of what to expect. My aunt, who is well into retirement, had no misgivings of camping for the first time in thirty-five years, and my son, just at the age when his enthusiasm for the role of navigator is matched by his capabilities as a map-reader, was looking forward to speaking French 'for real'.

'I am glad to say the whole five-day trip passed without a hitch or disappointment, in spite of heavy showers every day, and we had travelled exactly 1500 miles as we completed the journey at our home just outside York.

'As far as the ceremonies in Verrières were concerned, having made contact with the Deputy Mayor on Saturday evening, we were invited to each event, the first of which was a church service at 9.30 a.m. on Sunday morning. In spite of the teeming rain which competed against the cheerful chiming of the bells, there was standing room only once the service began. The predominantly bright red processional *maquis* flags added colour to the congregation. Although our French was not up to following much of the sermon, we were informed later that a main theme was the necessity of involving more young people in these remembrances, so that the realities of war, and the significance of local memorials and monuments, is not lost in the future.

'After the service the rain had eased a little and we joined the small gathering at the memorial to Lieutenant Twm Stephens, where the colours were lowered, a magnificent spray of flowers laid, and a prayer said. Then on to the memorial stone in the nearby forest where a large gathering was already assembled. The colours formed a guard of honour, the tricolour was raised on the adjacent flagpole, and a speech was made by the Mayor, Monsieur Lochon, including a mention of our small party from England. Several equally beautiful sprays of flowers were laid, including one which was presented to my aunt for her to lay, prayers were said and a bugler played the

Last Post. Also at this time, two survivors of the French *Résistance* in Verrières, Denis Chansigaud and Pierre Crest, were honoured by the Mayor. We were then escorted back to the Town Hall where a champagne reception took place, and much interest was shown in my aunt's photographs taken during her previous visit in 1948. This concluded the civic formalities.

'We now visited the War Graves Commission site in the cemetery at the village of Rom, 25 miles away, and made our own personal remembrances at the peaceful, immaculately-kept corner of the village cemetery where the gravestones of most of the British and a lone American stand in line, overlooked by the spire of the church, a little way away.

'The previous day, we had visited the tall pillar of stone, now with the names of those killed at its foot, erected at the site of the original graves in the forest of Saint-Sauvant. Once again, evidence that this apparently deserted place is well cared for.'

The memorial and burial sites at Verrières, Saint-Sauvant and Rom, are indeed well cared for and still honoured. For the 50th anniversaries of the tragic events, the municipalities of Verrières and Rom both organized commemorative ceremonies in July, 1994, attended by representatives of the British and French Armies and, at Rom, a pilot of the United States Air Force who had travelled from his base in Germany to recall the fate of Lieutenant Lincoln Bundy[1]. From the locality, Albert Dupont and Denis Chansigaud represented the *Résistance* fighters who had served with 'Bulbasket', while from England came survivor John Fielding; the sister, nephew and great-nephew of Richard Crisp; and the nephew and niece of Trooper Pascoe.

One final aspect of the events of 1944 must be placed on record and concerns the four men of 'Bulbasket' who have no known grave. The bodies of Troopers Ogg, Pascoe and Williams, the wounded men who were almost certainly murdered by lethal injection in Poitiers, were never discovered, but their deaths are recorded (somewhat tenuously) at Bayeux on the memorial to the missing of the invasion and Normandy campaigns. Yet the most that the families of Ogg and Pascoe had discovered of the fate of their loved ones came from the research for this book. News of neither the SHAEF Inquiry, Major Barkworth's investigations, nor the Wuppertal trial was passed down to them by the British Government, the official notification being only that the troopers were missing in action. James Robertson, who had waved Joe Ogg off to France from RAF Fairford, heard only a confused story as the SAS Brigade was disbanded in 1945. This suggested that his friend, along with Pascoe and Williams, had been given civilian clothes by the *maquis* in an effort to escape, but that they had been betrayed by informers. Their identity discs had supposedly sealed their fate and it was believed they were eventually shot by the Germans.

It had only been in April, 1947, that some of the truth emerged when Professor Villey again briefly picked up the trail of the three wounded in Poitiers. Villey had heard of the original trial findings at Wuppertal in respect of General Gallenkamp and Dr Hesterberg. Correctly linking the sentences to the events in Poitiers, the professor therefore passed the news back to the families of Ogg, Pascoe and Williams in Britain, but was then unable to investigate further before he moved to Brazil a few weeks later. For the families, there was no official notification of the trial, nor of the eventual amended sentences. As late as 1980 Joseph Ogg's family were still attempting to discover his fate, yet the reply of the Ministry of Defence to their enquiries still simply listed him as missing, presumed killed in action, in north-west Europe. There was not even confirmation that Joseph Ogg had served in the SAS, the Ministry's records only displaying the temporary parent formation of the Army Air Corps.

The fourth man, Trooper Biffin, disappeared when he parachuted into the town square at Airvault with Corporal Kinnivane's party. Rumoured to have been wounded and captured by the enemy, he was never heard of again and is even unlisted in the records of the Commonwealth War Graves Commission. But contrary to general belief, 'Biff' Biffin survived.[1]

---

[1] After publication of the first edition of *SAS Operation Bulbasket*, the SAS Regimental Association (SASRA) appointed a researcher to determine Biffin's fate. Several official record sources showed him as 'missing' and survivors of 'Bulbasket' had heard nothing further of him since the war. SASRA's diligent researcher, however, discovered a Private George Biffin in Red Cross records as a POW in Oflag 9C (Mulhausen) in March 1945. The Ministry of Defence was subsequently able to confirm that this George Biffin had been captured on 11th June 1944 and had then been a POW in German hands until repatriated to the UK in May 1945. A SASRA member then traced Biffin to his Dorset home and learned that, after immediate capture in Airvault, 'Biff' had then had the great good fortune to come under the care of a sympathetic *Wehrmacht* officer who ordered that he be treated as a normal POW. Only after publication of *SAS Operation Bulbasket* did 'Biff' join the reunion trips (supported by SASRA and superbly organised by 1st SAS veteran Major Joe Schofield) to the Vienne. 'Biff' was unable to join the last such SASRA tour in September 2008 due to ill-health and died shortly afterwards. The tour attracted nationwide press coverage in the UK and France.

ERRATA AND NOTES TO 2009 EDITION

Page 4

[1] The origin of the name of the Jedburg three-man teams is not known for certain. Several views are held, but it is most likely that 'Jedburgh' was simply the next available code word. The composition of the majority of Jedburgh teams was one British officer, one American officer and the third team member from the country in which they were to operate.

Page 7

[1] Contrary to the story that 'Bulbasket' had originated from Tonkin's nickname, it was one of a number of codenames with a biblical theme, other examples being 'Moses' and 'Lot'. 'Bulbasket' was an abbreviation of 'Bulrushes basket'.

Page 22

[1] Though clearly recalled and later recorded by Tonkin, I was unable to find the Châteauroux attic incident in the research for my biography of Maingard *Behind Enemy Lines With The SAS*.

Page 128

[1] Another account has the Dakota piloted by Major Stapel, rather than Colonel Heflin, and also carrying the SOE agent, Major Maingard ('Samuel'). This, however, is at odds with both Maingard's and Dane's recollections and SOE records of the date of Maingard's return to the UK.

Page 184

[1] Having had their attention drawn to the publication of *SAS Operation Bulbasket* the Bundy family, largely located in Arizona, USA, at last learned that Lincoln had a grave in France. Members of the family, including brother Atwood, have made emotional visits to the Vienne and met the Guillon family who harboured Lincoln before he was passed on to the SAS camp. In 2006 a US-published book, *Far from Cactus Flat* by Lyman Hafen, detailed Lincoln Bundy's life and tragic death. Further research revealed that, due to a mix up of the bodies during re-burial at Rom, an SAS trooper lies in the grave designated as Lincoln's, while the young pilot's remains are believed buried in one of the two communal SAS plots.

APPENDIX I

(**Author's note:** this report was written by John Tonkin within two days of his return to England on 7 August, 1944. It was produced purely from memory, aided by Lieutenants Weaver and Morris, Sergeant Holmes and Corporal Rideout. At that time, Tonkin did not have access to the radio log of 'Bulbasket', which is a far more accurate indicator of the dates and times of events. The main text of this book relies on the record of the radio log where it differs from the following text.)

REPORT OF CAPTAIN JOHN TONKIN, 1 SAS REGIMENT
OPERATION BULBASKET

Equipment: Very good on the whole, Michelin maps as issued are accurate and by far the best to work with, especially with jeep operations. The 100,000 maps are inaccurate and too detailed. There is no distinction between farm tracks and minor roads. Half of those shown on the maps ceased to exist years ago.

Small haversacks are essential, both for operations and for containing escape kits of MCR 1, medical wallet, and shaving kit. Rucksacks are too heavy to take across country if one has to travel fast.

Rubber soled boots are excellent if nailed AND sewn on, otherwise the rubber tends to break away.

Arms: A Colt automatic is definitely insufficient. Every man should have some long range weapon, either a .30 Carbine or a Bren gun.

I advise warm clothing, such as battle dress, for operating at night in a jeep is very cold.

MCR 1s [radios] work excellently.

Explosives: Fog signals were of no use in my area. All attempts to derail trains with fog signals failed as Jerry appears to have a scoop fitted in front of each engine. Pressure switches are very unreliable. The methods I can suggest are either Pull Switches or firing the charge electrically from a vantage point at one side of the line. It would be possible to have two parties on the line about one mile apart and to trap a train. German repair gangs take about 4 or 5 hours of daylight to repair the line. If good liaison with the RAF is available, Fighter Bombers could then finish the job.

Salt delay vibration switches hold great possibilities for convoys and trains. There are great possibilities in using camouflets sets [mines] on the *Route Nationale*. Care should be taken that *maquis* trucks are not destroyed.

Re-Supply: Interval between demand and supply is very quick. There were rare cases of French mail being sent to us etc. Sten guns are no longer wanted by the *maquis* and are not worth sending.

DZ: These should be chosen where possible, so that there is a view in daylight of 3 kilos or less. If the DZ can be seen for a long way around, then the fires should be sunk in shallow pits. A friendly farm nearby is essential, so that a bullock cart can be obtained. This is by far the easiest method of handling C containers as each bullock cart will hold up to 12.

With us, the RAF missed 7 out of 15 DZs which had 3 bonfires burning in them from 0001 hrs to 0330 hrs. One DZ was not lighted up [sic] due to enemy action. Of the total of 15 nights in which aircraft set out, there were only 7 successful drops.

Drill on the DZ is as follows:-

Immediately containers and panniers have dropped, douse the fires and then roll up the chutes. On one occasion we had a Night Fighter over the DZ ten minutes after the drop but the 'chutes were cleared and he didn't see anything. After that dispose of the containers, then check up at first light to see that nothing is left. With jeeps, it is essential to have a wood or thick scrub near in which to hide the cradles which are too big and heavy to bury. It takes longer to remove the jeep from the cradle than is expected here. It took us about three quarters of an hour. Parachutes are easily disposed of. The local people will willingly hide them for the cloth.

If possible, the ETA of the aircraft should always be given.

Camps: In my area choice of camps was limited due to lack of water in the area. This proved the main difficulty. I found that if I had a camp of my own, a camp guard alone was useless because Jerry rings the camp at a radius of 2 kilos and closes in in the morning. For a permanent camp, the guard must be all round the camp and a minimum of 5km from it.

The only solutions are, if operating alone, to move the camp every two or three days, thereby giving Jerry no time to plan an attack, or else retire inside a *maquis* guard where sufficient warning can be given.

Food: The food situation in my area was good. It was quite easy to live off the land. On the average the cost per day for 50 men was 1,000 francs. The main goods obtainable are eggs, bread, meat, some vegetables, potatoes, cheese, wine and fruit.

Co-operation with RAF: This proved surprisingly good. On one occasion on the 21st July [sic], fighter bombers were over the target four hours after it had been given to me by the *maquis*. On the 11th June they located and bombed some petrol trains 6 hrs after the message was received.

The results of this are very far reaching for the party concerned. The *maquis* entertain a greater respect and a greater desire for close co-operation. They will take trouble to bring authentic news of targets, and it is also the one method by which an expected attack in the area can be delayed or broken up. The attack on the barracks in Poitiers delayed an expected sweep of our area at a time when dispersal of the troop would have been most disastrous. That was the days immediately before the landing ground operations.

The ideal would be if some arrangement could be made, such as an S-phone, with the planes immediately over the target area.

Maquis: The *maquis* in the area could be split into two groups: The FTP or Communist *maquis*, and the FFI [sic]. Contrary to general belief, the FTP are singularly ill-disciplined. They do not wish to come under the FFI organisation, who were much the best to work with. They are all, however, friendly, good fighters, and very keen. For arms they need rifles, PIATs and Bren guns, Sten guns are of little use to them.

2" or possibly 3" Mortars would be invaluable provided there were trained personnel to instruct. They know little about explosives. We spent a lot of our spare time instructing them in Bren, explosives, unarmed combat and the PIAT. The Maquis we had in July were well armed, they were 500 strong and had 2 Brens, 1 PIAT, 1 Sten, and 6 rifles to a section of 10 men. They all came under central command and have a good system of inter-support. They have a certain amount of transport, but petrol is the great problem.

German defence in the area: For the defence of Lot 2 railway, SAMUEL [Maingard] reported sentries every half kilo, patrolling constantly. From observations, we found the line heavily patrolled by 3rd rate troops, who kept in the bushes and cover to one side of the line and did not appear on the permanent way. They were very nervous and constantly fired at bushes and shadows which made innocent operations distinctly dangerous. They did not use dogs.

Movement by day: This was quite possible in jeeps provided the jeep was not near the camp. The chief danger is that the locals' talk will reach the enemy through the village collaborator. A civilian car, which is fairly easy to get, is essential for movement near the camp.

Gestapo: This is a very real menace. Any unknown visitor should be regarded as suspicious and referred to the local *maquis*. 5 agents, including French women, were shot in our camp by the *maquis* during July.

Morale: One point to be watched carefully is the general state of alertness. It often happened that we went several days without a flap. Operations were successful. When driving around in daylight, all the villages were very friendly and the girls looked very nice. No Jerry was seen in the area, consequently the men tended to forget they were behind the lines and liable to be attacked at any moment. They wanted to stop in the villages and there was a general tendency to relax. They needed constant reminding of this point and the highest discipline must be maintained as regards wandering away from the camp. The British soldier's aptitude for scrounging will make him see 'no harm' in going to the nearest farm for eggs, whereas such a thing can be highly dangerous.

General: Tracks. The rubber sole leaves very distinct tracks. I don't think the enemy ever has the time to follow any and the advantage of silence far outweighs this disadvantage. It was, however, very useful to me on occasions in locating a man.

Passwords: All the *maquis* in our area had a password which was general to them and which changed every 24 hours.

Wine: The local wine and cider is stronger than one thinks. Kirsh or Schnapps is nearly pure wood alcohol.

APPENDIX II

REPORT OF CAPTAIN SADOINE
NO 3 PATROL, F SQUADRON, PHANTOM
OPERATION BULBASKET

(**Author's note:** as in Appendix I, this report was produced from memory by Captain Sadoine immediately after his return from France. Inconsistencies should therefore be treated with caution.)

On June 12th at 0230 hrs. No. 3 Patrol SAS Phantom was dropped over the area BULBASKET at 600 feet and 240 miles from the Beachhead.

The pilot had located the reception committee's fires and had then lost them again owing to patches of low cloud which covered the target area. Our orders were to drop so after 20 mins searching of the area, the pilot chose what looked like a good DZ and out we went.

The stick dropping consisted of 1 Officer, 1 Sgt, 3 Cpls and 6 O.R.s. Before leaving the airfield, I had decided to have two sticks and two run-ins over the DZ but this was changed to one stick of 11 over the Target Area, U.986412.

On arrival on the ground I hid my parachute, steel helmet, jumping jacket and kit bag in the hedge and started to look for my stick. After half an hour I found Nos. 2 and 3 but was unable to find any of the rest of the stick. Both were unhurt so we collected our ruc-sacs [*sic*] and started off in a Westerly direction to find cover. We marched for over an hour and when dawn began to break we found ourselves on the edge of a cornfield just beside a road junction which luckily had two signposts so that I was able to find myself on the map. We took cover in the cornfield, Q.005395, ate some chocolate and I wrote a message to send off by the pigeon which my No. 3 was carrying. The message being duly written and attached to the pigeon's leg, I launched the pigeon with perhaps more force than skill, for it circled us twice and made straight for the nearest big tree 50 yards away where it alighted. I believe it may still be there.

We then collected our packets and pushed on across country to a small river where I found a ruined mill behind which we spent the day, Q.030391. As no one came near us I decided during the afternoon to go up to the nearest farm (¾ mile away) which I had been watching through glasses, and ask if they could help. I contacted the cowman who was very voluble. He told me there were no Germans in the neighbourhood and offered to get his 'Patron' to bring us food. This they did. They also told me that they were getting in touch with the local *maquis* for us.

At 2200 hrs after much hand-shaking an elderly woman appeared who said that if we followed her we would be led to where the rest of the 'parachutists' were hiding. She took us a mile across the fields and crossing over a weir we were handed over to two men who were to be our guides. These two took us back to where our 'chutes were hidden. I wanted to do this first to prove that we were bona fide paratroops and secondly to make sure that the 'chutes were properly hidden. After a long march by small paths and side roads we eventually arrived at the farm, at 0330 hrs, where I found the rest of my stick under Sgt Eccles, Q.019434. He was very relieved to see us. Sgt Eccles 1st SAS is to be very highly recommended on the initiative he showed in organising search parties and himself going out in civilian clothes with the local *maquis* chief to look for us. He was also responsible for getting the 8 men and 12 containers collected and hidden away.

We stayed 3 days in the farm, Q.019434, sleeping in the hay-loft and being fed by the farmer. We were visited by many locals and the *maquis* chief who expressed great enthusiasm, gave us plenty of advice, accepted cigarettes and chocolate as if it came from heaven and all smelt to high heaven of garlic.

We moved next to a wood 1½ miles, Q.028443, from the farm where we dispersed ourselves in small parties of 2-3. This wood was on the edge of an excellent DZ and I had my first resupply. The wireless was now working well so I decided to start sending back information.

17 Jun to 22 Jun

After 5 days here we moved to another location, U.976451, 7 miles away.

The local *maquis* Chief was by now very much on our side and arranged a truck for transport. We moved at 2300 hrs arrived 2330 hrs, bedded down and moved into the camp at first light. Capt TONKIN visited me here (this was his second visit) and told me where he was located and where he was operating.

23 Jun to 25 Jun

My contact man (JOSEPH) then proposed that a youth from his village should cook for me. This youth was not what I required so I sacked him and a more reliable type (ex-Sgt from the French Army) came instead and proved very satisfactory. Joseph also produced another friend of his named ANDRÉ, (a post office operator) an intelligent type to whom I gave the job of organising road watching parties and procuring news. I had him a week and told him to see what he could do. I was then resupplied and we received our first mail (U.974445).

I had been just on three weeks in France by now so decided that we must become more mobile. I therefore asked ALBERT (local *maquis* chief) to get me a car. This he did (a Lincoln Zephyr) which served the purpose very well as I was able to transport the whole Phantom patrol and kit in one vehicle. We set up an MCR 1 in the back and used the car as an office, for coding and for listening to the broadcasts. We then moved another 8 miles to Q.073417.

1st Jul to 12 Jul

This new camp was the best we had. I went out daily to contact my information man, make recces of new DZs and dumps and find out as much as I could about general conditions in the area. I had no camp admin. worries as the cook did my foraging and procuring and buying of fresh rations and the wireless worked well.

Lt MORRIS from Capt Tonkin's party, came over and collected the remainder of the SAS personnel. Two days later I moved down to beside the *maquis* camp, Q.018449, 6 miles away, as there were rumours that the Boche was starting to comb the area. This was beside a DZ about one mile from my first DZ. I was resupplied here with 48 containers and four panniers by two aircraft. I was asked to pass a message that the potential strength of the *maquis* could be brought up to 1,200 if arms and amn. could be supplied. I was also informed of the collection by another *maquis* of two AAF aircrew.

Lt Morris came over again to collect supplies from my dump and on the way to it the jeep we were travelling in turned over. Lt Morris' left knee was injured and BROWN, his driver sitting in front, was also injured in the knee and shoulder, Q.003469. I had to place them in a farm for some days after they had been inspected and treated by the local doctor of the town LE DORAT, Q.0335. He was very relieved to hear that they had both had anti-tetanus inoculations as he confessed to me that he had only enough of this inoculation for 20 people and he was the doctor for a town of a population of approximately 2,000.

I had by then arranged for the placing of the two AAF aircrew in a safe place at U.869483, and on my way over to see them some days later I ran into an ambush. No casualties were caused to my party in the car. I moved again two miles away from where I was located, to wood Q.025498.

12 to 14 Jul

Then came the news of the attack on Captain Tonkin's party and I spent 3 days interviewing the *maquis* who had gone to his help and trying to find out whether Capt Tonkin was alive and how many of his party had escaped and where they were located. Lt Morris who had recovered from his accident went to contact SHIPWRIGHT who had in the meanwhile found Capt Tonkin and had informed London to this effect.

15 Jul

I then brought my W/T set and operators over to Capt Tonkin, went back and collected as much of the Dump as was possible, and acquired four more civilian cars for Capt Tonkin and joined him myself.

We stayed with Capt Tonkin just over four weeks, moving our location three times, the last time the day before we were evacuated by 'plane.

Details of the evacuation will no doubt be dealt with by Capt Tonkin and Lt Dane. I should like to add to anything they may say that the pilots of the Hudsons that brought us out deserve the greatest credit for the skill and nerve shown in landing and taking off of an unknown and flat field 200 miles behind the enemy lines.

Equipment: Personal equipment was first class and everything asked for before going was obtained. See attached list of kit taken by this patrol for small details and suggestions for improvement (Appendix 'A').

W/T Equipment: W/T equipment consisting of two complete Jedburgh sets and two separate MCR 1 carried by the patrol. None of these were damaged on the parachute landing. This was due to the fact that great care was taken in packing them into the top of the kitbags.

Jedburgh Sets: The Jed set proved very reliable and simple to operate. In two months operations one valve was broken and one generator burnt out. This latter was, I believe, due to the carbon brushes on the dynamo wearing out.

In the new type Jed set a spare aerial plug-in lead must be provided with each set.

MCR 1: Proved extremely good and with practice the operator becomes less ham-fisted when tuning to a station. The coils of range 1 and range 2 were never used for receiving the broadcasts by us.

The life of the batteries was longer than advertised. We had to change our first battery only after a month's working at an average of 3 hours per day.

Broadcasts: The 7205 m/c frequency proved unsatisfactory for reading owing to continual jamming.

The 9455 m/c frequency and the 6050 m/c frequency were good but jammed at intervals in turn. The Boche never appeared to be able to jam all three frequencies at the same time in our area. The news and news-reviews were regularly listened to and if warning was given, any new broadcaster was appreciated. The announcers are to be congratulated on their very clear diction.

The 0900 hrs broadcast during the day never had any messages on it of operational importance. I personally would have preferred the maximum number of messages early in the day in order to get them answered by the same evening. In my case the maximum number of messages seemed to be broadcast on the 1900 hrs and 2000 hrs periods. My last transmitting period during the day was at 2100 hrs. This gave me too little time to get the required answers and added to this the fact that the 2100 hrs transmission was our most difficult one owing to interference.

Sked Times: My transmitting periods daily were:

> 1300 hrs – 1400 hrs
> 1600 hrs – 1800 hrs
> 2100 hrs – 2200 hrs

Most traffic was passed on the 1600 hrs sked. The 2200 hrs sked began to fail as the nights became shorter and the day before leaving we were unable to repeat back and acknowledge at 2130 hrs a message transmitted at 2105 hrs. This was owing to fading and heavy interference.

Emergency Frequency: This link was found quite invaluable during the day. At night my operators were unable to get through although control could be heard at times strength 5.

One Time Pads: Found to be most adequate. We nearly always worked three on any long message. This saved time and was an aid to avoiding mistakes.

I suggest that new code books have perforated lines across the page for quick tearing out.

The total number of messages received by me was 100, the total number sent by me was 109. Of this total, only parts of 4 had to be sent back for re-enciphering.

Total number of messages sent over the broadcast to SABU 3 was 132, of which only two had to be asked for again. One of these was due to interference.

S-Phone: We only used this equipment once and it was very satisfactory. The maximum range was difficult to estimate, but the 'plane was out of hearing before the voice of the operator on the a/c faded out.

Eureka: This equipment proved very reliable for bringing the 'planes over the reception committee. The life of the batteries never exceeded 3 hours. I found it best to work the Eureka directly off the generator. The hum given out by the set could not be heard on a still night over 25 yards.

Rations – 24 Hour Packs: The biscuits and meat were never used by us. The sweets and chocolate were very popular with the French of all sexes and ages.

I would suggest that the chocolate be wrapped in wax and heatproof paper. Many boxes were split by the heat of the sun. Half the biscuits can be taken out and 5 or 10 cigarettes and book matches put in lieu.

Compo Cells Packing: The packing of compo cells was not carefully thought out, as we found in these cells that a half full sack of sand had been put in for weight. This is not to be tolerated in a country like France, where everything is in such very short supply that it is practically non-existent. Weight can be made up with arms, amn., articles of issue kit, more food, torches and batteries, condensed milk etc., all of which are quite invaluable to the locals.

Comp Cell Contents: There were far too many tins of biscuits sent. We used approximately 6 tins in 2 months (bread in our area was no problem).

The fruit cocktail and sultana puddings proved the most popular items with the troops. Sardines, although not so popular, had a very high barter value (one tin was worth a chicken or two to three dozen eggs). Stewed steak, M and V, and Irish stew although nourishing, became unbearable after the 4th day in succession. More variety needed and bully beef or, as a last resort, spam would have been better.

Tinned vegetables were good as in our area, the drought had been severe and there were very few fresh vegetables to be had. (We had our first new potatoes and runner beans a week before leaving, approx. Aug 1st).

The chocolate, cigarettes, jam, tea and margarine were adequate but more sugar is needed for the dehydrated tea.

I only saw 4 food cells smashed out of over 150.

Arms – Brens: Out of 10 Brens received, 4 were broken either at the magazine catch or the body-locking nut.

Stens: Of over a hundred Stens seen I never saw one broken from dropping by parachute.

American Carbines: An exceptionally good light weapon. Excellent for personal protection. I saw none damaged from dropping by parachute.

Note: Some form of webbing pouch to hold old spare mags. must be designed. Four spares should be carried per man, plus one on the gun, giving the total number of rounds per man as 75. (I personally found the Eureka battery pouches most useful for holding the spare mags.)

Fitness: The fitness acquired during training was quite adequate. The lack of sleep (approx 4 – 6 hrs per night with more sleep during the day) did not affect the troops. I believe that the mental fatigue of the operators and coders was considerable, not so much from coding and operating the W/T sets as from the general feeling of never quite knowing when and where the Boche might re-appear in strength. Feet had to be watched in hot weather and kept as clean as possible.

Lice: As we slept mostly in the open we were not bothered by these pests.

Fleas: Only encountered in the hay in barns and were kept away by regular and complete washing and sun-bathing when possible.

Snakes: I saw 3 during 2 months. I was assured by the locals that their bites were poisonous in the extreme.

Clothing – shirts: All shirts must have breast pockets.

Parachute Trousers: Very long-wearing but too hot for warm weather.

Boots: Started to crack after 6 weeks without greasing. Rubber soles excellent but a distinctive pattern should be avoided.

Sleeping Bags: Quite excellent. A much lighter waterproof cover must be designed instead of the present heavy one.

DZ and DZ Organisation: I found that the *maquis* was most useful in finding DZs for me and soon understood what was required (i.e. a long clear stretch of ground min. 800 yrds long by 200 yrds wide). It was necessary to have a small wood or cover to one side of the DZ for breaking down the containers prior to transporting to the dump which was anything up to 8 miles away.

For clearing the DZ of containers I used the *maquis* to hoist the containers, bullock and carts for transport to cover, and my own patrol for operating the bonfires, Eureka and signalling torch. My patrol also controlled the number of 'chutes brought in.

I found to start with that it was difficult to control the *maquis*' enthusiasm during a drop, but later on they became very good at it and quite understood the drill. The parachutes were given to the *maquis* or farmers who helped, for disposal. We kept quite a few ourselves for tents and barter.

DZ Lights: Three bonfires in a straight line at 100 yrds interval with a torch for the recognition letter was, I found, the most successful method. I used petrol to start the fires and to make them flare up as the aircraft approached.

Petrol Containers: The white containers with petrol in them were a great worry to us, as the only efficient way of hiding them was to bury them. They should be painted brown or black and only marked with a white P.

'Chute Failures: I saw only 3 container 'chutes fail to open and can give no reason for this. I consider this a very small percentage.

Any cell containers that were damaged, I found that only the bottom two cells were badly damaged. The remaining three were practically always intact. If, on the other hand, a petrol or arms container was damaged the contents were damaged and scattered as well. The crushable buffers on cell containers will take much more shock than the rubber buffers. The panniers were the least damaged; only 1 out of 12 that I saw had the material (a charging motor) smashed.

Maquis: NOTE (this only concerns the area in which I was)

The *maquis* were of the greatest possible aid to us in every way. They provided me with transport, rations (meat, bread, sugar and once coffee), guides, information, man-power on the DZ, and even boots. They should be treated unreservedly as friends and allies and the greatest trust can be put in them. Any mistakes they may make are from over-enthusiasm and willingness to help.

The organisation to start with was confusing but is now much more clear cut. Roughly speaking, the *maquis* consist of a series of groups, each group of from 80-200 strong. Each group is divided into a number of sections, each section under a *chef de section* who is a tried man and may more often than not be an ex-NCO of the French Army. Each group has its *chef* who is the person to deal with, as he has more authority than the *chefs de groupe*. All groups in our area were controlled by a *maquis* HQ (*Quartier Général*). The *Quartier Général* consisted of able officers with very strict disciplinary powers and organising abilities. These officers are not many and move about their area with a protection squad. In my area they directed the policy, discipline, training and operations of the *maquis* groups there. A very close liaison was kept between the SF representative and the *Quartier Général du Maquis*. The *Quartier Général du Maquis* also organised training cadres and recruiting.

Enemy Tactics: In this area the Boche was:-

1.Not moving about the country-side except in strength.

2.Planning a sweep of the whole area.

3.Using a large percentage of militia to a small percentage of himself.

Times of Attack: At first light, having moved into position the night before, Monday was always our 'flap' day.

Gestapo: The possibility of *Gestapo* agents was always a great source of worry to us; and although quite a number were reported to have been rounded up by the *maquis*, one was forced to view anyone not known to one personally with suspicion. The *Gestapo* were using a number of women as agents (I personally saw one being led off to be shot).

Militia: The *Milice* or Militia were the real 'bastards'. Having been hypnotised by the Boche in the early part of the war and having joined up they were drilled, disciplined, armed and injected with Boche frightfulness. Their position is now most unenviable as they are traitors to their own country and both they and the *maquis* know it. The *Milice* will hesitate at nothing.

Uniform: (not seen personally but explained in detail to me by a *guarde mobile* working with *maquis*)

Blue beret – blue shirt – dark blue skiing trousers – sometimes wearing a Sam-Brown. German arms.

Guarde Mobile: The three I saw were working with the *maquis* and struck me as being well disciplined and tough. They were mounted on a m/c combination with the French LMG.

Uniform: French DR helmets and goggles

Khaki shirts open at the neck

Sam-Brown with revolver holster and spare mag
pouches in leather

Khaki drill trousers and good boots

MISCELLANEOUS
Security: Only one bad breach of W/T security occurred. This was on a broadcast to me at 1400 hrs 6 August. Amongst groups of code the following phrases in clear were sent:-

Confirm ground OK
Priority 1st 2nd 3rd
Phantom patrol SAS Tps and Yanks

Dispatchers: My stick and myself were very grateful for the presence of a dispatcher. As we had made a total of 3 trips over the target area we were a bit unhappy about going out. Sqn Leader Norris' calmness and efficiency in getting us kitted up and ready for the jump made a very great difference to our morale.

Some points to note (this only applies to the area I was in as far as I know).

1.2 packets of cigarettes per person per month was the official ration (20 cigs per pkt).

2.Soap was practically non-existent.

3.No material was procurable except through the black market. (ie. material for clothes).

4.The farmers made their own oil for cooking from what looked like a very small bean.

5.The farmers always managed to have wine at every meal.

6.For special occasions, a local liqueur called 'gnole' would appear. It was very potent and I found it lit a fire much more easily than the heating elements provided with the 24 hr pack.

7.Parachutes were of untold value to the peasants as material for clothes.

8.Everyone shakes hands with everyone else at frequent intervals. Troops should be told about this so as not to offend local customs.

9.Money is still very important to peasants.

10.There are many bicycles but no new tyres to be had.

11.Petrol is non-existent and could be dropped in large quantities to the *maquis* for more mobility in getting to attack the Boche.

12.MICHELIN maps are easy to procure and much used by the *maquis*. Some system of map grid should be worked out so that locations etc. can be taken straight off the Michelin.

APPENDIX III

(**Author's note:** this was the task description discovered by John Tonkin in 1973. Hopelessly extensive for just Tonkin and Crisp, it had not reached Tonkin prior to his departure for France in 1944.)

TASK DESCRIPTION – 'BULBASKET' RECCE PARTY.

OBJECT	Two officers to Recce an area approx. L1403, Q1080, Q3083, Q3099 for its suitability as a safe base.
METHOD	By parachute, with SOE organisation.
TASK	Points to investigate:

	Partisans:	a) Strength and organisation of the partisans?
		b) Are they staying permanently in the area?
		c) Do they only come there to operate?
		d) If so, where do they come from?
		e) Will they provide us with guides?
	Enemy:	a) How strong are the German garrison troops in the area?
		b) How are they organised and how do they guard the country?
First Conclusion:		Is the area safe enough to be used as a base? How many SAS troops can be absorbed by the area?
	D.Z.	Investigate about suitable DZs for troops. Investigate about suitable DZs for supplies.
	Gliders	Investigate about suitable fields for gliders.

<u>L.G.</u>	Investigate about possible L.G. site.
<u>Second Conclusion</u>:	Is the area suitable for paratroops, and/or gliders, and/or aircraft?
<u>Movements</u>	Is it possible for small parties to move in day time?
	How many miles can a man, loaded, cover in day time?
	How many miles can a man, loaded, cover in a night?
	The area is closed by rivers navigable and canals. How much will these rivers and canals hamper our movements towards distant targets?
	Are they easy to cross?
	Where does the River Loire start to be fordable?
	Are there any other natural obstacles?
	Would it be possible to use jeeps and to what extent?
	Is it possible to find motor cars in the area?
	What do they require mostly to be in running order:

> Petrol?
>
> Lubricant?
>
> Tyres? and what size?

	Are pack animals available and can they be used?
<u>Operations</u>	Our main task being to deal with L of C: what are our prospects in the area? How many men can be employed; the area being limited to the East by the River Loire? Would it be possible to operate with jeeps?
<u>Other Dumps</u>	Investigate for Operational Dump sites to the South, S.E. and S.W. of BULBASKET.
	Could these dumps be built up from BULBASKET?
	Should they be built by dropping direct into them?
<u>Last conclusion</u>:	
	Is the area easy to operate from or is it impossible to reach the targets owing to the ground or other conditions?
<u>Miscellaneous</u>:	
	Can the country provide food?
	Up to what extent?
	Is money of primary importance?

What are the local diseases?

CODE NAMES

Operation GAIN will be used when general reference to 1st S.A.S. Ops. against Railways is necessary.

LOT 1   Railways LIMOGES – VIERZON L74

LOT 2   Railways POITIERS U47 – TOUR P76

LOT 3   Railways in area TOUR – ORLEAN F62 South of River LOIRE.

LOT 4   Railway NIORT – PARTHENAY – THOUARS – SAUMUR

LOT 5   Railways PARIS – ORLEANS – TOURS (North of River LOIRE)

Emergency code letter for D.Z. if proper code letter is not given over: W/T is "K" but is NOT to be used except in dire emergency.

LIST OF AERODROMES IN YOUR AREA

	Name	Grid Ref
x	BOURGES	L 9933
x o	CHÂTEAUDUN	W 2860
	CHÂTEAUROUX/DECLS.	L 5305
	CHÂTEAUROUX/LA MARTINERIE	L 5802
x o	ORLEANS/BRICY	W 5349
	ORLEANS/SARAN	W 6245
	ROMORANTIN	L 5159
x o	TOURS	P 7869
	ST. YAN	S 3 5
	LIMOGES/FEYTIAT	V 1991
x	ANGERS	O 8181

x = means of particular importance at present
o = means scheduled for bombing

APPENDIX IV

HITLER'S *KOMMANDOBEFEHL*

1. For some time our enemies have been using, in their warfare, methods which are outside the International Geneva Conventions. Especially brutal and treacherous is the behaviour of the so-called Commandos, who, as is established, are partially recruited even from freed criminals in enemy countries. From captured orders it is divulged that they are directed not only to shackle prisoners, but also to kill defenceless prisoners on the spot at the moment in which they believe that the latter, as prisoners, represent a burden in the further pursuit of their purposes, or could otherwise be a hindrance. Finally, orders have been found in which the killing of prisoners has been demanded in principle.

2. For this reason it was already announced, in an addendum to the Armed Forces report of 7th October, 1942, that, in the future, Germany in the face of these sabotage troops of the British and their accomplices, will resort to the same procedure, that is, that they will be ruthlessly mowed down by the German troops in combat, wherever they may appear.

3. I therefore order:
From now on, all enemies on so-called Commando missions in Europe or Africa, challenged by German troops, even if they are to all appearances soldiers in uniform or demolition troops, whether armed or unarmed, in battle or in flight, are to be slaughtered to the last man. It does not make any difference whether they are dropped by parachute. Even if these individuals, when found, should apparently be prepared to give themselves up, no pardon is to be granted them on principle. In each individual case, full information

is to be sent to the O.K.W. for publication in the Report of the Military Forces.

4. If individual members of such Commandos, such as agents, saboteurs, etc., fall into the hands of the military forces by some other means, through the police in occupied territories, for instance, they are to be handed over immediately to the S.D. Any imprisonment under military guard, in P.W. stockades, for instance, etc., is strictly prohibited, even if this is only intended for a short time.

5. This order does not apply to the treatment of any soldiers who, in the course of normal hostilities, large-scale offensive actions, landing operations and airborne operations, are captured in open battle or give themselves up. Nor does this order apply to enemy soldiers falling into our hands after battles at sea, or to enemy soldiers trying to save their lives by parachute after air battles.

6. I will hold responsible, under Military Law, for failing to carry out this order, all commanders and officers who either have neglected their duty of instructing the troops about this order, or asked against this order when it was to be executed.

Adolf Hitler
18th October 1942

APPENDIX V

38 GROUP RAF
SUPPLY AND TROOP DROP OPERATIONS

DATE	Nos AIRCRAFT	OPERATION	RESULTS
7/8th June.	1 aircraft.	Troop drop.	Successful drop of main recceparty – Lt Stephens + 8.
10/11th June.	1 aircraft.	Troop drop.	Successful drop of 'Lot 2' parties – Lt Morris + 3 and Sgt Holmes + 2.
" "	1 aircraft.	Troop drop.	Inaccurate drop of 'Lot 4' parties – Lt Weaver + 3 and Cpl Kinnevane + 2, one man captured.
" "	1 aircraft.	Troop drop.	Main party. Unsuccessful – DZ not located.
11/12th June.	2 aircraft.	Troop drop.	Main party drop – one aircraft on target, one dropped 25 kms away.
14/15th June.	1 aircraft.	Resupply (Sadoine).	Cancelled – weather.
15/16th June.	1 aircraft.	Resupply (Sadoine).	Cancelled – weather.
16/17th June.	1 aircraft.	Resupply (Tonkin).	Unable to locate DZ.
" "	1 aircraft.	Resupply (Sadoine).	Successful.

SUPPLY AND TROOP DROP OPERATIONS

DATE	Nos AIRCRAFT	OPERATION	RESULTS
17/18th June.	5 aircraft.	Jeeps and troops (Tonkin).	Successful.
19/20th June.	1 aircraft.	Resupply (Sadoine).	Cancelled – weather.
20/21st June.	1 aircraft.	Resupply. (Sadoine).	Lights lit but not seen. Unsuccessful.
21/22nd June.	1 aircraft.	Resupply (Tonkin).	Unable to locate DZ. Unsuccessful
" "	1 aircraft.	Resupply (Sadoine).	Successful.
22/23rd June.	1 aircraft.	Resupply (Tonkin).	Unsuccessful – no lights lit on DZ due to enemy presence in area.
23/24th June.	1 aircraft.	Resupply (Tonkin).	Unsuccessful – DZ believed not manned.
24/25th June.	1 aircraft.	Resupply (Tonkin).	Unsuccessful – no lights seen from DZ. Tonkin moving camp.
27/28th June.	2 aircraft.	Resupply (Tonkin).	Cancelled – DZ location given too late.
28/29th June.	2 aircraft.	Resupply (Tonkin).	Cancelled – weather.
29/30th June.	2 aircraft.	Resupply (Tonkin).	Cancelled – weather.
" "	1 aircraft.	Resupply (Sadoine).	Cancelled – weather.
30th June /1st July.	2 aircraft.	Resupply (Tonkin).	Cancelled – weather.
" "	1 aircraft.	Resupply (Sadoine).	Cancelled – weather.
1/2nd July.	2 aircraft.	Resupply (Tonkin).	Cancelled – weather.
" "	1 aircraft	Resupply (Sadoine).	Cancelled – weather.
2/3rd July.	2 aircraft.	Resupply (Tonkin).	Cancelled – weather.

SUPPLY AND TROOP DROP OPERATIONS

DATE	Nos AIRCRAFT	OPERATION	RESULTS
" "	1 aircraft.	Resupply (Sadoine).	Cancelled – weather.
3/4th July.	2 aircraft.	Resupply (Tonkin).	Cancelled – no confirmation from Tonkin.
" "	2 aircraft.	Resupply (Sadoine).	Successful.
7/8th July.	2 aircraft.	Resupply (Tonkin).	Cancelled by SAS.
8/9th July.	2 aircraft.	Resupply (Tonkin).	Cancelled by SAS.
13/14th July.	1 aircraft.	Resupply (Tonkin).	Successful.
15/16th July.	1 aircraft.	Resupply (Tonkin).	Successful.
16/17th July.	1 aircraft.	Resupply & S-phone.	Successful.
17/18th July.	1 aircraft.	Resupply (Tonkin).	Successful.
24/25th July.	1 aircraft.	Resupply (Tonkin).	Unsuccessful, reception not spotted.
27/28th July.	1 aircraft.	Resupply (Tonkin).	Cancelled by SAS.
28/29th July.	1 aircraft.	Resupply (Tonkin).	Successful, Surrey Dane and supplies.

TOTAL SORTIES: 53

SUMMARY:

Successful and accurate troop/jeep drops	9
Successful but inaccurate troop drops	2
Successful supply drops	7
Successful S-Phone flight	1
	19
Abortive troop drop	1
Cancelled – weather	17
DZ not manned / lights not lit	3
Cancelled by SAS	9
Unable to locate DZ	4
	34

APPENDIX VI

2 GROUP AIR OPERATIONS
IN SUPPORT OF
OPERATION BULBASKET

<u>11th June 1944 – Attack by 12 Mosquito FB VI on 11 petrol trains in sidings at Châtellerault.</u>

487 Squadron RNZAF (140 Wing), RAF Gravesend.

HP924	EG-T	W/C I S Smith, F/L R A Marsh
NS964	EG-S	S/L J L W Ellacombe, F/O R Peel
NT180	EG-Y	F/L W G Runciman, F/O E R G Jones

464 Squadron RAAF (140 Wing), RAF Gravesend.

NS994	SB-F	W/C R W Iredale, F/L J L McCaul
MM403	SB-V	S/L T McPhee, F/L G W Atkins
HX914	SB-?	F/O R G Rowell, F/O C E Davidson

107 Squadron (138 Wing), RAF Lasham.

NS820	OM-P	W/C M E Pollard, F/O J M L Drummond
NS912	OM-C	S/L H G Brittain, F/O G Stephenson
NS853	OM-G	F/L B G Slip, F/O F E Thomas
NT207	OM-B	F/L J Whittle, F/O D W Shanahan
NT136	OM-A	W/O R A Martin, F/S T G Patterson
NS886	OM-Q	F/S H S Ross, F/O J R Green

464 Sqn RAAF reported trains on return journey between Châtellerault and Châteaudun. Two Mosquitos of 21 Sqn RAF therefore attacked from RAF Gravesend.

14th/15th July 1944 – Attack by 14 Mosquito FB VI on barracks of 17th SS *Panzergrenadier* Division at Bonneuil-Matours.

Attack led by Wing Leader and Wing Commander (Flying), 140 Wing, RAF Thorney Island.

| NS840 | EG-X | G/C P G Wykeham-Barnes, F/O A E Chaplin |
| HX920 | YH-M | W/C R Reynolds, F/L E B Sismore |

21 Squadron RAF (140 Wing), RAF Thorney Island.

NT174	YH-V	W/C D F Dennis, F/O R J Grantham
NT197	YH-X	S/L J Murray, F/L G S Bliss
LR291	YH-B	F/L D Bell-Irving, F/O A Holt
NT124	YH-F	F/O Fielding-Johnson, F/L J Blyth

487 Squadron RNZAF (140 Wing), RAF Thorney Island.

HP924	EG-T	W/C I S Smith, F/L R A Marsh
HP933	EG-U	F/L W J Runciman, F/O E R G Jones
LR333	EG-R	F/L J H W Yeats, F/O A F Howlett
NT184	EG-P	F/L G D Thorpe, F/O N Pountney

464 Squadron RAAF (140 Wing), RAF Thorney Island.

NS944	SB-F	W/C G Panitz, F/L R S Williams
HR187	SB-S	S/L R W Hyem, F/O E J Brayne
NS926	SB-G	F/L W D Parsons, F/O E Ramsey
HX919	SB-P	F/O J R C Walton, F/O C H Harper

Mustang III fighter escort provided by 12 aircraft of 65 Sqn RAF (122 Wing) from French coast to south of Rennes.

1st August 1944 – 23 Mosquito FB VI attacked Caserne des Dunes barracks, Poitiers.

Attack led by Wing Leader, 140 Wing, RAF Thorney Island.

| NS840 | EG-X | G/C P G Wykeham-Barnes, F/L E B Sismore |

21 Squadron RAF (140 Wing), RAF Thorney Island.

NT174	YH-V	W/C D F Dennis, F/O R J Grantham
NT197	YH-X	S/L J Murray, F/L G Bliss
NS978	YH-J	S/L J P Lloyd, F/O W Roe
LR291	YH-B	F/L M Forbes, F/O L Halliday
HP150	YH-?	F/L J Martin, Sgt H Herman
HR194	YH-K	F/L J Freeman, W/O J Lindsell
NS183	YH-T	F/L D S Mussett, P/O H Burrows *
LR348	YH-P	F/L G Murray, F/O H G Batt
NS884	YH-A	Flt/Off R M Seage (USAAF), F/S A Halliday

NS965	YH-?	F/O W R C Smith, F/O A H McKee

487 Squadron RNZAF (140 Wing), RAF Thorney Island.

HP924	EG-T	W/C I S Smith, F/L R A Marsh
NS988	EG-S	S/L J L W Ellacombe, F/O R Peel
NT144	EG-A	S/L W J Runciman, F/O E R G Jones
NT184	EG-P	F/L G D Thorpe, F/O N Pountney
NS963	EG-H	F/L J L Mason, F/O F J Roe
NS834	EG-G	F/L R J Coombs, F/O W G Judson
PZ164	EG-K	F/L W G Gasquoine, F/O P E Prior
HR144	EG-J	F/L R D Watt, F/S K C Dorman
NT180	EG-Y	F/O H G Edwards, F/O W L Webster
HP931	EG-N	F/O E C Heaton, W/O K G Mason
NS964	EG-E	F/O C D B White, F/O C B Ball
NS829	EG-W	P/O L D Gilbertson, F/O S A J Askew

Reserves (did not attack):

HP931	EG-O	F/O A N Wilson, F/O E O Davies
NT135	EG-U	P/O K C Bacon, F/S A R Watkins

Mustang III fighter escort from 122 Wing provided by 12 aircraft of 19 Sqn RAF and 8 of 65 Sqn RAF from French coast to the target.

* NS183 YH-T of 21 Sqn RAF crash-landed in France, F/L Mussett and P/O Burrows evaded and returned to squadron 21.9.44.

2nd August 1944 – Attack by 17 Mosquito FB VI and 1 Mosquito IV on Château du Fou, living quarters of 17th SS *Panzergrenadier* Division.

107 Squadron RAF (138 Wing), RAF Lasham.

(1st wave):

NS833	OM-V	S/L W F Wallington, F/O G H Briggs
NS836	OM-U	Lt/Cdr K Skavhaugh, F/O A H Bobbett
LR257	OM-F	F/O D Swale, F/S M L van der Helstraete
NS820	OM-P	F/O W M Taylor, F/O A K Aiken
NS910	OM-T	F/O P Slayden, F/O N L Gilson
NS952	OM-S	F/S F D Hawkins, F/S E F Waring

(2nd wave):

NS912	OM-O	W/C W J Scott, W/O N A Barry
NS946	OM-E	S/L D N Wellings, P/O W D Hemmings
NT226	OM-G	Capt A A Brown, W/O I J Self
NS958	OM-R	F/L A J Ripon, F/S T A F Ridout
NT207	OM-B	F/L J Whittle, F/O D W Shanahan
NS934	OM-K	W/O L H Rogers, F/S H B Pounder

(3rd wave):

NS908	OM-N	F/L J McLurg, F/O H W Parkinson
HX832	OM-D	Capt T A Hunt, F/S V M Collins **
NS852	OM-Q	F/O J M Ballachy, F/O J F Arnold
NT136	OM-A	F/O L Gasson, F/S L C Etheridge
HJ771	OM-J	F/O O D Staple, F/O D Wimmers

+ F/L Hester, F/O Oakley in Mosquito IV of RAF Film Production Unit – poss. DZ414.

** HX832 OM-D crash-landed at RAF Thorney Island after returning on one engine at 2340 hrs. Crew unhurt.

N.B. Possibly as a result of intelligence from Operation Bulbasket:
12th/13th June 1944 – Attack on Poitiers railway station and marshalling yards by 112 Lancasters and 4 Mosquitos of 5 Group, RAF Bomber Command.

APPENDIX VII
SAS/PHANTOM/RAMC PERSONNEL

CAPTURED, AIRVAULT, 10/11.6.44, FATE UNKNOWN.

1)   Tpr G Biffin   No. N/K   Age N/K

CAPTURED P.O.W.s AT ST. BENÔIT, POITIERS, 28/29.6.44.
EXECUTED, FORÊT DE SAINT-SAUVANT, 7.7.44. BURIED AT ROM.

2)	Sgt D Eccles	2735399	Age 24
3)	Cpl K Bateman	5572359	Age 24

CAPTURED WOUNDED AND KILLED, VERRIÈRES, 3.7.44. BURIED AT VERRIÈRES.

4)	Lt T W M Stephens	95606	Age N/K

CAPTURED WOUNDED P.O.W.s 3.7.44. PROBABLY LETHALLY INJECTED, POITIERS KOMMANDANTUR, c.13.7.44.

5)	Tpr J Ogg	11006397	Age 21
6)	Tpr H Pascoe	5729548	Age 26
7)	Tpr J Williams	2066732	Age 23

CAPTURED P.O.W.s 3.7.44 AND EXECUTED, FORÊT DE SAINT-SAUVANT, 7.7.44. BURIED AT ROM.

8)	Lt R Crisp	303259	Age 20
9)	Sgt R E Heavens	820065	Age 31
10)	L/Sgt J R Jessiman	1468628	Age 23
11)	Cpl W W Allan (RAMC)	2031580	Age 23
12)	Cpl R Chick	7895914	Age 23
13)	Cpl J C W Govan MM	3057065	Age 30
14)	Cpl J Kinnevane	6094156	Age 26
15)	Cpl L C Long	6019123	Age 26

16)	L/Cpl J H M Baker	2615455	Age 22
17)	Tpr E Y Adamson	4399392	Age 22
18)	Tpr A G Ashley	5729859	Age 24
19)	Tpr J Aspin	10602266	Age 21
20)	Tpr M J Brophy	6353031	Age 22
21)	Tpr G H F Budden	7958191	Age 21
22)	Tpr G O Cogger	5729670	Age 24
23)	Tpr L R Eades	14542517	Age 22
24)	Tpr D Gray	320068	Age 25
25)	Tpr R Guard	2929492	Age 24
26)	Tpr H Hill	6298443	Age 29
27)	Tpr D M Livingstone	3324838	Age 29
28)	Tpr A McLeod	2822451	Age 26
29)	Tpr H Mullen	2935098	Age 29
30)	Tpr D Phillips	5498990	Age 23
31)	Tpr W E L Richardson	92635	Age 26
32)	Tpr S J Ryland	5729976	Age 29
33)	Tpr E Simmons	124047	Age 26
34)	Tpr A J Spooner	6216295	Age 20
35)	Tpr V O White	6011364	Age 26

SURVIVORS EVACUATED BY RAF HUDSON 7.8.44.

36)	Capt J E Tonkin	44)	Tpr J Fielding
37)	Capt R Sadoine (Phantom)	45)	Tpr L Keeble
38)	Lt H Morris	46)	Tpr A McNair
39)	Lt P Weaver	47)	Tpr R Smith
40)	Sgt J Holmes	48)	Tpr S Smith
41)	Cpl G Rideout	49)	Tpr W Smith
42)	Tpr A Brown MM	50)	Sgnm E Armitage (Phantom)
43)	Tpr T Cummings	51)	Sgnm W Plumb (Phantom)

SURVIVORS EVACUATED BY USAAF DAKOTA 10.8.44.

52)	Lt D Surrey Dane	54)	Sgnm J Bell (Phantom)
53)	Cpl D Stephenson (Phantom)		

HOSPITALISED, POITIERS, 22/23.6.44,
LIBERATED BY ALLIED TROOPS 8.9.44

55)	Tpr A O'Neill

MAQUIS OF THE FTP 'AMILCAR' GROUP, ATTACHED TO 1ST SAS 'OPERATION BULBASKET' AT VERRIÈRES.

1) Pierre Lecellier – ('Pierrot') Killed, Verrières. Age 20.

2) Jean Desvignes – Killed, Verrières. Age 19.

3) Albert Sola – Killed, Verrières. Age 21.

4) André Quintard – Killed, Verrières. Age 20.

5) Pierre Bonneau – Killed, Verrières. Age 20.

6) Albert Choisy – Killed, Verrières.

7) Maurice Salmoni ('Pierrot le Corse') – Killed, Verrières.

8) Lieutenant Jean Dieudonné ('Maurice') – Escaped at Verrières, survived.

9) Marcel Weber ('Marcel') – Wounded at Verrières, escaped and survived.

10) Denis Chansigaud ('Henri') – Escaped at Verrières, survived.

11) Pierre Crest – Wounded at Verrières, escaped and survived.

12) Godefroy Koenig ('John') – Slightly injured in jeep accident with Lieutenant Morris' party. Survived.

USAAF EVADERS ASSISTED BY 'OPERATION BULBASKET'.

1) Lt L D Bundy. 0-804996. Captured, Verrières, 3.7.44. Executed at Saint-Sauvant, 7.7.44. Buried at Rom.

2) Lt W A Bradley

3) Lt F D Harper } Evacuated by RAF Hudson, 7.8.44.

4) Sgt J T Norton

5) Lt T H Scott

6) Lt W Banks } Evacuated by USAAF C-47, 10.8.44.

7) Sgt J G Gros

8) Sgt Hitchcock

APPENDIX VIII

SUMMARY OF SAS OPERATIONS

	DATE	TARGET	PERSONNEL	NOTES
1)	10/11th June	'Lot 2' railway south of Châtellerault	Lt Morris + 3	Blew both tracks over a culvert. Tpr Brown originally missing, later rejoined.
2)	" "	'Lot 2' north of Châtellerault	Sgt Holmes + 2	Removed 15-20' of line under road bridge.
3)	" "	Recce of petrol trains at Châtellerault	Lt Stephens + French civilian	Trains located and reported to England for air attack.
4)	" "	'Lot 4' near Airvault	Cpl Kinnevane + 2	Unsuccessful. Fire fight with enemy troops, Tpr Biffin wounded and believed captured.
5)	11/12th June	Railway south east of Montmorillon	Lt Stephens + ?	Road bridge over railway half destroyed.
6)	12/13th June	'Lot 4' near Parthenay	Lt Weaver + 3	Cut line, de-railed train.
7)	" "	Road in Fôret du Défant	Lt Crisp + ?	Mined *Route Nationale* (N147).
8)	13/14th June	Locomotive in station at Le Dorat	Sgt Eccles	Blew front pinions of engine.

9)	" "	Railway south of Le Dorat	Cpl Bateman	Destroyed points.
10)	15/16th June	Railway south of Le Dorat	Sgt Eccles, Cpl Bateman	Destroyed points following repairs.
11)	20/21st June	'Lot 2' north of Poitiers	Lt Stephens + ?	Line successfully cut.
12)	" "	'Lot 2' south of Poitiers	Lt Crisp + ?	Line cut and points blown.
13)	22/23rd June	Railway in Poitiers	Capt Tonkin, Maurice Dieudonné and 1 Tpr	Line cut.
14)	" "	Railway east of Poitiers	Capt Tonkin Maurice Dieudonné and 1 Tpr	Line cut.
15)	" "	'Lot 1' railway south west of Eguzon	Sgt Jessiman + ?	Line cut in two places.
16)	23/24th June	Railway at Fleuré	Capt Tonkin + ?	Line cut.
17)	24/25th June	'Lot 2' railway north of Poitiers	L/Cpl Smith + 1 Tpr	Line cut.
18)	" "	'Lot 2' north of Vivonne	Sgt Holmes + 1	Line cut.
19)	24/25th June	Road south of Vivonne	Sgt Jessiman + 1	Mined *Route Nationale* (N10).
20)	28/29th June	'Lot 2' rail junction at St Benoît	Sgt Eccles, Cpl Bateman and 1 Tpr	Line cut but Eccles and Bateman captured.

21) 1st July	Châteauroux airfield and railway	Lt Morris, Tpr Brown and Godefroy Koenig	Unsuccessful due to accident in jeep.
22) 2/3nd July	'Lot 2' south of Voulon	Tpr S Smith, Tpr R Smith and Tpr Fielding	Line cut.
23) 11/12th July	'Lot 1'	Capt Tonkin, Sgt Holmes, Tpr Cummings	Line cut.
24) 12/13th July	'Lot 1'	Capt Tonkin, Sgt Holmes, Tpr Cummings	Line cut.
25) 20/21st July	'Lot 2' north of Epanvilliers	Sgt Holmes + ?	Line cut.
26) 22/23rd July	'Lot 2' south of Le Coureau	Capt Tonkin, Tpr Fielding, Jean Dieudonné and Lt Harper (USAAF)	Unsuccessful – line guarded by sentries.

(Order to cease operations received 24th July)

APPENDIX IX

BIBLIOGRAPHY
AND
DOCUMENTATION SOURCES

<u>Publications:</u>

(English language)
CARVE HER NAME WITH PRIDE. R J Minney.
Chivers Press 1983. ISBN 0-86220-521-2
COLONEL PADDY. Patrick Marrinan.
Pretani Press 1983. ISBN 0-9503461-4-4
DAS REICH. Max Hastings.
Michael Joseph Ltd. 1981. ISBN 0-7181-2074-4
FLIGHT MOST SECRET-AIR MISSIONS FOR SOE AND SIS. Gibb
McCall. William Kimber & Co Ltd 1981. ISBN 0-7183-0038-6
RESISTANCE. M R D Foot.
Paladin Books 1979. ISBN 0-586-08277-8
ROGUE WARRIOR OF THE SAS – Lt-Col "Paddy" Blair Mayne.
Roy Bradford and Martin Dillon.
John Murray (Publishers) Ltd. 1987. ISBN 0-7195-4430-0
SAS OPERATIONS. James D Ladd.
Robert Hale Ltd. 1986. ISBN 0-7090-2372-3
SECRET WAR. Nigel West.
Hodder and Stoughton Ltd. 1992. ISBN 0-340-58029-1
THE SAS. Philip Warner.
Warner Books 1993. ISBN 0-7515-0829-2
THE SAS AT WAR 1941-1945. Anthony Kemp.

John Murray (Publishers) Ltd. 1991. ISBN 0-7195-4890-X
THE SECRET HUNTERS. Anthony Kemp.
Michael O'Mara Books Ltd. 1986. ISBN 0-948397-35-7
THESE MEN ARE DANGEROUS. D I Harrison.
Blandford Press 1988. ISBN 0-7137-20492
WINGLESS VICTORY. Anthony Richardson.
Odhams Press Ltd. 1950.

(French language)
A L'OMBRE DE SAINT-MARTIAL (LA CLANDESTINITÉ EN VIENNE SUD JUSQU'AU 6 JUIN 1944). R Jovelin.
Privately published 1948.
ARMÉE SECRÈTE DANS LES FORCES FRANÇAISES DE L'INTÉRIEUR - RÉGION 5. Jacques Blanchard.
Privately published 1993. ISBN 2-9506436-1-2
L'ODYSSÉE DES PARACHUTISTES SAS DU CAPITAINE TONKIN ET DES MAQUISARDS DU CAPITAINE DIEUDONNÉ. A Marnais.
Privately published 1973.
LA RÉSISTANCE DANS LA VIENNE ZONE SUD. Camille Olivet.
Privately published.
LA VIENNE PENDANT LA SECONDE GUERRE MONDIALE. Gaston Racault. C.R.D.P. de Poitiers 1987. ISBN 2-86632-208-8
LA VIENNE DANS LA GUERRE 1939/1945. Roger Picard.
Éditions Horvath 1984. ISBN 2-7171-0337-6
LE PICTON magazine, editions 47 and 48, 1984.

<u>Documentation sources:</u>

Public Record Office, Kew:
AIR 25 /40 (May/June)
    /41 (July)   } 2 Group Ops book
    /42 (August)
    /586 – 38 Group Ops book
AIR 26 /181 – 122 Wing Ops book
    /199 – 138 Wing Ops book
    /204 – 140 Wing Ops book
AIR 27 /254 – 19 Squadron Ops book
    /264 – 21 Squadron Ops book
    /595 – 65 Squadron Ops book
    /845 – 107 Squadron Ops book

/1068 – 161 Squadron Ops book
/1154 – 190 Squadron Ops book
/1649 – 298 Squadron Ops book
/1924 – 464 Squadron RAAF Ops book
/1935 – 487 Squadron RNZAF Ops book
/2134 – 620 Squadron Ops book
/2159 – 644 Squadron Ops book

AIR 37 /714 – 2nd TAF Ops book

DEFE 3/171 – Ultra signal intercepts

WO 218/114 }
       /115 } HQ SAS Troops
       /187 – SAS/RAF liaison

WO 219/2329 – SHAEF liaison with Special Forces HQ
       /2342 – SAS summaries
       /2389 – SAS operations

WO 235/293
       /294 } – Wuppertal Trial, papers of the Judge Advocate
       /713 }   General's Office

WO 309/226 – NW Europe War Crimes Group
       /474 – SAS regiment War Crime Cases
       /488 – SAS war crimes extraditions
       /830 – Poitiers case

WO311/627
      /628 } – SAS War Crimes Investigation Team
      /629 }

INDEX